THE MIND OF MENCIUS

Trübner's Oriental Series

CHINA
In 5 Volumes

THE MIND OF MENCIUS

POLITICAL ECONOMY
FOUNDED UPON MORAL
PHILOSOPHY

E FABER

Routledge
Taylor & Francis Group

LONDON AND NEW YORK

First published 1882 by
Trübner & Co Ltd

2 Park Square, Milton Park, Abingdon, Oxfordshire OX14 4RN
711 Third Avenue, New York, NY 10017

*Routledge is an imprint of the Taylor & Francis Group,
an informa business*

First issued in paperback 2018

Transferred to Digital Printing 2007

Copyright © 1882 E Faber

The publishers have made every effort to contact authors/copyright holder
of the works reprinted in *Trübner's Oriental Series*.
This has not been possible in every case, however, and we would
welcome correspondence from those individuals/companies
we have been unable to trace.

These reprints are taken from original copies of each book. In many cases
the condition of these originals is not perfect. The publisher has gone to
great lengths to ensure the quality of these reprints, but wishes to point
out that certain characteristics of the original copies will, of necessity, be
apparent in reprints thereof.

British Library Cataloguing in Publication Data
A CIP catalogue record for this book
is available from the British Library

The Mind of Mencius
ISBN 978-0-415-24488-6 (hbk)
ISBN 978-0-415-86567-8 (pbk)
China: 5 Volumes
ISBN 978-0-415-24287-5
Trübner's Oriental Series
ISBN 978-0-415-23188-6

THE MIND OF MENCIUS

OR

POLITICAL ECONOMY FOUNDED UPON MORAL PHILOSOPHY.

*A SYSTEMATIC DIGEST OF THE DOCTRINES OF THE
CHINESE PHILOSOPHER*

MENCIUS,
B.C. 325.

The Original Text Classified and Translated, with Notes
and Explanations,

BY THE REV. E. FABER,
RHENISH MISSION SOCIETY.

TRANSLATED FROM THE GERMAN, WITH NOTES AND EMENDATIONS,

BY

THE REV. ARTHUR B. HUTCHINSON,
CHURCH MISSIONARY SOCIETY, HONGKONG;

*Author in Classic Chinese of the " Primer of Old Testament History;"
" A Parallel Harmony of the Four Holy Gospels;" " The Athanasian Creed;"
In the Dialect of Kwantung, " The Book of Psalms;"
" The Complete Book of Common Prayer, with Ordinal, &c.;"
In English, " Chapters of Chinese Philosophy," &c. &c. &c.*

LONDON:
TRÜBNER & CO., LUDGATE HILL.
1882.

" Reason itself points out that, in the long-run of years, *the moral standard* of a city or a nation is the grand secret of its prosperity. . . . The sinews of a nation's strength are truthfulness, honesty, sobriety, purity, temperance, economy, diligence, brotherly kindness, charity among its inhabitants, and consequently good credit among mankind. . . . And will any man say that there is a surer way of producing these characteristics in a people than by encouraging and fostering, and spreading and teaching, *pure scriptural* Christianity? "—*Primary Charge of the Right Rev. the Lord Bishop of Liverpool.*

TRANSLATOR'S PREFACE.

It seems proper, in introducing to the English public the following work, that I should briefly state the reasons which induced me to undertake this translation.

Most students of Chinese have, I suppose, felt the hitherto well-nigh insuperable difficulty of obtaining anything like a clear and orderly view of the principles underlying and imbedded in the Confucian philosophy. Yet such a view, most necessary to the statesman, is well-nigh indispensable to the missionary. He certainly will find himself at an immense advantage in making use of whatever principles of eternal truth are already recognised by those to whom he is sent. Finding in this work of the Rev. E. Faber the very key required to unlock the mysteries of Confucianism, I felt I should be doing good service to my brethren in the Chinese portion of the mission-field by making it easily accessible to them in an English dress. Being warmly encouraged in my undertaking by two well-known missionaries and Sinologists, I have at length accomplished what I hope

will prove to be a work of permanent utility to all really
interested in the Chinese. Whilst neither statesmen nor
philosophers will find the system of Mencius perfect,
either as to its political economy or its moral teachings,
the one will respect that economy as having proved practical in its working for nearly 3000 years, whilst the
other will confess that it contains more morality than
others besides the Chinese have ever been able fully to
grasp or completely to carry out. In his researches into
human nature, Mencius will be found to have anticipated
many of the results of modern psychological study. The
appeal made by both Mencius and Confucius, in support of
their alleged Divine mission, to the conformity of their
doctrines with the essentials of the human mind as discovered by observation, rather than to any external
credentials, may suggest one reason why the appeal to
the miracles has generally such little weight in China.
Whilst agreeing in the main with the opinion of my
friend Mr. Faber, I have not thought it necessary to
indicate the few cases in which my personal convictions occasionally compel me to differ from the view
he takes. My share in the work having been carried
out in the brief intervals of rest afforded to a missionary
on furlough by deputation-work (comprising in thirty
months some thirty thousand miles of travel, and nearly
six hundred addresses from pulpit and platform), will
account for any inaccuracies which, in spite of every

endeavour to avoid them, may possibly have crept in. In returning to the missionary field, as I hope shortly to do, I shall be sufficiently rewarded if my labours are found eventually to have contributed in any degree to the much-to-be-desired transference of the Chinese from the sway of the "mind of Mencius" to the easy yoke and rightful dominion of the "mind of Christ."

EXETER, *November* 1881.

PREFACE.

MENCIUS has already been translated into several European languages. Notwithstanding this, the doctrines of this ancient Chinese philosopher are almost unknown; the reason of which is the general lack of system which prevails amongst Chinese authors. One may often read through the production of a Chinese mind, and receive various impressions from it, but yet find it hard to get a systematic view of the whole. Nevertheless it is to be supposed that the embodied thoughts of the most important of Chinese authors is in itself a coherent whole. Of course the Chinese did not think scientifically, in the modern sense; we find, therefore, that instead of a well-arranged system, there is an all-pervading affinity in the truths they proclaim. Each intuition stands in intimate connection with the others. This is especially true of Mencius. So far none but slight attempts have been made to give a characteristic view of the teaching of Mencius. The necessity for a more thorough displaying of this has become increasingly perceptible to me during my literary labours for the Chinese in the last few years. The educated Chinese have, indeed, no practice in the systematic treatment of any subject, but yet such strikes them forcibly when they meet with it. Still it was not this consideration which induced me to present the Chinese with a systematic exposition of the doctrine of Mencius, but

rather the desire of bringing about a well-founded reversion
to dogmas universally and well known throughout China.
Mencius is better suited than any other Chinese author to
serve as a foundation for an explanation of the doctrine of
the Gospel in harmony with the mind of China. In the
year 1872 the plan of this work was commenced, and it
has since been gradually carried out. The first idea was
to proceed in a similar way to that pursued with the
" Digest of the Doctrines of Confucius." [1] The conviction
soon forced itself upon me that it would be better to go
more into detail. In the first place, it was necessary to
find a practical arrangement. It did not appear desirable
to lay down any known plan as a basis, because the
foreign matter would become so much misshapen. Mencius should himself speak, and his teaching find the most
natural, yet well founded and easily recognised grouping.
How far this has been successful the reader now has the
opportunity of proving. Only it should be borne in mind
that the present work is only an extract from a much
larger yet unpublished work, intended for Sinologists. I
hope at a later date to issue a supplement with the
necessary additions in Chinese character. In that the
translation, as far as is necessary, will be supported by
proofs, and antiquarian and historic notices will find a
place.

The quotations from Mencius in the text have subjoined
the page of Dr. Legge's edition of the " Chinese Classics."

This is undoubtedly the best of all the translations that
have been made. Notwithstanding this, I have often felt
obliged to depart more or less from it. The reason is that
Dr. Legge follows only the explanation of Choo-fu-tsze.

[1] " A Systematic Digest of the Doctrines of Confucius." E. Faber.
London, Trübner & Co.

I, on the other hand, have followed the newest and best
commentary, the Mang-tsi Ching I. Although this work
in nine volumes is new, there are very few new views
brought forward in it, but the oldest explanation, that
of Chow Ki, circa 108 A.D., is renewed, established,
strengthened, and used throughout against Choo-fu-tsze,
who lived fifteen hundred years after Mencius, and introduced his Buddhistic philosophic notions into the work of
Mencius. Of course, individually obscure passages are
not lacking; there is, and remains for the interpretation
of such, a possible difference of explanation. Still such
doubtful explanations and translations occur but rarely
in this work. The doctrinal passages are not influenced
thereby.

The translation would be characterised by a critic as
authentic and precise throughout, and generally as adher-
ing, as closely as possible, to the original. Unfortunately
brevity obliged me to leave out many interesting extracts
from the complete commentary before mentioned. That
volume is more suited to students than to the public
generally. On this account many paragraphs of less
importance are omitted here. The titles of these are,
however, given in the table of contents. The complete
rendering of these paragraphs will add to the interest of
the future supplemental volume.

It is to be regretted that Dr. Legge's annotations on
Mencius are so scanty. The later volumes of the Classics
are, in this respect, much better throughout. Dr. Legge's
own remarks in his notes to Mencius show that he has
very little philosophic sympathy with the author.

In the present work the reader is afforded every facility
by its arrangement for understanding the peculiarity of
this Chinese philosopher. The system would very pro-

bably have taken another form in its various parts at the
hands of other labourers. Apart from details, which might
perhaps be improved, I have, for my part, done what I
could, and consider the division into groups the most
natural and correspondent with the matter. The same
may be said for my explanations. But I would have it
kept in mind that I write here for the public at large,
and not merely for Sinologists. I therefore enter more
into the thought which Mencius puts before us in the
text, and seek to bring home the same to the reader's
comprehension. It has likewise been my endeavour to
bring out other and cognate thoughts. I am convinced
that no one who reads thoughtfully will lay down the
book without strong inducement. I must guard myself
at the outset against undue stress being laid on single
passages. It is impossible in every place to say everything that the subject properly requires, in order to render
misconception impossible. The necessary additions or
limitations will generally be found in another paragraph.
It is hardly necessary to add, that I do not profess to
have mastered all the ground covered by the text, with
its peculiar explanations concerning political science, so
as to have been able to handle the subject exhaustively.
I venture one more remark on this head. A twelve years'
study of Chinese in China itself, and a residence, chiefly
as a solitary European, in the town of Fumun, near the
Bocca Tigris, south of Canton, together with unhindered
intercourse with Chinese of all ranks in my place of
residence, as well as when travelling in the interior of the
province of Kwantung, have helped me considerably in
arriving at a correct judgment, a sound conception and
a full comprehension of the philosophy of Mencius, re-
presenting generally the mind of China at its best.

The understanding of modern Chinese is, of course, not all that is required for the explanation of an ancient author. One has to be on one's guard in this respect. Chinese scholars and graduates readily assume a learned expression of countenance to hide their ignorance. Exact study is a very unusual thing in China. The Sinologist who wishes to take up any subject will have to take great trouble, and expend both time and money in finding the necessary material. It appears to me, in reference to obtaining a well-founded understanding of these old classics, urgently necessary, that the whole period of mental activity in China, which reaches back to about 250 B.C., should be mastered on all sides. One old writer sheds light upon another. Properly these should be treated in historic succession. That is, however, very difficult, as there are but few workers. Another way is to begin with an author like Mencius, who is so plain and full of detail. Other necessary works can then follow this as convenient. My plan is nothing less than to go carefully through the collected works of the most ancient times up to about 250 B.C., specially with reference to the doctrine they contain, and then to publish the results as opportunity shall offer. Thus the scheme laid down in the " Digest of Confucius " will, D.V., be carried out, and a sound basis be afforded for a history of the mental life of China.

E. F.

CONTENTS.

BOOK II.

THE PRACTICAL EXHIBITION OF MORAL SCIENCE.

BOOK III.

*THE RESULT AIMED AT IN MORAL DEVELOPMENT:
THE ORGANISATION OF THE STATE.*

INTRODUCTION.

I.

THE FAR-EASTERN QUESTION.

CHINA at the present time is drawing the attention of other nations to herself in a marked manner. Already there is in process of development a Far-Eastern Question that will soon surpass in importance the present Eastern Question. It is very noteworthy that in both cases Russia forms the axis upon which revolves the wheel of events. Besides this, in the far East, as in nearer Asia, Mohametanism is the motive element which tends to bring about the final crisis. Let us not deceive ourselves about the sick man. We must clearly distinguish between Mohametanism and the Turkish Empire. Turkey may perish, Mohametanism, mightier than it has been for a hundred years, is now steadily advancing throughout Africa and Asia. A spark may cause the explosion of its dynamite-like fanaticism, terribly shatter the dominion of England in India, place the possessions of Holland in peril, cost the lives of innumerable Christians, and subjugate at least all Asia and Africa to the Crescent. Mohametanism is a Great Power, not owing to a national principle, for it is international; not owing to material interests—it is the power of Faith which inspires it, whereby it binds together savage and inimical tribes. Monotheism is the truth upon which Islam stands, and

A

fatalism the two-edged sword in its hand. We see in it the antichristian bitterness of Judaism re-aroused, and endued with greater power than of old. Fixed monotheism has yet its mission in the world, so long as polytheism exists. Mohametan fanaticism serves as the scourge of God, whose corrective task cannot be entirely completed whilst in the presence of a degenerate Christendom, paralysed amidst its external forms, dragging on its existence without inner spiritual life, and offering, as of old under Byzantine rule, a Christianised heathenism, earthy and sensuous.

Russia stands ready, like the Byzantine Church risen from the grave, sorely chastened yet not killed, a brazen wall against which break the waves of Mohametanism, crimsoned with Christian blood.

The overpowering position of Russia in Europe may arouse feelings of jealousy, especially in her German neighbours; the proximity of this Colossus may fill them with horror; we may abhor this imperial-papal despotism, because it compresses all religious life in iron bands, and makes impossible all higher development, all spiritual freedom. Nevertheless Russia has in Asia a future full of promise. Were Russian influence to extend farther westwards, it would be hurtful not only to Europe but to Russia herself. The natural destiny of Russia is back from Europe towards Central Asia. But before all things Russia needs a higher spiritual elevation, which must come from herself by the placing of the Evangelical and Romish Churches on a footing of equality with the Russo-Greek, and also from the fostering of all noble scientific and philanthropic endeavours. The spectral dread before all parties is superstitious. No state is injured by the presence within its territories of conflicting religious and scientific schools, nor even by political parties, so long as the aim of all is a moral one, and right and justice are paramount in every department of government. Russia has a great future if she only understood how to grasp it.

We are obliged to glance at Russia as the power amongst modern states which seems called upon to seal the destiny of Mohametanism in Europe. The European Eastern Question might conveniently solve itself best alone, but not so the more recently propounded Central Asiatic problem, nor the Far-Eastern Question.

England has at present a more powerful position in Asia than has Russia. England is also much in advance of Russia as the oldest Protestant state; she stands at the head of European civilisation, possesses excellent laws, a body of officials of the highest class, an able government, public and well-managed administration of justice, free commerce, and she seeks also the elevation of Asia. But in English colonial policy, civilisation is not itself the aim; it is only the means for furthering the interests of commerce. The Asiatic is offered protection and individual freedom; but with these, owing to the superiority of English industry, he is degraded to a beast of burden merely to prolong his existence. England becomes wealthy, India ever poorer. Her government itself has often declared that it cannot do without the profits resulting from the opium monopoly. The many millions of dollars which China pays yearly for opium must help to defray the cost of English civilisation in India. India, one of the most beautiful, most fruitful of all countries, is unable, under English dominion, to raise enough to support its own government! No wonder that this sort of civilisation is not loved or admired in the East. Neither England nor Englishmen are popular in Asia. Who does not know this? England seeks, indeed, to win the confidence of her subjects, and that successfully, in small things; but in great matters destroys everything by her utilitarian, self-seeking, retail policy. It is seeking, so to speak, the friendship of the Bengal tiger, the trying to ameliorate the condition of the Mohametans in India until everything shall be transformed to their views. Indeed it is not so long since there was, under Christian rule, full freedom for the propaganda of Mohametanism, whilst Christian missions were hindered and even forbidden.

In opposition to Mohametanism, Russia has ever followed a plain and firm policy. Thence it is, notwithstanding this, the most beloved of all the great powers, at least in China. England is only feared, and that simply so long as she is powerful. France is hated. Her policy in Asia is simply to be the representative of the interests of the Church of Rome. Therefore it is that the Asiatic fails both to appreciate and understand it. The United States represent hitherto a policy which we can really call one of free Christian conviction, in foreign lands as well as in America itself. Unfortunately the organisation of the consular service is very defective, depending upon the change of President : in this respect the English system has the advantage. Germany has already commenced to look after her interests in Eastern Asia. In Germany philosophy and politics yet go hand in hand, and just now the philosophy of the Unknown has in a manner the upper hand, so that we ought not to wonder if Germany should represent in Asia, as in the East, the policy of the Unknown.

China has now in the north a long frontier line common to Russia, which latter has already won in the Amoor territory a commanding situation, just as in Ili in the west. By means of the Siberian railway, Russia has established connections with the headquarters of her power, and is prepared to make the full weight of that power perceptible in the farthest East in the shortest space of time. In the West the Anglo-Indian empire already extends to China. France, through her colony in Cochin-China, has already become a near neighbour. The long sea-coast stands open to all navies. Japan appears to desire to raise herself into the position of the Britain of the East. The long diplomatic negotiations of France with China concerning the Tientsin massacre, of England about the murder of

Mr. Margary (and the yet unratified Chefoo Convention), of consuls and explorers for a direct overland channel for commerce to and from India, of Germany *in ré* the piracy of the merchant ship *Anna*, and of all the representatives of the West, which resulted in an audience of the Emperor, are well known. China is thus surrounded on all sides by powerful but diversely constituted states, and begins herself to be a factor in European affairs. The times when any people can go their own peculiar way are over. International intercourse will ever henceforward be a condition of existence for states in modern civilisation. The stream cannot be turned back again to its source. The barriers with which China sought to defend herself against the rolling waves of foreign intercourse are destroyed. China henceforth must be included in the common civilised life of the Western Powers. But against this China struggles. One meets at first with stubborn opposition. Chinese civilisation is unique, and has come down from the Chinese themselves. They hold fast to it as to their very existence. Other relations are found at least unpractical, and many wrong. China sees only the bright side of her own civilisation; and whilst feeling at times its pressure, she lays the onus, not upon the system, but upon the age or upon some individual. She sees much of the dark side of our Western civilisation, and has little opportunity of studying accurately and learning to appreciate the beautiful and good belonging to it. In a word, she fails to comprehend the foreign. In order to pave the way for this, a medium of communication from our side is necessary, a comparative explanation of the principles of our civilisation with those of the Chinese. In order to the carrying out of this in a thorough and convincing manner, we must ourselves first acquire a thorough knowledge of the Chinese nature. It is not enough to learn to recognise in a general way the difference between the present and the past forms of social and political life. The characteristic of China is her constant and continuous intimate connection with her oldest antiquity. Her language, her literature, her religion, her justice, her science, even her manners and customs, always base their validity upon a reference to the most ancient writings which embody the spiritual life of China. The ancient, the classic, is yet the authoritative in China, and even when not strictly obligatory, is still the moral law. Therefore it is that an accurate acquaintance with the contents of the classic writings of Chinese antiquity is not only of antiquarian value, and of extreme scientific interest, but is of the greatest practical importance. One can make daily use of it in China, and that with success.

The Chinese are conservative in the fullest meaning of the word, and as such are born enemies to all innovation, but they are in nowise disinclined (as they are often thought to be) to the widening of the social edifice upon the ancient well-proved foundations. Every innovation is not necessarily a step in advance, nor is every step in advance progress. This is only the case when it results from or attaches itself to that which is already recognised as good, and has stood the test of proof. The Chinese wishes everything to become Chinese to him, *i.e.*, to lead him back to Chinese foundation principles, and thence prove to be either a higher development or the correction of a deviation.[1] This desire has its value. Where several apparently opposing views come into contact, it is necessary to find a common platform, then to bring forward the common numerator from the midst of the various ideas, and thus slowly and surely lead to the climax of the representative view. Evangelical missions in China are working out this problem. Men may think of this as they will, and have this and that to censure in individual missionaries; they are

[1] In reference to the teaching of evangelic faith and practice, the author has worked this out in his Commentary on St. Mark, 5 vols., Religious Tract Society, Hong-Kong; likewise in German Educational Principles, 1 vol., and On Education, 1 vol., Rhenish Mission House, Canton, and Library, Shanghai. These works are all in classic Chinese (Wen-li).

but men. One thing is certain. Evangelical missions are the bearers to China of the genuine human international spirit of Christendom. All evangelical salvation for the religious and moral life of the individual and the community must be brought about for the common weal of all peoples and languages, by no other power than that of the Word and the Spirit. Protestantism, in spite of all its divisions, shows itself in this respect as one evangelical Church, as a spiritual and Divine power for the regeneration of the world.

II.

OF THE IMPORTANCE OF CHINESE TO MODERN SCIENCE.

China forms a world in itself. The Chinese language and literature is the ideal impression of this world. Every language is the result of the spiritual development of the human community which uses it. In the language of a people their history lies embodied in a peculiar way. By means of its language a people stands likewise in intimate connection with the whole of the rest of mankind. In this our day hundreds of languages are spoken, of which many do not appear to have the slightest trace of resemblance to one another. The science of language has nevertheless already accomplished much towards bringing back these apparently opposed tongues into their radically relative groups. In reference to the Aryan and Semitic groups we have already attained to firm scientific laws, and at the same time to the end of inquiry in many directions. With the confusion of the languages of Eastern, Central, and North Asia the task is more difficult, although even here the clue already begins to unwind itself. The Aryan group offers the inestimable advantage of an established grammar as a firm starting-point for comparative examination. The same is also the case with the Semitic, but it is quite different in regard to by far the greater number of agglutinative languages. Still more difficult is the inquiry where, as in the Chinese, grammar is entirely wanting. Yet the Chinese may possibly supply the key to many unsolved problems in the study of languages, both on account of its being one of the oldest of languages (certainly the oldest of living tongues), and because in many ways it remains in its primitive condition.

Chinese is, in the first place, a general term, like Indian or European. We may, indeed, rightly speak of a Chinese written language, but not of one Chinese spoken language, because there are many such. These several languages in China have hardly been scientifically studied, certainly not sufficiently so. We require, in the first place, the fullest possible collocation of the same, in order that, by comparison of the values of words and their phonetic relations, we may be assured concerning the radical words still existing in Chinese—possibly also be enabled to find their oldest forms, and thus fully and securely lay down the laws for the changes in pronunciation. It is important, in the next place, to compare the positions of words in the formation of sentences, and so obtain a view of the variety in the construction of the Chinese languages. We should thus be placed in a position to pronounce with some degree of certainty what was the original construction and what the later development. Only when Chinese is studied in this way can it be placed on an equal footing with other great groups of languages with a view to scientific results.[1]

To study Chinese in this way is not so difficult as it appears at first sight. At the present time there are educated Europeans dwelling in nearly all the provinces

[1] China's Place in Philology, and Introduction to the Study of the Chinese Characters, are the best works on this subject, but yet very unsatisfactory on account of the lack of the necessary preliminary information. The Syllabic Dictionary of the Chinese Language, by Dr. S. Wells Williams, may also be mentioned here.

of the empire, as well as in the neighbouring countries. These might be induced to engage in the requisite preliminary work. The stimulus is all that is lacking. Besides this, it is indispensable for such work to have a qualified director of solid practical experience—one who should understand how to value rightly the material accumulated; and thus another want is indicated.

In Chinese literature there is for us another matter of great scientific interest. It has effected many transformations. By means of it we can travel back through a period of at least 4000 years, of which we otherwise know but little. The most ancient characters, of which there are only about 200, supply us with so many outlines of the natural and social history of that venerable antiquity. It has recently been discovered that resemblances occur between the composition of several of the characters and those of ancient Egypt and Babylon.[1] In all three of these kinds of writing, derivatives are formed by the union of the primitive with the classifier or radical.

The literature of China has, besides its antiquarian interest, much to engage the attention of the modern world. As throughout this the Arabic numerals are almost universally used, being pure symbols without reference to their sound, so might a modified Chinese writing become the most proper medium for universal intercommunication. For this are required only about from 1000 to 2000 selected signs for as many ideas (not forms of words). The form of each sign being so given that the idea could be recognised, writing would be easy. On the other hand, Chinese writing is altogether unsuited for the various departments of science. Present endeavours in that direction must soon increase the number of characters to a million (*e.g.*, for every plant a separate character, &c.).

The literature is one of the oldest and comprehensive

---

[1] Cf. L. de Rosny and G. Schlegel, Sinico Aryaca, and Dr. R. K. Douglas, The Language and Literature of China.

in the world, that of our own day of course being excepted.[1]

For the study of natural history it contains a mass of important observations of numberless natural phenomena, astronomical,[2] meteorological, and geological; also many notices of plants and animals. The scientific study of China might every way become of greater importance, especially for geology and palæontology.

For practical medicine, agriculture, and many branches of industry there is abundance of most valuable material in both ancient and modern works.[3]

Chinese literature is also a rich storehouse of information on topography, folklore, and history, not only of China proper, but also of all Central Asia, Eastern Asia, and the territories to the north, even into Siberia.[4] On the south, also, a portion of the islands comes into consideration. The literature of China is almost the only source of information concerning the people, the language, and ancient history of this extensive territory. The value of Chinese in this respect is well understood, but at present a beginning has hardly been made towards mastering its treasures. It is singular that the history of the laws and governments of these the oldest states in the world have been so little studied.[5] Much could be extracted from it of importance for the circumstances of our own day. China has successfully treated many social problems which are only commencing for us. We find there first the old feudal

---

[1] *Vide* Schott, Entwurf u. Beschreibung der Chin Literartur, and that most comprehensive work of Wylie, Notes on Chinese Literature.

[2] On Chinese astronomy Biot treats, Précis de l'Histoire de l'Astronomie Chinoise; and G. Schlegel, Uranographie Chinoise.

[3] There are a few monographs by Porter Smith, Dr. J. Dudgeon, St. Julien, P. Champion, Leon d'Hervey St. Denys.

[4] Cf. the new edition of Marco Polo, the works of Philipps, C. Bret-schneider, Von Richthofen, Bastian, G. Pauthier, A. Pfzmaier, W. F. Mayers, besides many papers in the China Review and Missionary Recorder.

[5] Dr. J. Hein. Plath's Essays in the Royal Academy of Sciences at Munich contain a few studies of this kind. Also the translation of the penal code of China by G. T. Staunton. Cf. Warn. König, Juristische Encyclopädie, and China das Reich der Mitte, by Gustav Klem..

system, then a number of almost sovereign states surrounding the supreme authority; later still a monarchy, gradually extending towards universal dominion. Amongst her statesmen various principles are represented; various opposing parties amongst the people, which coming into conflict with each other, have modified the government. Free associations have existed for a long time amongst the people, enabling them to protect themselves against their officials (executive) and fellow-citizens, as well as beggars and thieves, or great bands of robbers and pirates. There are united societies for mutual help and for savings, some having a philanthropic aim, others of a political tendency, others again devoted to literary undertakings. There are commercial corporations, guilds, and all kinds of clubs. Generally speaking, there has existed a many-sided, consolidated social life throughout the empire, which one finds scarcely mentioned in those works which up to the present have been written on China.[1]

The philosophy of China and its development is for the most part unknown. The works of the most important writers for this purpose have not only not yet been translated,[2] but so lightly is that which has already been published passed over, that it is held of no account whatever; and learned professors, in their histories of philosophy, generalise thus, "The philosophy of China is properly no philosophy." Of course the Chinese have not undertaken

[1] The present social life of the Chinese has been well treated of by W. Williams, F. Davis, De Huc, J. Doolittle, Nevius, &c.

[2] At present it is only the works of the Confucianists which are reckoned canonical which have been translated. Of philosophers proper, only Lau Tan has been thus honoured. Abel Remusat writes well of him. St. Julien gives a good sound translation, collecting the text and notes from several commentaries. The German work of R. V. Plaenkner gives us his own ideas, but scarcely those of Lau Tan. That of Herr V. Strauss is much better, in several places very good, but throughout there is too much foreign colouring. The assumption that Lau has been misunderstood by all the Chinese, and first rightly comprehended by Herr V. Strauss, is worthless. Monographs by Neuman and Meadows have appeared on the philosophy of China in the middle ages, and in Canon M'Clatchie's The Chinese and their Rebellions. No sinologist has yet treated of the philosophy of the last 650 years. See also my Digest of Confucius.

those researches into the regions of theoretical knowledge which too frequently seem to be taken as the only standard. In spite of this, it is a matter of great interest to learn upon what problems the Chinese mind has generally been engaged. For that it must have thought we cannot but suppose, for the great literature of China has not grown upon its trees nor arisen out of chaos. Some interest there would be in seeing which ideas have come into prominence from the thinking of these Chinese, and on what basis they have sought to establish their speculations. We may be sure, and the system of Mencius will make it plain, that the ideas contained in Chinese philosophy are scarcely inferior in importance to those of the Greek. The form is, of course, of importance in a system of philosophy, but it does not constitute its nature, which is found in its ideas, thoughts, and principles.[1]

Chinese Buddhism, with its abundant literature, is of special importance for the history of religion. This is partly translated from the Indian (Sanskrit) and partly original, and its value has already been recognised.[2] The religious elements which are occasionally met with in the more ancient literature have not yet received sufficient attention.

Even the wealth of poetry is almost unknown, save that recently the department of fiction has been diligently worked.[3]

We see that there lies before us in Sinology a broad and fallow field, yet scarcely any other territory is so uncared for. The cause is easily ascertained. The merchants and officials of Europe and America who reside in China

[1] Specially worthy of note is Chwang - tze, the most important thinker of the classic period, contemporary of Mencius. His style is often obscure, and requires the close consultation of several commentaries. No translation has yet been published of this writer.

[2] Cf. the works of Rev. S. Beal, St. Julien, and Dr. E. J. Eitel.

[3] By St. Julien, Bazin Aîné, and many others. Cf. On the Poetry of the Chinese, Sir J. F. Davis. Proverbs, which form a kind of didactic popular poetry, have recently been collected by the Rev. W. Scarborough ; see also P. Perny and Sir J. F. Davis.

take, with very few exceptions, no interest in earnest
studies. Missionaries, who have hitherto accomplished
the chief work, have yet too many claims on them from
their vocation. One ought not on this account to reproach
missionaries, as is often done in no gentle way by their
opponents. The proper *rôle* of the missionary is not the
opening out of scientific paths. He is a channel for
certain ideas.[1] He has the department of morals and
religion as his field of labour. From this point of view
he is to be regarded as a worker, and not to be classed
with the mass of foreigners. Still, as a means for the
working out of his great problem, the missionary will
study closely his field of operations, regarding as factors
Chinese life and thought, the everyday manners and
customs, and the literature. Thus missions have yielded
many fruitful results for science (the present work being
one such). The missionary is also seldom in the most
favourable position for having recourse to a good library
of the best literature. It is to be hoped that the example
of France, recently followed in England, may be copied
also in Germany. Should the cultivation of Chinese by
representatives in the universities be at present impossible,
yet a gifted professor like Abel Remusat, Biot, or others,
might secure in part a well-grounded treatment of the
language. It is most important that the results of many
individual researches which are embodied in magazines
and fugitive papers, or in rare and costly volumes in Latin,
French, English, German, and Russian, should be collected
together and made available for public inspection. Thus
the student would be enabled to see quickly what has

[1] The most important literary
achievements of the missionary undertaken for the Chinese ought here
to be taken account of. Much has
already been done in this way; not
only are little tracts published in
Chinese, but the whole of the
Sacred Scriptures in various versions, many comprehensive theolo-
gical works, with translations or
original compositions in nearly all
departments of science. Such works
form already a library. What, on
the other hand, have the opponents
of missions done—the thousands of
well-to-do merchants and officials,
with their friends and adherents?
Even if men have no love for missions, let them be just in their opposition.

been done, and provide himself with the best equipment for pressing forward into the yet unexplored territory. The reflex action upon European science would be speedily perceived by the advantages secured.

III.

A BRIEF CONSPECTUS OF CHINESE CLASSIC LITERATURE ANTERIOR TO MENCIUS.

At the head of the classics of China stands " The Book of Documents," simply called "The Book." It contains imperial decrees and ministerial orders from about 1200 years B.C., or even a little earlier. This book is specially valuable for the history of the ancient laws and government of China. " The Book of Odes " contains popular poems and sacrificial hymns belonging to the same period as that of the documents. It presents us with many glimpses of the social and national life of those days. These two works form the foundation of the collected ancient literature and developed civilisation of the Chinese. China ever remains in most intimate connection with the ideas of these two books, for they form the plan for the mental training of the Chinese both of ancient and modern times, being constantly subjects for examination. Concerning "The Book of Changes"[1] I have treated in the " Digest of Confucius." This work began first to influence Chinese literature in the time of the Han dynasty, which rose about a century after Mencius. It first brought Taoism into harmony with Confucianism. The same experiment was tried later on by the Tung philosophers, who first introduced their ideas derived from Buddhism into the obscurity of the diagrams of " The Book of

---

[1] The translation of this by Dr. Legge, for his invaluable Chinese Classics, is now in the press.

Changes," and then proved out of it that Confucianism had long had the truth of Buddhistic doctrine. It would at that time have been easy to have withstood the error, but a good many Buddhistic ideas were in this way transferred to orthodox Confucianism. Mencius does not mention this book in a single case, but, on the other hand, he frequently quotes the "Documents" and "Odes." "The Chronicles of the State of Lu," and especially the three commentaries upon it, form the bridge between the "Documents" and "Odes" and our philosophers. There were also several other historical works, which have been lost, a remnant only being preserved in the later great history of the Chinese Herodotus, as we may call Sze-ma-tsin.[1]

As in Greece philosophy did not begin with Plato and Aristotle, so in China Lao Tan and Confucius were not the first. Of the more ancient philosophers there only remain a few sentences, but nothing collected. Confucius and Lau likewise only left behind them fragmentary sayings, so that it is not easy to give a clear and systematic representation of their doctrine.

Lau was a contemporary of Confucius. His doctrine is mystico-pantheistic. His school soon placed itself in open opposition to the orthodoxy of Confucius. The pantheism of the master soon fell into shameless sensualism (sensationalism) in the hands of one of its chief representatives, Yang-shu. In the time of Mencius this section made a great noise and spread rapidly. On the other side of the school of Lau the chief thinkers lost themselves in scepticism, *e.g.*, Lih-tze and Chwang-tze, and the crowd soon plunged into the depths of superstition.

Confucius, on the other hand, represented the standpoint of humanity. To him man was the worthiest object of thought and action. He regarded men not in a one-sided or abstract way, but in their individual as well as in their social and political relations. Political economy is

[1] A translation of this is in hand, with a commentary, by my friend and colleague, Rev. W. Dilthey.

therefore the constant aim and corrective of his philosophy. Ethics were to him so closely bound up with external forms or rites, that his disciples for the most part lost themselves in the rites and neglected the morals.

Besides these schools of thought, and soon in opposition to them, stood a third, not less interesting, viz., socialism. Mih Teh, the most important representative of Chinese socialism, lived about the same time as Confucius, circa 450 B.C. The common weal was to be placed in the foreground; the highest moral act of the individual was found in making sacrifices for all. All art was to be cast away as luxury; simplicity was insisted upon, also equality and indiscriminate love. His followers went farther, until the extremest communism was reached, not only of goods, but of position and occupations also. Every one, princes not excepted, was to build his own granary and make his own clothes.

The advocates of socialism and communism were getting the upper hand after the death of Confucius. Then stepped forward to oppose them in the field, and with them the other extreme of sensationalism, a doughty warrior from the camp of Confucianism, or political conservatism. That was Mencius. He lived from B.C. 372–289, and was the contemporary of Plato and Aristotle. Mencius is the most important representative of the Confucian school, which then had broken up into several discordant parties.

The doctrines of Mencius were collected by his disciples without regard to order and published. This work received at a later date canonical recognition. We can indeed say in all truth that Mencius is now the darling of the Chinese. Out of the whole range of their literature there is no other work which is such a living reality as Mencius. As a schoolbook it is learnt by heart by the little children, and its style is such, that even if they are not thorough scholars, it is in a measure intelligible to them. For the examination of the scholars it offers a favourite text for essay-writing (besides the writings of Confucius in a wider sense). The chief *dicta* of modern Chinese ethics and politics are mostly taken literally from Mencius, or adhere closely to his teaching. The teaching of Mencius is even more fully and comprehensively contained in the canonical books than is that of Confucius. His style is lively and interesting, the form being for the most part either dialogue or narrative. In many places he is quite racy in his discussions, again he is mystical or metaphysical. In this, however, he is decidedly inferior to his contemporary Chwang, the most important thinker of that time.

Mencius is, like his master Confucius, simply a teacher of political economy. To him the State is the sum of all human endeavours, natural and civilised, working together as a united organisation. Through his direct opposition to the socialist, and in lesser degree to the sensationalist, Mencius saw himself necessitated to base his political economy upon ethics, and his ethics upon the doctrine of man's nature. The ethical problem is for him the utmost development of all the good elements of man's nature. The problem of the organisation of the state is, under what conditions can the highest aim be set before it? and then that the government shall consciously endeavour to bring about those conditions.

IV.

DETAILED ANALYSIS OF THE SYSTEM OF MENCIUS.

BOOK I.

THE ELEMENTS OF MORAL SCIENCE.

PART I.—PROPERTIES.

CHAP. I.—MAN'S ESSENTIAL NATURE.

(*a.*) *Defined.*

ART.

1. All experience is founded on phenomena.
2. "Life" too vague and comprehensive a term.
3. "The appetites" an improper term.
4. Form and beauty constitute man's nature.
5. Not of many kinds, but homogeneous and good.
6. The type of each and all found in kind and likeness.
7. Permits neither of increase nor of diminution externally.
8. It is inherently connected with heaven.

(*b.*) *Man's Nature Developed.*

9. Diversity depends upon the degree of development.
10. Perversion to the earthly.
11. Natural development differs from artificial treatment.
12a. The law within is opposed to influences from without.
12b. The energies of man's nature destroyed from without.
13. Diversity of action has its cause within.
14. Freedom of choice : (*a.*) internal decision ; (*b.*) external.

Chap. III.—Heaven.

The Relation of Heaven to Man.

(a.) *Its Gifts.*

ART.

36. The life of man ; the cause of causes.
37. The senses and the understanding.
38. The highest nobility and its constituents.
39. The throne, officials and revenue.
40. In these Providence declares itself for the people.
41. Misfortune.
42. Man can avert misfortune by a change of mind.

(b.) *Heaven's Action.*

43. In all spontaneous growth.
44. In the harmonising of occurrences.
45. In that which is impossible to man.
46. Overrules men, also their evil intentions.
47. Corresponds to the mind of the people (vox populi).
48. Governs states.
49. Prepares for itself the proper individuals.
50. Perfects that which man (the superior) has commenced.

(c.) *Human Conduct with Regard to Heaven.*

51. Recognition of the heavenly.
52. Delight in and fear of heaven.
53. The service of heaven.
54. Cultivation of the heavenly nobility.
55. Men fellow-workers with God.

(d.) *The World of Spirits.*

56. Spirits are men a degree higher than the holy.
57. The spirits of the land rank between the people and the ruler.
58. The tutelary spirits are punishable.
59. Besides these there are a hundred kinds of spirits.
60. They are from God.

Chap. IV.—Tao, or the Universal Reign of Law.

(a.) *Laws of Various Kinds.*

Art.

61. The Law of Yaou and Shun, filial piety and brotherly kindness.
62. Of the ancients, not eating and drinking.
63. Of the student, to seek the lost heart.
64. Of the difference between wealth and benevolence.
65. Of bravery, or the acquiring of an unmovable heart.
66. Of women, submissiveness.
67. Of the people, dependent upon nourishment.
68. Of communism : princes ought to obtain food and clothing by their own labour.
69. Of art and skilled labour, not contrary to the master.
70. Is a maxim of business.
71. Several deviations from duties.
72. Amidst the variety of law (Tao) the aim the same.

(b.) *Of the Tao (Law) which ought to Guide Men.*

73. The true *Tao* is only one.
74. It consists in affection for sublime virtue.
75. In benevolence.
76. In the five social relations.
77. In filial piety and brotherly kindness.
78. The *Tao* is near to man.
79. The recognition of the same is easy.
80. No compromise therein.
81. Personal example is important.
82. It makes a difference to the realm whether *Tao* rules or not.
83. Variety of individual conduct.
84. Only *Tao* can save a falling state.
85. Benevolence belongs to *Tao* as its completion.

Chap. V.—Destiny.

86. There is a destiny for external things (determination).
87. The right destiny is conformity to *Tao*.

BOOK II.

THE PRACTICAL EXHIBITION OF MORAL SCIENCE.

PART I.—THE INDIVIDUAL CHARACTER.

Chap. I.—The Scholar.

PART II.—THE ETHICO-SOCIAL RELATIONS.

CHAP. I.—FATHER AND SON.

(a.) *The Father.*

(b.) *The Son.*

(c.) *Reciprocal Relations of Father and Son.*

CHAP. II.—BRETHREN, ELDER AND YOUNGER.

CHAP. III.—FRIENDS.

CHAP. IV.—MAN AND WIFE.

CHAP. V.—THE SOVEREIGN AND THE MINISTERS.

SECT. I.—THE SOVEREIGN INDIVIDUALLY.

Art.

346. Preachers of humanity and righteousness are to be supported.

347. Leaves blood-revenge to the people.

SECT. III.—THE RULER AS FEUDAL PRINCE OR EMPEROR.

(a.) *Feudal Princes.*

348. A fief is an office dependent upon the Emperor.

349. Feudal princes are rewarded or punished by the Emperor.

350. A confederation of princes.

(b.) *Feudal Princes may aspire to Imperial Dignity.*

351. Unity is strength.

352. There ought to be no wrong perpetrated on that account.

353. The people the political foundation for the Emperor.

354. The people gather round him who protects them.

355. Humane government is the only way to power.

356. Inhumanity loses what humanity gains.

357a.Humanity wins the heart of men.

357b.No enforcing of goodness.

358. Neither great family influence nor long time is requisite.

359. Humanity finds no enemy.

360. An adverse criticism on the *Shoo King*, based on the above theories.

361. No military operations are required.

362. The virtue of humanity is characterised by its effects.

363. The examples of Tang and Woo.

364. At times a humane prince is able to serve another smaller state.

365. Previously excepted imperial prerogative is no hindrance.

(c.) *The Ruler as Emperor.*

366a.Inspection of the feudal princes.

366b.This should not be a pleasure excursion at the cost of the country.

C

Sect. IV.—Ministers.

1. Their Prerequisites, Duties, and Failures.

(a.) *Preparation of Ministers.*

(b.) *Minister seeking Office.*

BOOK III.

RESULT OR AIM OF MORAL DEVELOPMENT: THE ORGANISATION OF THE STATE.

ART.

428. Times to be appointed for agricultural operations (the calendar).
429. The government is answerable for the welfare of the people.
430. Inspection of public husbandry necessary.
431. No neglect of work to be tolerated.

(b.) Commerce.

432. The essential condition of this is the division of labour.
433. The motive is the value of the product.
434. Chief requirements are markets, bridges, roads, &c.
435a. Luxury and extravagance are to be prevented.
435b. In time of need, human food not to be given to cattle.

(c.) Taxes.

436. The tenth, for the necessary requirements of a civilised state.
437. Better in the form of performance of work (socage) than in a direct share of goods.
438. The ancient agrarian system.
439. The doubling of taxes (fifths) to be strongly condemned.
440. Taxes at the boundaries.
441. Customs to be abolished—free trade.
442. Marshes and ponds ought to be kept common.
443. The leading principle is that true wealth does not consist in gold and silver.

CHAP. II.—NATIONAL EDUCATION: ITS THEORY, SCHOOLS, TEACHERS, METHOD, AND MUSIC.

(a.) Theory.

444. Moral culture as well as physical is indispensable to the state.
445. Education is not a suppression but a drawing out.
446. Therefore the people fear good government but love good instruction.
447. Guidance of the people by personal example.

THE MIND OF MENCIUS.

Book I.

THE ELEMENTS OF MORAL SCIENCE.

PART I.—CONCERNING PROPERTIES.

CHAPTER I.

MAN'S ESSENTIAL NATURE.

(*a.*) *The Idea Defined.*

1. "It is only from phenomena that the world draws its conclusions;" it fails to apprehend their causes or fundamental realities [1] (p. 207). But, unfortunately, it often happens that delusive inferences are drawn from the facts observed, and thus false conclusions are arrived at instead of the truth.[2]

2. Kaou, one of the philosophers of that day, maintained that man's essential nature consisted in life. Mencius replied, "'Is life, then, to be called the essential nature, just as white is called white?' Being answered in the affirmative, he continued, 'Is, then, the white of a white

---

[1] The numbers in brackets throughout refer to the page in Dr. Legge's Chinese Classics—"Mencius."

[2] Dr. Whewell has pointed out the difference between the ultimate *causes* of the facts themselves and the *laws* which govern the occurrence of phenomena generally in his "Philosophy of Inductive Sciences," ii. 260.—Tr.

feather like the white of snow, and this again as that of
a gem?' Kaou again replied, 'It is.' 'Then, verily,' said
Mencius, ' the nature of the dog is the same as that of the
ox, and the nature of the ox the same as that of man ' "
(p. 272). It is well shown by the illustration that "life"
as a definition is too universal, *i.e.*, it is too comprehensive,
and fails in the determination of characteristic differences.

3. Upon the same philosopher, Kaou, affirming that "the
appetite for food and the sexual appetite constitute man's
nature" (p. 273), Mencius vouchsafed no answer, for he did
not consider the lower sensualism worthy of his attention.
It was, indeed, already confuted by the simple fact that
the sensual appetites and enjoyments are not the highest
of which human nature is susceptible. The capacity for
higher things is the characteristic of humanity.[1]

4. Mencius maintained, on the contrary (p. 348), "Form
and beauty constitute our heaven-imparted nature; but
one must first be a holy man, then can he manifest the
(true) form." The external corresponds to the internal,
at least in its main features. Man is no dualism of body
and soul, but as man he possesses an essential unity of
nature, even if his origin be dualistic. In Europe this
fact has long been overlooked, that every organ of the
body corresponds to some peculiar attribute of the soul,
or, in other words, the body and the soul mutually condition each other. But in saying this we do not affirm the
one to be the cause of the other. They are neither opposites
nor are they identical, and neither are they the internal and
the external of the same things. The Chinese fall into this
latter mistake when avoiding the former.

5. Men have not various natures, but the nature of all

---

[1] "Among these [principles of
action by which a man may be led]
we must give a high place to the
propensity to seek that which is
known to communicate pleasure and
avoid that which is expected to in-
flict pain, and this in regard either
to ourselves or others. But they
take a miserably defective view of
man's nature who represent him as
incapable of being swayed by any
other motive, better or worse "
(M'Cosh, *Divine Government*, p.
416).

men is homogeneous and good. Kung-too, one of his
disciples, by bringing to the notice of Mencius the principal opinions of that day concerning human nature,
obtained from him a fuller explanation (p. 277). (*a.*)
" Kaou affirmed that the nature of men was neither good
nor the reverse " (consequently there is only necessity, no
freedom); (*b.*) " another maintained that man's nature may
be made good or the reverse through external influences "
(this is distinct from good and evil unknown, but artificially caused from without) ; (*c.*) " a third maintained that
there are good natures and evil natures," and he adduced
as examples from ancient time, that the best sovereign
had a bad minister; the most reprobate father had a most
excellent son ; a tyrant of a ruler, being an elder brother,
had noble younger brethren as his subordinates. (This
indicates the immutability of one's nature.) Every man's
nature retains its original direction notwithstanding circumstances the most unfavourable for its preservation.
Of these opinions the third is directly opposed to the
second; the possibility of such absolutely contradictory
views clearly manifests their deceptive one-sidedness. The
disciple continues, " If it is now affirmed that man's nature
is good, then each of these views is altogether wrong."
Mencius replied, " As far it concerns the emotions, it is
possible for one to do that which is good ; it is this which
is termed good. But if one does that which is not good,
it is not the fault of his disposition. The three former
views display a lack of reflection." According to the
Commentary, men have emotions of two different sorts ;
those from within, which arise from man's real nature
and which are good, and others which come from without
through the senses and tend to that which is not good.
He who wishes to define the idea of a genus or of a species
has, in the first place, to discover amidst the multiplicity
of phenomena that which is most perfect, and therefore
most characteristic, and with this to establish the type.
Then every deviation appears not so much a development

as a variety occasioned by many circumstances preventing or modifying the full manifestation of the original type itself. In the holy or ideal man, Mencius, like Confucius, contemplates this original type (of humanity).[1] Of this more hereafter.

6. The type consists in kind, hence the resemblance between all individuals (p. 280). "All things of the same species have on that account an all-pervading resemblance to each other; why, then, should we doubt that this is also the case in reference to men? The holy are of the same kind with ourselves." The context elaborates this idea, viz., that there is an analogy between human nature and "the form of the feet, the taste of the mouth, the hearing of the ear, the sight of the eyes." Mencius closes with this *résumé:* "Therefore I say that (with all men) the mouth has the same relish as to taste," *i.e.*, perceives salt to be saltish, sweetness to be sweet, &c., "the ears have the same perception of sounds, the eyes have the same impression as to colour. Shall it be given to hearts alone to be without anything in common? What is it then which is common to all hearts? This is 'the ideas and righteousness.' Holy men apprehend sooner than others that which is common to our hearts. Therefore our heart rejoices in 'ideas and in righteousness' just as our mouth enjoys the flesh of fatlings." The Commentary says, by way of explanation, "The mouth, ears, nose, &c., are the organs for external impressions, and the heart is the organ for ideas and righteousness. These are likewise not external, *i.e.*, not through the senses. Those organs of sense are able everywhere to distinguish impressions of taste, smell, &c. The heart is able everywhere to arouse to action 'the ideas and righteousness.' Thus the natural disposition which man has from heaven becomes perfected. It is not hereby asserted that man's nature generally consists in that which is common to all, but in that which their hearts have in common in ideas and a sense of right

---

[1] Not in the *monkey* or *ascidian*, as do some modern philosophers.—TR.

(righteousness), *i.e.*, in that which constitutes the continuity of humanity. The bodily organs then obey that which is noble, pure, and archetypal." This passage limits in the right direction the often misapplied quotation, *Quod ubique, quod semper, quod ab omnibus creditum est, hoc est vere proprieque catholicum.* Error is to be found amongst men more frequently than truth, selfishness than love, the sensual both more common and more obtrusive than the spiritual. But the spiritual (ideal) is the higher; therefore it is that Faust in Auerbach's cellar stands in a loftier position than the guests. But, as has been already particularly described, the germs of these higher principles exist in all men. The relation of righteousness to the ideas is treated by the commentator in the following way : —Ideas, and their carrying out into action, ought to correspond, but men in so doing ought to start from the correct instead of from the corrupt. This gives rise to active controversy. In opposition to the mystical school it is observed, " The most important point with Laotsze is the compassing of both unity and freedom from passions. According to Chwangtsze it is the repose felt by the holy men, so that the universe is insufficient to occasion disquiet to the heart. For vacuity, repose, indifference, silence, inaction are the peace of heaven and earth, the culminating point of the Tao-teh [1] (principle and beneficence). Yet this is not the true standard of conduct. The heaven-implanted ideas govern the desires of men but do not suppress them. One may have desires; when restrained they occasion no transgression. But selfishness is begotten when the desires go astray, and darkness reigns if the understanding misleads itself. The desires are begotten from flesh and blood; knowledge springs from the heart. By reason of selfishness desire becomes sinful, and

---

[1] Mr. Faber writes *Tao-Virtue;* but if the second character be translated, why not the first also ? A careful perusal of the Tao-teh King suggests that these are Laotsze's formula for the internal and the external, the spiritual and the material, the idea and its execution, God in his essence and his working.—TR.

therefore also flesh and blood. By reason of its darkening the knowledge becomes sinful, and thence also the heart." In this definition of man's essential nature as ideas and righteousness, idea signifies the participation in the eternal idea, and righteousness is the innate perception of that practice which is most conformable thereto, or its application to the varying circumstances of human life.

7. This nature permits neither of addition nor subtraction from without. "The superior man," says Mencius (p. 335), "desires extensive territory and numerous subjects, yet his enjoyment consists not therein. His enjoyment consists in this, to stand in the midst of the realm and to ensure the stability of the people within the four seas, but that which is to him his nature consists not therein. The occupying of himself in great matters (as emperor) adds nothing to that which is the real nature of the superior man, and his continuing in poverty (as a beggar) detracts in nowise from it, for his portion is fixed. That which the superior man regards as his nature is benevolence, righteousness, propriety, and intelligence. Their root is in the heart; their manifestation is a peaceful expression of the countenance, a fulness of contour in the back, and a something imparted to the four limbs which make it known without words." Their nature reveals itself involuntarily in the entire personality of men, on every side, and in everything. External circumstances cannot form the internal nature, but simply offer a temporal sphere of operation for the self-made ideal personality, *i.e.*, already complete in its very self. This idea of the great importance of man's individuality was also frequently brought forward by Confucius. The superior man finds entire satisfaction in his own moral nature.[1] External possessions or entire lack of these, a high position or lowly estate, are unable to make any change in this. All that these can do is to show what the man is in himself.

----

[1] See Systematic Digest of the Doctrine of Confucius, 105–111.

8. Yet this nature has a still more profound connection. Man stands not alone, an isolated being. Mencius says (p. 324), " He who has fathomed his heart knows his nature; if one knows his nature he also knows heaven." The heart is therefore the oracle by which human nature is revealed, that is to say, its medium of communication with the external world. But it is well to observe that not only the external world, but somewhat of the specifically human, manifests itself in the heart. This peculiar humanity is nevertheless only a portion of the celestial nature, or, more generally speaking, of heaven (God). From this point of view human nature passes as the image and at the same time the oracle of heaven. This is, again, a yet more important idea, but one which, alas! is only just hinted at. The attainment of anything like an exhaustive treatment of this subject is only possible from a theistic standpoint.

(b.) *Of Developing or Perfecting Man's Nature.*

9. If all men have the same nature, whence come those real diversities which we perceive amongst them? Mencius answers (p. 279), " Seek, so shalt thou find them; neglect, so shalt thou lose them (*i.e.*, benevolence, righteousness, propriety, and intelligence). That men are distinguished from one another by having of these either as much again, or five times as much, or an incalculable amount, arises from this, that they do not fully develop their natural faculties. Everything has in itself its own (normal) principle ; this is what the people lay hold of, therefore they love this sublime virtue."[1] From this we see that Mencius only conceived of this diversity as quantitative, as the measure of the development of the essential nature. But the complete highest ideal lies concealed in every breast, remaining amongst the mul-

[1] Legge's Shi King should be consulted here, part. ii. p. 541, note on this passage.

tiplicity of phenomena, the one constant standard owing
to which the people pay an involuntary tribute of respect
to all genuine virtue.

10. But there are also things which draw aside men's
hearts from the heavenly and give them an earthward
direction. Mencius used the growth of wheat to illustrate
this (p. 280), "One sows and harrows it; if the soil is
uniform and the time of cultivation the same, it rapidly
shoots up and grows, until at the right time the *whole* is
ripe. Should there, however, be diversity, it is owing to
inequalities in the richness and poverty of the soil, in the
nourishment afforded by rain and dew, and in the amount
of labour bestowed upon it." Because human nature is
not perfect from birth onwards, but must develop itself,
it happens that external circumstances interfere in a most
important manner, unhappily chiefly in the direction of
disturbance, too often destructively.

11. Yet natural development is quite different from
artificial treatment. This truth Mencius stoutly upheld
in opposition to his before-mentioned opponent, Kaoutsze
(p. 270), "Kaou said, ('Human) nature is like the willow-
tree, righteousness is like a bowl; as a bowl is made from
a willow, so are love and righteousness out of man's
nature.' Mencius answered, ' Can you, sir, agreeably to
the nature of the willow-tree, make it into bowls? The
willow must have violence done to it in order to become
a bowl' (*i.e.*, the bowl does not *grow* out of the willow).
Had one in like manner to do violence to men in order
to produce love and righteousness, all men universally
would regard love and righteousness as sources of misery."
It is not the form which man imparts to the wood of the
willow, that indicates its nature, but that which it has the
power to give itself under favourable circumstances. So
is it with men. It is most important that this idea be
firmly grasped.

12*a*. In the same way the law within acts differently
from the influences which are without with regard to

modification. Kaou comes again with his view (p. 271), " Human nature is like a reservoir of water ; if one makes an outlet on the east, the water will flow eastwards ; if one makes the outlet to the west, it will flow westwards. Human nature is indifferent with reference to the good and not good, just as water is indifferent with reference to east and west." Mencius answered, " Water is indeed indifferent to east and west, but is it so in reference to the above and below ? Good, to human nature, is like the tendency of water downwards. Man (as man) has nothing else than good, just as water has nothing but a downward tendency (*i.e.*, gravitation). Now if one strikes and splashes water, it is possible to make it go over one's head ; if one constrains and guides it, it can be brought over a mountain. Is this also the nature of water ? The force (exerted) makes it thus ! Even so is it with human nature when man is induced to do that which is not good." We will add to the above another passage which it in some measure serves to explain.

12*b*. The energies of man's nature and external destructive influences. Mencius said (p. 282), " The trees of the New Mountain were once beautiful, but being on the borders of a great state, they were hewn down, and how could they retain their beauty ? Yet still owing to the productive energy (at work) day and night, and the fertilising influences of rain and dew, they could not do otherwise than put forth new leaves. There came also sheep and cattle and browsed upon them; thus the mountain became so entirely barren. When men see its barrenness, they think that it never could have been a beautiful object. Is this, then, the nature of the mountain ? Can it, nevertheless, possibly be that amongst men there is no sense of benevolence and righteousness ? The cause of their losing their integrity of heart is like the case of the axe in the wood ; can it, whilst being daily hewn away, remain beautiful ? But that which by day and night shoots forth and rises in the peaceful daydawn—the predilections and antipathies—

D

stands in far closer connection with man (with his innermost nature), only they are too weak, so that they become
entangled or neglected amidst the daily occupations of
life. This entanglement repeating itself continually, the
night-time is insufficient for its restoration. When the
night-time is no longer sufficient to restore it, the distance
is not great between man and the brutes. When men
perceive their animal nature, they think that they never
had any other disposition. But can this possibly represent
the energies of humanity? Therefore there is nothing
which receives nourishment that does not grow; and there
is nothing which misses its nourishment without decreas-
ing." It is well known how every one shuns solitary converse with himself, a proof how rarely one is in a position
to find his better self, and how yet more rarely one therefore attains to union with the powers of heaven or with
God, the prototype. One seeks dissipation in order to get
away from oneself, and the getting lost amid (the multitude of) things we call pastime, in which there is nothing
of eternity to be felt. Silence is necessary! concentration in the depths of pure humanity. Only when the
passions are still, when the rush of the day's avocations
ceases its distracting tumult, does the sense of the primor-
dial nature bestir itself in the soul. Thence at such a
moment are good resolutions formed, which yet seldom
take root sufficiently deep, and soon become stifled by the
pressure of the following hour, by the lusts and desires
arising from our connection with nature around us. At
last one arrives at that point when he holds sensual enjoyment to be the only problem of life, and regards every
virtue as mere hypocrisy or narrow-mindedness. Man develops his animal nature by the neglect of humanity proper,
and then with savage delight appears in exact conformity
with the brutes around him. Piety and virtue generally
require cultivating, just as much as talents, intellect, or
memory. Every human disposition allows itself to be
developed by means of corresponding exercise, but also to

be spoilt by neglect or violence, ofttimes indeed to be well-nigh annihilated.

13. Mencius again (p. 275), in reference to the sense of right, which the philosopher Kaou held to be something drawn from the external world, carried on a lively conversation, in which he handled sensualism very severely. Neither things nor the impressions of them are the standard for man, but his conduct in reference to them, which corresponds to the sense of right within him. That is the cause of righteousness, and therefore likewise the expression of man's essential nature. The impression made on the senses is only the motive.

14*a*. That man has a twofold nature is still farther explained by Mencius (p. 294). On one side stand the senses and desires, on the other is the heart as the sum total of the higher motives, especially of thought. " Thinking attains to it (the truth) ; if one does not think, he attains to nothing. This it is that heaven has given to us. Let one first be established in thought (which here is called the greatness of human nature), and the little (the sensual) cannot tear it from him." ' Thought' here signifies not abstract or ideal thought, but deliberation in regard to action. By this reflective capacity that which is within man places itself in apposition with the impression of the senses received from without. Nevertheless deliberation (or reflection) can only take place when a normal rule is also contained in man's inmost nature. Mencius entertained no idea of calling that which is contained in the intellect great in comparison with that which the senses offer us. Therefore he did not, like the Buddhists, call the impressions of the senses. evil, but asserts that only their influence over the ideal is so. (Thus literally the commentary.)

14*b*. Yet man has not only the power of choice within, differences arise also from without (p. 294). Mencius says, " There is both a heavenly greatness and a human greatness. Benevolence, righteousness, truth, faith, delight in goodness without weariness, this is heavenly greatness. To be a duke, a minister of state, a privy councillor, this is human greatness. The ancients cultivated heavenly greatness, and human greatness followed thereupon. Those of the present day cultivate heavenly greatness in order to seek human greatness; if they obtain the latter they despise the former. They labour consequently under an intense delusion, which can result finally in nothing but destruction." Unfortunately, it is now still worse in modern China and in other modern states; men just begin with human greatness, and let the heavenly go entirely and altogether uncultivated. By examinations that alone can be estimated which is on the paper, the quality of the essay not that of the heart. The result is the destruction of internal morality by external display. Mencius hints in the following chapter at that "honour which one has in oneself," for the sake of which one can do without that from without, from other men; indeed, he speaks of "a satisfaction derived from benevolence and righteousness which is independent of food from a royal kitchen."

15. But practice is necessary to attain to this; its nature is to harden (p. 323). Hence Mencius makes a "threefold difference" between men. Pure physiology explains this as follows :—There are genial, richly endowed natures which are so deeply imbued with religion and morality that to them development in the highest degree is a painless progress. Others have to struggle with difficulties, yet through the energy which they exert it comes about that they arrive pretty nearly at an equality with the first. Others have nothing particular in themselves, either from natural endowment or personal culture, but they well know how to take advantage of opportunities. These only recognise selfish aims, and are often not very particular as to the means they employ. One can still take pleasure in persons like these if they but employ good means exclusively. We come, then, to that ordinary morality which

is not to be despised, but also must not be too highly
esteemed (see pp. 371 and 342).

16. But the cultivation of the personal must be perpetual and symmetrical. Mencius said (p. 291), " Every
one who wishes to grow timber of one or two handbreadths
in circumference knows how he must attend to its nourishment. Does one then not know in reference to his own
character how that is to be cultivated? Is it possible
that he does not love himself as much as timber? What
a great lack of reflection!" One treats things according
to the view one takes of them ; in other words, according
to the purpose which they ought to serve. This is specially
important in regard to education. He who will educate
must have a clear idea of that to which he wishes to
attain, and calculate the means employed accordingly. It
is, alas! to be deplored that the only learning met with
in the great majority of cases in China and elsewhere
to this very day still betrays a great lack of reflection.
That every faculty ought to become developed Mencius
farther indicates (p. 292) by the analogy of the "human
body," which one also cultivates symmetrically. In the
same way "the gardener likewise cultivates his plants."
Unfortunately, owing to the great division of labour, even
in the territory of the spirit, one drifts ever farther away
from this, the result being misjudgment and misconception. Mencius brings forward yet another important point
concerning symmetrical treatment (p. 285). He says,
" Although anything grows in the easiest way in the
world, yet if one expose it for one day to the heat and for
ten days to the cold it can never thus thrive. It is just
so with men when various influences work together against
them. Although they put forth somewhat, of what good
is it?" (See Art. 12*b*.) Fluctuation between extremes
is destructive to progress. To secure successful development constant attention is necessary. This is observed
by Mencius (p. 286). " A celebrated chess-player taught
two pupils, of whom one gave his whole heart to the

study, the other was thinking about a swan, and, of course, could not make the same progress." The energies of the soul must be concentrated upon the subject in order that they may be able to receive a correspondent impression and the clearest ideas possible.

17. We have already spoken, Art. 12, of silent concentration and right cultivation of the soul. Many, indeed, remember the silent concentration, but forget the cultivation required for the superior humanity. Men know how to avoid unwholesome food for the body, but their imaginations are crowded with all sorts of sickly pictures, the fruit of bad literature. It is miserable to perceive how, through pestilential reading, so many noble spiritual gifts are distorted, the moral perceptions blunted, the noblest energies weakened. Let this be much more thought of, the advancing by means of reading of every noble trait of human nature. Let us oppose most vigorously every book, every publication which nourishes the lower motives, anything that tends to excite or foster man's passions. Such pages, for instance, as treat with scorn and derision the "Holy place " and the "Holy of holies" should fill us with horror, for they are murderous attempts against all that is true in humanity.

CHAPTER II.

THE HEART.

(a.) *Psychological Idea.*

18*a*. THE heart is the immediate locality of the revelation of man's nature. In reference to this it has been already mentioned that it is thinking which determines its office. (Art. 14*a*.) For the heart is with the Chinese as with others of the ancients, especially the peoples of the East, not only the seat of emotion, but generally the centre of spiritual life.[1]

18*b*. (See Art. 5, *ante*.) The contents of the heart are the will and the motives (p. 64). " The will is the leader of the motives; these are the fulness of the bodily organism. The will is supreme and the motives are its subordinates; wherefore it is said, ' Restrain the will, but do no violence to your motives.' If the will is concentrated, it imparts activity to the motives; but if the motives are concentrated, they impel the will." In this place a word is employed in the text which it is extremely difficult to translate into another tongue by the exact equivalent, viz., "breath." The characteristic idea of breath is twofold—a streaming forth and a drawing inwards. To these correspond expansion and contraction, or attraction and

---

[1] It may be as well to quote here a statement which may be taken as a fair representation of modern European thought on this subject. Dr. M'Cosh on Divine Government, p. 265, says, " We have in this book to do with the emotions, the will, and the conscience, as constituting what may be appropriately called the motive powers of the mind," and these three are all included in the popular word " heart," and in the still looser phrase " feeling."—TR.

repulsion. The cause of this phenomenon is, to the Chinese mind, one and the same in all departments of nature and psychology, and is expressed by the word "*Hi*." In the case of nature, therefore, we find it best to translate "*Hi*" by the word "*powers*" because the singular "*power*" is too abstract. Everything that stirs within the heart of man, as well as the motives, is comprised in the word "powers." The will stands to these motives as their regulator, and therefore as the ruling principle over them. It is a deep psychological view which Mencius here takes. With this is also correctly opened out the problem of man's freedom. Freedom consists not in the independency of the motive powers, but in the possibility of imparting to them a definite direction. In the will all the motives ought to find their centre of agreement, and through it alone their practical realisation. Mencius seems, however, not to have recognised that the will has never attained, nor in this world ever can attain, to perfect mastery over the motives in any man. From his standpoint he could in no case have been able adequately to explain the cause of this phenomenon. The direction of the will is not in this place treated so fully as by Confucius.[1]   (See *Digest Confucius*, p. 56 and *seq.*)

19 and 20. Of the other contents of the heart we have already treated in Arts. 6, 12, and 17, *ante*.

21. The fourfold description of motive (p. 78) is most important. Mencius maintained "that every man has a heart sensible of sympathy, shame, tenderness, and conscientiousness, and he who is without these is simply not a man." A beautiful example illustrates this. "If men

---

[1] It is very significant that we find nothing about conscience here. But on a comparison with a note by Dr. M'Cosh, p. 273, we see that Mencius had anticipated the philosophy of the West. "The motive should be divided into two parts, that which is without the will, and that which is within the will : the latter of these being, we maintain, the main element." And Leibnitz seems to include conscience amongst the motives when he says, "The motives comprehend all the dispositions which the mind can have to act voluntarily, &c." See Reid, by Hamilton, pp. 610, 611, note.—Tr.

suddenly see a child approach a well, they all exhibit excitement and distress of heart, and they do this neither to recommend themselves to the parents of the child, nor to earn the praise of friends and neighbours, nor from a disinclination to the reputation" (of being unfeeling). He continues (p. 79), " The heart of sympathy is the germ of benevolence, the heart of modesty is the germ of righteousness, the heart of tenderness is the germ of propriety, and the heart of conscientiousness is the germ of wisdom." This paragraph opens out a wider field of action beyond what has been already said concerning essential nature. Mencius is a determined opponent of the mechanical conception of human nature. Man is no *tabula rasa ;* his heart contains its own peculiar life, and brings forward germs capable of development out of its very inmost nature. These germs manifest themselves in the case of all men under all circumstances. External circumstances only condition the kind of appearance and the degree of perfection belonging to the development. But everything human lies dormant in men from their very birth, just as the plant in the grain of seed. Soil and climate may modify the development, but the specific character cannot be imparted from without.

(b.) *Moral Definition of the Heart.*

I. *Subjectively Considered.*

22. Mencius never remains standing upon mere physical or psychical grounds, but always unites the moral with them. Therefore he continues (p. 79), " The *Ego* of every man contains these four germs; if he knows how to develop and to perfect them, it is as when fire begins to burn or the spring first gushes forth. If one is able actually to complete them (fully to mature or perfect them), they are then ample to provide for all within the four seas ;[1] if unable to mature them, it is not enough for

[1] The whole Empire is signified by this term.

the service of one's parents." As ethical maturity in its
fullest scope flashes upon Mencius in dominion over nature,
it comprises and includes the inferior part of humanity.
Of this more later on.

23. Cultivation of the heart is necessary on account of
"the desires for the enjoyment of external things" (p. 341).
We remark the important distinction between culture,
which applies itself to the nourishment and development
of the ideal humanity and that enjoyment of external
things, to which everything belongs that has the senses for
its medium, as well as those nobler forms such as art and
science, in so far as they draw man away from the former,
which is his proper vocation.

24. Therefore, says Mencius (p. 373), "For the culture
of the heart there is nothing better than the diminution of
our desires." The desires, like weeds amongst the wheat,
absorb the best nourishment.

25. But the growth of the good cannot be busily pressed
forward. Mencius warns us of this by an illustration (p.
67). "Be not like that man of Sung who, being sore troubled
that his wheat would not speedily grow to full height,
went and pulled at it. Quite exhausted, he returned to
his home and said to his people, 'I am weary to-day; I
have been helping the wheat to grow.' His son ran off
quickly to see it—there was the corn all withered. There
are a few in the world," adds Mencius, "who do not help
the corn to grow. These few hold it (such labour) to be
useless, and do not trouble themselves in the least about
it; they do not weed between the corn. Those who help
the corn to grow pull out the germ, and are therefore not
only useless but injurious as well." It is clear from this
that the nature of men, as it reveals itself in the heart,
indicates a natural growth which follows its inherent law.
Yet man finds himself placed in opposition to himself,
either as disturbing this growth or as freeing it from its
hindrances. If now the nature of man consists in that
growth itself, or, more exactly, in the good which grows

up, what is then that other which distinguishes and plucks
out the weeds ? Mencius overlooks this problem. It is,
nevertheless, important to keep these facts clearly before
us. Again, if it could be proved that some animals had
all faculties in common with man, and that there are only
degrees of difference, little would be thereby either gained
or lost. The placing of himself in opposition to himself
or to some part of his consciousness, and the possibility of
his varying his action towards the same, belongs only to
man—that is what constitutes humanity.

26. But the good part, alas! is rarely chosen. Mencius
is a vigorous preacher of repentance (p. 288). He argues,
" Were life dependent upon a portion of soup and a plate
of rice, and these were to be offered in a harsh way,[1] no
traveller would receive them ; if offered insultingly, even
a beggar would not care for them. But one receives ten
thousand loads of corn without any regard to propriety
and righteousness. What can ten thousand loads offer
me ? It is for the adornment of official and private
dwellings, to secure the services of wives and concubines,
and in order that my poor acquaintances may receive
support from me. In that case one declines to receive
anything to save his body from death, in this he does it
for the sake of adorning his official and private dwellings ; in that he receives nothing to save his life, in
this· he accepts, seeking the attendance of wives and concubines ; in that he receives not, even to save his life, in
this he accepts so that his poor acquaintance may receive
his assistance. Could one not also decline in such a case
as this ? This is termed losing the original attributes of
the heart!" And again (p. 290), " Benevolence (love) is
the heart of man, righteousness the way. It is pitiable
for man to abandon his way and not follow it, to let slip

---

[1] In Art. 82 Mr. Faber translates
this, " A man who walks in the Tao
would rather suffer death than unworthy treatment." This latter
rendering differs from that adopted
by Dr. Legge, which is as above,
but it is more in accordance with the
context, besides being literally exact.

his heart and not know how again to seek it. When people's fowls or dogs stray away, they know how to seek them again; they have an erring heart, yet they know not how to seek that again. The aim of studies and investigations consists in nothing else than this, only and altogether the seeking of the erring heart." According to Mencius, study is carried on not so much for the sake of much and varied knowledge, nor for the acquisition of a technical readiness for some terrestrial vocation, but rather, and above all, for the elevation of the heart. Many modern so-called Christian professors could learn something from Mencius. Of this more anon (Art. 444). Mencius continues, " Is a man's finger crooked, yet without sickness or pain or hindrance to his work, he still regards the way from *Ts'in* to *Ts'oo* as anything but far if there only be some one who can make it straight, because his finger is not like that of a man. If his finger is not human, he knows how to feel abhorrence; but if his heart is inhuman, he knows not how to feel abhorrence at it. This is termed misunderstanding the idea of species (the type in kind)." [1] Know thyself and seek thyself, not the delusive self-seeking, but the noble Ego, the very image of God (within). Of himself, says Mencius (p. 160), " I wish also to improve the hearts of men, to put a stop to destructive doctrines, to oppose strange behaviour, to banish unseemly language, in order to act as representative of the three holy ones. Is it because of a taste for controversy? I cannot do otherwise."

27. He therefore also praises sincerity (p. 326). "Everything is provided within us (in the Ego). To find one's self sincere by self-examination is a joy unequalled." All

---

[1] It is curious to note the results of this teaching in the neighbouring country of Japan. By the kindness of the Rev. H. J. Foss of Kobe I am enabled to give the following quotation from the Shin-ga-ku-to-wa, or talk about the way of instructing the heart—

" Men are many, people say,
Yet among the many, pray,
Are there many men?
Listen to me then,
Be a man thyself, O man!
Make as many as you can."

should be natural in men, that is to say, correspondent to the peculiar natural disposition. Every possible relation to the external world is conditioned by the ego, in which they are all interwoven. The Ego is the responsible central organ. Therefore the delight is so great, when its entire management of external matters leads to no contradiction between these and the internal.

28. That "to err is human" was also known to Mencius. He says (p. 323), "Men for the most part go astray, and at first are able, after so doing, to reform. They are grieved in their hearts and oppressed with anxiety, and act accordingly; it shows itself in their complexion, breaks forth into utterance, and then becomes plainly declared. Thence one discerns that life results from affliction; misery, and death, on the contrary, from rest and bliss." Mencius, nevertheless, did not affirm the necessity of error (see Art. 7), but he speaks only of the actual circumstances of life. Adversities, however, should not discourage, but so direct the mind to the truth as to occasion conversion. Prosperity, joy, and bliss nourish the thirst for pleasure, and causing men to relax their efforts, draw inevitable ruin after them. The struggle with adversity steels the energies against it, and leads to a buoyant elevation instinct with life.

29. Constant activity, however, is needed; therefore, says Mencius (p. 20), "By weighing we discriminate the light and the heavy; through measuring we discern the long and the short. It is so with all things, and much more so with the heart." Mencius says farther to his opponent, the oft-mentioned philosopher Kaou, "The footpaths of the hill-passes, if much used, become highways; but if for a long time unused, grass encumbers them. Your heart is now encumbered with grass." It concerns us, therefore, to promote the voluntary, *i.e.*, the freely determined action of the heart in order thereby to keep down the superabundant growth of the involuntary appetites (the passions). In the province of the heart it

is with the *laissez faire* system of indolent inactivity as with the same applied to the cultivation of the soil—it only produces weeds.

30. Motion results in commotion (see Arts. 14 and 28). All progress is conditioned by the activity of the bodily and spiritual organs. Although this activity is seldom freely determined upon, it nevertheless effects and makes possible the complete execution of difficult problems.

2. *Objectively Considered.*

31. The culture of the heart is not only of subjective importance for the life of each individual, but it exerts also an important influence upon human matters in the mass, upon the political welfare of the community. It was so in the case of the kings of antiquity, their beneficent government was simply "the result of their benevolent heart," p. 166. (Cf. Art. 317 ff.)

32. Stability of heart, that is, a contented heart, a mind satisfied with goodness on the part of the people, results in quiet, peaceful living and consequent general stability (p. 23).

33. On the other hand, those evil things which have their origin in the heart injure also the body politic (pp. 67, 159). These he considers, so to speak, as political heresies. Mencius mentions sensualism and communism. These heresies always have their ultimate cause in erroneous moral or religious theories. It is by no means a matter of indifference what kind of theoretic convictions are entertained by members of the Government. Theories influence opinions and these govern actions. Yet it is not always open wrong-doing which is thus committed; often it is simply a thoroughly lawful inclination towards helping in establishing one's favourite view in opposition to that which is less appreciated. This may also happen if only sufficient elbow-room be given to the legislators.

34. From heart to heart is likewise a truth recognised of old. Mencius says (p. 72), "He who subjugates men

by force subdues not their hearts; external force is
inadequate. He who by virtue brings them into submission rejoices their inmost heart and really subdues
them, just as the seventy disciples submitted themselves
to Confucius." It is well known that men only yield a
temporary submission to brute force, but, on the other
hand, give way willingly to spiritual superiority, especially
to moral qualifications. Yet in this case the virtue of
benevolence is meant to be understood. Many of the
other virtues tend rather to the alienation of hearts. The
idea of virtue expresses more than that of cultivation,
which plays such an important part in the present day.
Industry by itself simply awakens covetousness, envy, and
pleasure-seeking; it makes *one* happy and many others
yet more miserable. It is only where virtue, the higher
cultivation of the spirit, makes equal progress with material
culture, that a people becomes truly blessed and contentment reigns in their midst.

35. Satisfaction of the heart by pious observances with
regard to the defunct (pp. 97 and 135). This depends
upon the dead being properly interred in coffins. Mencius
recommended "a thick double coffin, not for the sake of a
beautiful exterior, but because then first the heart of those
who remain becomes satisfied." Mencius says by way of
conclusion, "To cover over the corruption of the corpse
and not to let the earth touch the body, is not that a
source of joy to the human heart?" The Chinese even to
this present day have a great horror of cremation, and
this notwithstanding the fact that the corpses of Buddhist
priests are so treated. Underlying this feeling is a simple
natural sentiment, a kind of illusion, whereby one thinks
of those lying in the grave as being bodily present. Still
the Christian faith in the resurrection [of the body] is in
no way dependent upon the treatment to which the dead
are subjected; whether the ashes of the martyrs are
scattered to the winds or cast into the stream that shall
bear them to the ocean, matters nothing. The resurrec-

tion body has its germ in the spiritual. The soul, by means of her inherent divine power, forms out of the elementary matter of the purified earth her purified body, a perfect instrument for the enjoyment of her new existence. (See Arts. 159 and 288.)

CHAPTER III.

HEAVEN.

ALTHOUGH man is the centre of the Chinese conception
of the universe, yet the more thoughtful, and amongst
these Mencius, cannot forbear the recognition of a higher
power, which projects itself into and lays hold of the life
of man.

THE RELATION OF HEAVEN TO MAN.

(a.) *Its Gifts.*

36. The cause of causes (p. 135). "Heaven produces
things, in that it appoints them one originating cause."
This was spoken in the first place of parents, of whom
men are born in the natural course of things. Yet a
universal idea underlies this as a basis. "Heaven" stands
here for God. He brings everything to pass, yet not
without means; only the first beginnings of things are
instituted without means. These are the causes which
are ever energising in the world. In and through these
the power of God ever works, investing them with permanence, for besides God there can be no *perpetuum
mobile.* It is owing also to the ever-pervading influence
of the Absolute Cause upon all conditioned causes that the
operation of the various powers in the universe, and their
co-operation in a given direction, never fails. Both kinds
of causes are necessary to the satisfactory explanation
of the existence of things, and especially of ourselves.
Science, alas! soon loses the one, the Cause of Causes, in

E

human limitations, and the others, the second causes, soon come too short.

37. (Cf. Art. 14.) The "senses" and the "understanding" spring from Heaven.

38. (Cf. Art. 14b). It has already been mentioned that the same holds good of the "highest nobility," which consists of "benevolence, righteousness, truth, faith, delight in goodness."

39. Also from Heaven are appointed the regal power, with officials and revenue (p. 254). According to the Chinese view, Heaven lends these to those who are worthy.

40. This is an act of Providence (p. 32). The *Shoo King* is quoted to the effect that, "When Heaven brought forth the lower classes, it made for them rulers and leaders (teachers), making manifest the purpose that they should be fellow-workers with God." We see that Providence refers not only to the maintenance of the bodily existence, but pursues a higher aim, the spiritual cultivation, that is, the moral improvement, of the people. The higher classes, the leaders of the people, are here alluded to, as being what they should be everywhere, examples to the people both spiritually and morally. Their duty it is, likewise, to bring the lower classes to a consciousness of that good which slumbers concealed in their hearts, and which is readily brought to light and perception by a very small degree of enlightenment. This truth forms that thread of life on which depends the long existence of the Chinese commonwealth. Where, on the other hand, the perpetual rejuvenating of the higher life comes to an end, and the object of cultivation is more or less exclusively sought in mere material interests, there self-seeking becomes rampant, and, as a consequence, that spirit of party which, in its remorseless revolutions, crushes the state to atoms.

41 and 42. "Misfortune" also comes from Heaven, yet man is able to avert it by means of "change of mind," and by walking in the thoughts and ways of God (p. 75). In this the Chinese have by means of errors and per-

versions fallen into many superstitions. That the same, indeed, has happened also to Christians is not the fault of the absolute right idea, as it has been declared to be, but of selfish folly and want of judgment. ·

(b.) *Of Heaven's Action.*

43. Through this there is "spontaneous growth" in nature and history, such as everything which is apart from or in advance of human influences (p. 235). Ancient Confucianism differs from the modern school of Choofootze in occupying this vantage-ground. Whilst this latter is degraded into simple naturalism, to Mencius there stands above Nature a moral spiritual power which energises in and through her. Now with us offence is frequently taken at this, particularly on account of modern philosophy having busied itself almost exclusively with theories of knowledge. Laws for man's will are almost unknown, because the original moral germs are principles and not laws.

44. Beyond this there is the harmonising of all occurrences (p. 231) : "Heaven does not speak. It manifests itself only and alone by means of the conduct (of the ruler) and by what happens." The explanation is given by the recital of the history of the imperial choice of *Shun.* There we see results put down as the characteristic work of Heaven. Anyway, results in many, possibly in most cases, are not in the power of men; in fact, the most insignificant circumstances frequently lead to results contrary to all calculation. The immediate result cannot always be calculated upon : the heavenly characteristic does not always appear to retain to the end the upper-hand; yet this must really be the case if results generally (as in special cases) are to be regarded as effected by Heaven. This necessitates a higher wisdom than the Chinese possess.

45. Heaven effects that which is impossible to man

that is, it gives time sufficient [for the production of results] (p. 232). Men of the present day are ready to exclaim, "Chance." Chance is properly only a recognition of our ignorance. In a universe regulated and governed by law there can be no such thing as chance, but simply cause and effect,—ethically termed, means and aim. Mencius thinks teleologically : he believes in final causes.

46. Heaven, we further learn, overrules men as well as their evil intentions (p. 53). "Some one may be able to occasion promotion, or may stand as an impediment in the way, but promotion or hindrance is not in the power of man. . . . That is from Heaven." It is only the religious position of real and blameless piety which can contemplate those disappointments it has endured, and which it has yet to endure, as guidance from above. Surely neither materialistic nor pantheistic conceptions by way of explaining the daily path will suffice us here. Had Heaven really no intentions apart from those of men which serve as second causes, and were Heaven consequently not a willing and consciously governing power, such a faith would be simply inconceivable. Nevertheless, inasmuch as this faith in predestination or the divine controlling of affairs, spite of other and false theories, is held by the leading spirits amongst all peoples, ancient and modern, it is the expression of an inherent and universal truth. He who cherishes this faith is every way preserved from despair. We must also here remark that although men act consciously, they are yet at the same time unconsciously serving a higher will.

47. The action of Heaven corresponds to that of the people: *vox populi, vox dei.* "Heaven sees as my people see; Heaven hears as my people hear" (p. 233). What is here said is true only of that which is permitted. Even evil comes under this head ; else indeed there would be no possibility of evil in the world. Hence is it that the favourite appeal to the *vox populi,* as well as to the permission of

Heaven or of God, is in no way a criterion of the moral
rectitude of what is done. This must be estimated according to the pure principles of goodness, righteousness, &c.
Only thus would it be, according to Mencius' own teaching. In the preceding case matters had gone on in due
course without any violation of what is right.

48. "No man nor emperor can bestow an empire, but
only Heaven alone" (p. 230). One man alone has no
power over other men, *i.e.*, over thousands and millions;
it must be given him from above. As there are born
artists, philosophers, and generals, there are also born
rulers. Culture only assists these. The natural disposition is from God (Heaven). Besides this, there is also
needed the special guidance of God through external circumstances.

49. Heaven prepares its own agents (p. 323). "When
Heaven is about to impose an important office upon a
man, it first embitters his heart in its purposes; it causes
him to exert his bones and sinews; it lets his body suffer
hunger; it inflicts upon him want and poverty, and con-
founds his undertakings. In this way it stimulates his
heart, steels his nature, and supplies that of which the
man would else be incapable." Here, again, we see Heaven
as a conscious and free agent. Amongst all people the
belief obtains that great men are especial instruments of
the providence of Heaven—rather of God. Such have
also usually passed through a course of training peculiarly
full of suffering.

50. Heaven also "perfects" that which (the superior)
man has commenced (p. 51). (Cf. Art. 480.) The heart
of man beats on in its path, but it is of the Lord that
it goes beyond.[1] That which is really good is never
lost, but works on for generations; its fruit oft makes
its appearance long afterwards, like the seed which has
become a tree, yet is forgotten when the time of fruit

---

[1] "Our hearts, like muffled drums, are beating funeral marches to the
grave."—*Longfellow.*

arrives. It is always thus; the fruits yield no advantage to the seed. Besides which, both kindly soil and favourable weather are requisite as well as natural energies. Man lays a solid foundation for his own prosperity and for that of his successors by means of that beneficence which springs from a benevolent heart. This is especially the case with rulers. (Cf. Art. 317. Cf. also Digest of Confucius, pp. 44–46.)

(c.) *Human Conduct with Regard to Heaven.*

51. In the first place, we have naturally the knowledge of Heaven. As already said, the knowledge of Heaven begins with the knowledge of self. "He who has fathomed his heart knows his nature; if one knows his nature, he knows Heaven" (p. 324.) (Cf. Art. 8.[1]) Hence it follows that our knowledge of God is altogether anthropomorphic (of a human form), but this is only because man is in the form of God (the image of God). Only we must not forget that this is man in his ideal nature, and not in his ruined condition.

52. Delight in and fear of Heaven (p. 31). "He who (as ruler) serves the small with the great delights in Heaven; he who with the small serves the great fears Heaven; he who delights in Heaven protects the realm; he who fears Heaven protects his state." (See Art. 134.) In both cases one's own wishes are sacrificed for the good of the community. Thus we recognise the divine way. This teaching is specially important to feudal states; but how greatly was the simple law perverted in the great and small states of Germany until 1870! The delight spoken of in the text refers, in the first place, to that which is good, the higher culture, improvement of customs and

---

[1] Cf. Al Gazzali, a Mohammedan philosopher, A.D. 1010. "A knowledge of God cannot be obtained by means of the knowledge a man has of himself or of his own soul. The attributes of God cannot be determined from the attributes of man. His sovereignty and government can neither be compared nor measured."

laws, which the smaller possibly effected before the greater, and which this on its part respected. The fear refers to the display of power by the greater, which could coerce the smaller state. In either case there ought to be no recourse to external force, but the inner ability should by its exertion gain for itself the mastery. (Cf. Art. 351.)

53. The service of Heaven is thus explained (p. 325): "Inasmuch as one preserves his heart and cultivates his essential nature, one serves Heaven." Such a service is more than sacrifice. We find here the fundamental idea of the Evangelical Church already hinted at. The essence of religion, especially of Christianity, consists, not in the offering of objective forms (*i.e.*, such as stand in no necessary connection with the person of the offerer),[1] but in the presentation of the entire personality. The more this becomes conformed to a correspondence with its prototype, so much the more can the divine and God Himself dwell in them, and through them work with reforming influence upon the world. All else that is called divine service is only a means to this end. The great majority of men, alas! cling to the means but lose the reality under the sign, carrying on an idolatrous service without any clear consciousness of aught beyond. This is true, not only of the various forms of heathenism or of the ritual, &c., of the Romish and Greek Churches, but also amongst Protestants there is quite enough of so-called divine service which is nothing but the apotheosis of some form which is accompanied by no Holy Spirit who may transform the worshipper into His own divine nature.

54. We have already (Art. 14*b*) spoken of the cultivation of the heavenly nobility. That the heavenly is placed in opposition to the human nobility points to the fact that both are not of necessity coexistent in this world; and although the moral problem remains of striving for this,

---

[1] Cf. Office for Holy Communion in the Prayer-Book of the Church of England: "Here we offer and present unto thee, O Lord, ourselves, our souls and bodies, to be a reasonable, holy, and lively sacrifice unto Thee."

this result is, according to Mencius, very seldom attained. To the question "Why?" he has no satisfactory answer. He might indeed have exclaimed: Men have altogether deviated from heaven and become incapacitated; there is none who does good (fulfilling the will of Heaven), no, not one.

55. That the magistrates serve Heaven as "fellow-workmen with God" we learn in Art. 40. This knowledge, that the magistrates are appointed as fellow-workers with God in the education of men for the heavenly idea, one would scarcely expect from a heathen. Modern political economists, who are unable to grasp this, have consequently not yet attained to the position of a civilised heathen. Besides the celestial powers there exists yet an invisible world.

(d.) The World of Spirits.[1]

56. They are men a degree higher than the holy (p. 366). "He who is great and incomprehensible is termed a spirit." The text as well as the commentary indicates that under the term "spirit" are to be understood spirits, and with these the most highly developed men, whether living or dead.

57. The tutelary deities of the land stand in rank between the people and their ruler (p. 359). "The people are the most important; next come the spirits of the land; the ruler is of least importance;" and "If a prince brings these guardian spirits into danger, he is to be deposed." The spirits of the land are considered as the channels for the blessings of Heaven. It is very peculiar that their action is made dependent upon the conduct of princes. The people are in the position of minors; the ruler alone is responsible.

58. But the tutelary spirits are also punishable (p. 360). "When the sacrificial victims are perfect, the corn in the vessels pure, the sacrifices at their proper times, and yet

[1] Cf. Digest of Confucius (p. 47 ff.)

there arise drought or flood, then the tutelary spirits must be changed." We here see the character of the worship of the spirits very plainly set forth. The spirits, in spite of their superhuman efficacy, both are and remain dependent upon men, and are also subject to human weaknesses. In this place we have neglect of duty plainly mentioned. In extreme cases there should be a deposing of the spirits, and that by the prince. Thus the spirits are vassals of princes, the living, consequently, standing higher than the dead ; men above spirits, and these only called to the service of man. There we have the caricature of an idea which in itself is right, which is Scripturally explained as follows : The angels, *i.e.*, the celestial, not human spirits, stand in a rank below that of man (who is in the likeness of God), and are for the service, but not at the command, of sinful men. That departed holy men obtain such offices is absurd ; for before their day and during their lifetime there was just such growth, and rain, and sunshine, &c., as after their death is to be dependent upon their efficacy as mediators.

59. Besides the tutelary spirits, there are a "hundred (*i.e.*, many) kinds of spirits " (p. 232). These are the invisible mandarins of the unseen world, who are just as open to bribes as those of the visible world.

60. Concerning God, Shang-ti, we find a classic quotation in Mencius (p. 206). "Although any one be a bad man, if he fasts and is collected, bathes and washes himself, he may indeed offer sacrifice to God." Besides this place, Mencius only uses two quotations from the old classics in which the name of God is used—the one already mentioned from the *Shoo-King*, that the magistrates are fellow-workers with God, the other from the *Shi-King*. God had "already issued the decree that the new dynasty of Chow should assume the office of the old one of Yin " (p. 173). After these passages from Mencius, there can be no doubt about one point, viz., that the most correct term for God [Elohim] is *Shang-te*, and in no case *Shin*

(spirits). *Shang-te* is, according to these few places—(1.) The Supreme Ruler, who, as to kings, sets up one and puts down another. (2.) He desires the physical and moral health or well-being of men. (3.) He is holy, so that no uncleanness dare approach Him. (4.) He is nevertheless gracious to the penitent. Against such a doctrine concerning God there is nothing to be advanced, as although it is not exhaustive, yet it contains the essential elements of the Old Testament doctrine of God. It is to be regretted that nowhere is there a hint given that He is the Creator; but, on the other hand, He nowhere appears as a created being.

CHAPTER IV.

OF TAO, OR THE UNIVERSAL REIGN OF LAW.

ACCORDING to the Chinese, there is only one universal
law that makes itself known in all the unities throughout
the course of the universe. Physical nature or spirit
life makes no difference. Each follows in its way a
fixed, ordered course, a series of occurrences, in which
cause and effect, or means and end, stand in an appointed,
ever-recurring relation. In the reality of life, then, are
there so-called surroundings to be considered which directly
modify the result ? The Tao regards not so much the
results or the surroundings as the means and end, bringing sometimes the one, sometimes the other, to the front,
but expressing only the law or fundamental relation
between them. In the conduct of men, it signifies the
maxims of business as well as the proceeding to be
observed in special cases. (Cf. Digest of Confucius, pp.
94–101.)

61–72. We pass by the various kinds of law (Tao) for
the sake of brevity, and consider only that which should
guide men generally. (For classified titles of Arts. 61–72,
see detailed analysis, *ante.*)

73. The true Tao is only one (p. 110). That is, there
can only be one direct way, because it is the shortest line
of connection between the subject and its true aim. Other
ways are not necessarily erroneous; very often they are
right, but must be more or less circuitous.

74. This one *Tao* is indicated by "an affection for

sublime virtue" [virtue in the abstract] (p. 279). Virtue only appears as such when it is a step onward in the path towards an appointed end.

75. It shows itself in "benevolence," *i.e.*, human benevolence, or that which is from man to man (p. 361). (Cf. Art. 136.)

76. Also in the "five human relations" of father and son, ruler and minister, husband and wife, elder and younger brothers, and friends (p. 127). (Cf. Art. 276.)

77. In "filial piety and brotherly kindness" (p. 301).

78. "The *Tao*," says Mencius (p. 178), "is near, and is often sought after. Duties lie in that which is easy, and are frequently sought in what is hard. Let every one treat his relations as relatives, his superiors as superiors, and the whole realm will have peace." The root of many social and of yet more political evils lies in this, that men are only willing to do and to see great things, whilst they neglect and despise the small. If there is the honest fulfilling of the nearest and the smallest duties, the great will soon offer of themselves.[1]

79. As a consequence, the knowledge of the same is also easy (p. 302). "The *Tao* is like a great road. Is it perhaps hard to recognise it? The evil of men is that they do not seek it." This evil, alas! is always at work, and not only among the Chinese. Men do not inquire about that problem of life which most concerns them.

80. Mencius abhors all false compromises in reference to the same. (Cf. Art. 99 and p. 350.) "A disciple once said to him, 'The *Tao* is so majestic and sublime, it is just as if one would ascend into heaven; it appears unattainable. Why is it not made comprehensible to people, so that they may daily give themselves some trouble about it?' Mencius answered, 'A great employer does not on account of

---

[1] It is refreshing to find here a recognition of the duty implied in the ten commandments, and unfolded in the Catechism of the Church of England in her answer to the question, "What is your duty to your neighbour?" Some moderns question whether men have any "superiors" or "betters."

a stupid workman alter or dispense with the levelling line. E (the great archer) did not alter the pull of his bow on account of a stupid archer. The superior man draws but does not let fly; as if playing, he takes his position in the midst of the *Tao;* he who can follows him.'" (Cf. Art. 464.) It is the part of teachers and preachers to present the highest ideal. He who is able to receive it, let him receive it. He who is lacking in endowments will by righteous zeal be enabled to make something of it. The old saying may again and again be uttered even in this present day, " The too hard and too difficult depend upon a deficiency of will." To him who will not learn every problem is too hard. It is so in science, in morals, and yet more so in religion. By all means in instruction let the understanding of the taught be had regard to; let the commencement be made with that which is easy, and be careful also that the eye never lose sight of the subject as a whole, else one is only cultivating superficiality. The history of literature and art as well as of religion is a proof of this.

81. But for the carrying out of the *Tao* personal example is necessary (p. 358). " Mencius said: If any one does not himself follow the *Tao*, neither does it take place with his wife and children. If one does not manage men according to the *Tao*, he cannot do so with his wife and children." In every case personal example effects more than talking and ordering. There are very few men who do not recognise this, but notwithstanding there are only a few who carry it out in practice. Our innate egoism (selfishness) nowhere more plainly manifests itself than in the fact that every one willingly vindicates for himself a ground of excuse, knowing well what others should do, but for himself, seeking to avoid that which is personally disagreeable or troublesome. That is an infirmity which often becomes hardness and injustice.

82 and 83. It makes a great difference to the realm whether *Tao* governs it or not, and the conduct of officials

possessed of decision of character testifies to this. Mencius says (p. 350), " If there is *Tao* in the realm, one identifies himself with *Tao*" (*i.e.*, places himself in the service or under the direction of *Tao*). "If there is no *Tao* in the realm, one identifies *Tao* with himself. I have never even heard of one identifying other men with *Tao* in death" (*i.e.*, *Tao* perishes not with men). He farther says (p. 289), "A man who lives according to *Tao* rather receives death than unworthy treatment." Consequently the Chinese possess character; unhappily, however, decided characters are rare in China, and elsewhere they are not abundant. But by *Tao* we must never understand pet plans, or democratic, socialistic, or conservative theories, &c., or individual or national prejudices, and suchlike, but rather an ethically regulated, law-abiding course (of life or action). In our days, alas! religion and morality are very often sacrificed to many other and less important considerations.

84. "Only *Tao* can save a falling state" (p. 183). Benevolence and righteousness are here meant. Our present race of politicians indeed know many means of doing this, means which for the most part are good, but which rarely reach to the root of the evil. Beneath all there is a degeneracy of human nature which absolutely needs elevating.

85. But the very *Tao* of ·the best models as rulers is "insufficient without a benevolent disposition" (p. 461). The proceedings of other rulers are not to be externally imitated. The condition of the people and their needs are at all times various. With high officials and sovereigns everything depends upon the natural disposition and a right spirit. Therefore the effect of the gospel of Christ is full of blessing to the life of the state, yet without any desire on that account to cause the disruption of any realm.

CHAPTER V.

DESTINY.

This is an idea which gives much trouble to all Chinese, both in philosophy and actual life. They desire to learn beforehand what is predestined in individual cases, and on this account have recourse to many absurd practices. Confucius himself was not free from these, as we see in the doctrine of the Mean, chap. xxiv. Mencius, at least in theory, was possibly as enlightened as any of the Chinese.

86. There is a destiny of external things which is not the right one (p. 326). "If one by seeking finds, and loses by neglect, the seeking is useful for finding: that which is sought is in ourselves (the *Ego*). If the seeking is according to *Tao* (established rules), and the finding is destined, then the seeking is useless for finding: that which is sought is external."

87. On the contrary (see p. 325), "The true destiny and not the false is to be willingly received. He who thus recognises destiny does not place himself under an overhanging wall. To die in fulfilling one's duty (*Tao*) is the right destiny. To die in fetters (as a criminal) is not one's true destiny." Every externally happy lot which is possible to us as men is not consequently the proper one. The destiny of man which is of importance to him is the ideal of his personality. External circumstances only modify the kind of fulfilment. We should keep our aim constantly in sight, and so preserve ourselves from receiving unnecessary injury from external things, which are

no ways connected with our work. Consequently we should not recklessly run into danger, neither should we like cowards start back horrorstruck at it, if only duty demands that we meet it.

88. Cultivation of one's self confirms our destiny (p. 325). "He to whom a short or a long life is all one, he cultivates himself and awaits (the predestined); he establishes thereby his destiny." From those external circumstances which only in the smallest degree are in the power of men come the most important: he mentions life and death. Whether life shall only last a few years or many is a matter of indifference to the ethical mind. It depends upon the use which man makes of his lifetime whether he labour for the accomplishment of his personal destiny or stand in opposition thereto. The divine pre-destination extends beyond individuals. The individual himself, however, is firstly to be considered as of chief importance. Self - improvement lays the foundation, appropriates to itself the objective individual destiny in a subjective manner, and thereby prepares itself for accomplishing the objective universal destiny. This consists in the improvement of the world until it be in perfect harmony with the universe, and God be all in all.

89. "Fortune and misfortune are dependent upon individual (moral) conduct." [1] Our experience of things around seems to contradict this; it requires inner experience, an enlightened spiritual perception, in order to attain to such knowledge. Everything depends upon what makes us happy, and whether we truly become so.

90. Finally, there is yet an intimation given us by Mencius concerning the relation which exists between nature and destiny. He says (p. 365), "The relation of the mouth to taste, of the eye to colour, of the ear to sound, of the nose to odours, of the four limbs to rest, is nature

---

[1] "Honour and shame from no condition rise;
Act well your part, there all the honour lies."

(being), but is destined; the superior man does not call it essential nature. The relation of love between father and son, of righteousness between ruler and minister, of propriety between guest and host, of wisdom with the talented, of the holy man in reference to the heavenly *Tao* is destined, but it is natural (essential); the superior man calls it not destiny." The first part treats of the senses and their peculiar organisation; they are the " nature," but not the specific human nature. Mencius here declares himself very plainly in opposition to sensualism, and in the second half he confesses himself decidedly on the side of idealism. This is the territory of moral freedom, on which account neither the superior man nor the sage dare to call it destiny, although, as is plainly indicated above, it is the higher destiny. The lower destiny is the course of things, the laws of nature, almost independent of the action of the individual. As a conclusion to this section, I will recapitulate the principal points, viz.: Destiny is to human nature as a plan, according to which, whatever there is of moral grandeur has been achieved. There is a difference between hearts upon which the external world exerts an influence. There is a contact of man's nature with the Divine Being (Heaven). The will in its central position is the proper personality in the being, in which it should be the regulator of the energies and appetites. Consequently moral freedom is recognised. The moral perfection of human nature is the service of God, as well as the path which leads to our true destiny. We have in these, some contributions towards the Christian doctrine of man being the very image of the personal God. Personality is, of course, not considered as a barrier to, but as the absolute perfection of, moral consciousness. In man, His likeness, will God find Himself; in him rest, or even dwell. Men becoming God and God becoming man condition each other. The destiny is the standard of the highest development or completed representation of the Divine image, so that it

F

becomes a reflection of the glory of the prototype. The way to this is pointed out by the example of the Son of Man. It must, nevertheless, be here borne in mind that these deeper doctrines have become quite strange to the consciousness of the modern Chinese. They require long and patient explanations before these thoughts can be understood; but it is possible finally to attain to this (in some cases with joyful concurrence) among the Chinese already prepared for it. The progress is, however, step by step; only in rare cases is it suddenly, as by a Paul. What is presupposed is not simply a craving of the intellect, but also of the moral and religious consciousness.[1]

[1] The incarnation and our becoming "partakers of the Divine nature" are two parts of one great truth, which is only made clear to us by revelation.

PART II.

VIRTUES AND CORRESPONDING DUTIES.

———o———

CHAPTER I.

VIRTUE IN CONDUCT.[1]

(*a.*) *In Conduct in General.*

91. FROM abstaining from evil one goes on to doing good. Mencius says (p. 333), "Do not what he did not, desire not what he desired not; this is enough." This is to be referred to the conduct of that ancient holy man, *Shun,* who for a long time dwelt amongst savages without allowing himself to become barbarous through their influence. Emphasis is here laid upon opposition to external evil influences. The same thought recurs also on p. 197, "If men understand ceasing (leaving undone), they can then understand also what is to be done." It is at first easier to cease from evil than to do the good; this was formerly too lightly esteemed by many moral philosophers as a negative or passive virtue. It should, of course, only be the preparation or starting-point of activity in what is good.

92. Diligence in what is good. Mencius says (p. 340), "He who rises at cockcrow to occupy himself diligently in good things is a disciple of Shun. He who does so for the sake of gain is a disciple of the (robber) Chih. If one

---

[1] See Digest of Confucius, p. 59.

wants to know the difference between the holy man and the robber, it is nothing else than the distance of selfishness from goodness." Zeal alone is not virtue,[1] else even the greater number of evil-doers themselves would be to be praised; the zeal must be directed towards that which is really good.

93. But perseverance also is required (p. 342). "Activity is to be compared to the digging of a well; if a man digs nine fathoms deep without reaching water, he may as well be without the well." It often happens that work, especially that of self-improvement, has been commenced with great zeal and then left suspended. One not only through this misses gaining anything, but also incurs loss, and that the greater the longer the work has been carried on. Many opponents of Christianity have in past days given up this work in mind and spirit too soon, and thereby have become such as we now see them.

94. Beyond this, it is requisite that virtue be thorough (p. 358). "A bad year cannot ruin him who is always making money. A perverted world cannot destroy him who is thoroughly virtuous." Much may be acquired by circumspection. He who takes precautions in a good season can stand in the time of need. Investments or sources of help must, however, be of many kinds, so that if one leaves us in the lurch another may come to the rescue. So is it with virtue. One virtue alone, even if developed to the highest degree, never satisfies and is speedily destroyed. Thoroughness, on the contrary, imparts a firm and restful security; therefore is religion better than mere morality, for it is many-sided and central.

---

[1] Misdirected zeal, however, on the part of ecclesiastics, seems to be an exception, judging from the measure of praise dealt out so largely to the Ritualists of England of late years on account of the zeal they exhibit.

(b.) Virtue in Things which are to be Avoided (Negative).

95. Indecision is injurious (p. 204). "Where one ought to receive and also to decline, receiving injures one's abstinence; where one ought to give and also to withhold, giving injures one's goodness; where one ought to die and also ought not, death injures one's courage." Where one hesitates, it is in most cases safest not to act. Action always loses its moral value if it proceeds from a divided heart. Whatever is not of faith is sin.

96. Mencius is opposed also to narrow-minded one-sidedness (p. 341). "To hold the mean without weighing (the surroundings) is also one-sided. That which is to be shunned in the holding firmly to one point is the injury it does to the *Tao;* one lays hold of a single point and neglects a hundred." All heretics plead for some single truth, but apprehend it in a one-sided and often most dangerous manner. Although we must keep ourselves clear from such perverseness, it is nevertheless just as perverse to reject what is good because it has the appearance of being such (heretical). One should rather have regard to the various extremes, and seek to supply the defects of each by the others, keeping oneself to a spiritually active, living medium, instead of dead and rigid orthodoxy.

97. Going to extremes. Mencius said (p. 197), "Confucius never acted in an exaggerated way." To maintain a well-balanced moderation in all things is often a hard task, yet to be thoroughly virtuous is only possible upon this supposition; the one helps to the other.

98. Perversity, *i.e.,* the doing of what is right in the wrong place (p. 351). "He who stops short where he ought not, stops short in everything; he who is niggardly where he ought to be liberal is mean in everything. He who advances rashly retreats precipitately." There is really a great deal of mischief in the world caused by the

occupying of oneself in good in the wrong place. But it is also often quite an open question what really is the best to be done. Five kinds of considerations present themselves: The object; the surrounding circumstances; the means at our disposal; the manner of applying these; and, lastly, there are the immediate result and the remote effect to be calculated upon. He who does this acts wisely in the great as well as in the little events of life.

99. Still Mencius is no friend to cringing, bending, and bowing; these are all to be avoided. (Cf. Art. 80.) " He who bends himself can never make others straight" (p. 140). One ought not to give way to his perverted nature lest he should destroy himself without being of use to any one. But firmness is different from obstinacy and self-will. Firmness is objective, and serves as a universally valid principle. Self-will is subjective, has no mind for anything but its own opinion, and clings to that, neither owning nor recognising its perversity.

100. Pharisaic appearance of holiness (p. 375). " Mencius was asked, 'How is it with those who may be styled honest country folk?' He answered, 'Just this, wherein they are so vainglorious: their words have no reference to their conduct, their conduct has no reference to their words; so they say, The ancients! the ancients! how peculiar and reserved was their conduct! Born in this age, we do as does the age; to be good may suffice. Treating the world exceedingly well, these are your honest country folk.' The disciple replied, 'Their whole village calls them honest folk, they everywhere in everything proclaim themselves such. Why does Confucius hold them to be thieves of virtue?' He answered, 'If one blames them, there is no proof; if one criticises them, there is nothing to lay hold of; they swim with the stream [of public opinion], and agree with an impure world; their demeanour resembles that of truth and faith, their actions seem to savour of moderation and purity; the whole multitude without exception is pleased with them; they

themselves hold that they are right, and because of this
one is never able to tread with them the way (*Tao*) of
Yaou and Shun (*i.e.*, the ethical ideal). On this account
they are called the 'thieves of virtue.'" Unhappily the
great majority of men consists of such honest country
folk, and that not merely in the country. Christ found
the same difficulty in dealing with the Pharisees as did
Confucius and Mencius with people of this sort. In the
present day it is no easier to bring moral and religious
influences to bear upon such wily glib-tongued people.
In China especially does this operate against the missionary. The Chinese are always boasting of their ancient
learning, and think that they have no necessity to learn
anything, but that their hearts and their country are
perfection, just as they themselves are. If one speaks
to them of other lands, it is said, "That is no concern
of ours;" if one appeals reprovingly to antiquity, they
say, "The times are changed;" if one enlarges upon the
loss they experience, this is explained away as either
natural or inevitable; if one appeals to their consciences
and their higher moral requirements, this will generally
be granted, but they hold these as too difficult—"We are
verily not holy sages," &c. This alone accounts for missions
being more fruitful amongst savages than amongst so-called
civilised people. Happily we now and then meet with
exceptions, and China must yet change.

(*c.*) *Individual Positive Virtues.*

101. Kindness, truth, benevolence (p. 129). "To impart
to men of one's possessions is kindness; to direct men in
goodness is truth; to find a man to benefit the empire, this
is called benevolence." This definition is given first with
reference to political life, but it has also a general value,
and indicates very strikingly the peculiar characteristic of
each of the three virtues. Kindness hastens to the relief
of immediate necessities, truth to the moral improvement

or spiritual culture of the individual, and benevolence embraces both in view of the common weal.

102. Sincerity (p. 179). " The most thorough sincerity has never yet remained without influence, but insincerity cannot possibly acquire influence."

103. Sense of shame. Mencius said (p. 327), " Men should not be without a sense of shame. Shame on account of shamelessness brings no shame " (disgrace); and " Shame is most important to man. He who carries on mischievous intrigues requires no shame. He who is not ashamed at not being equal to others, what has he in common with men?" True shame always reveals itself at some defect in the exhibition of that individuality which our inborn destiny demands from us through the voice of conscience. The conscience desires that which the noblest men before us have accomplished. He who does not recognise such types, and does not make them the standard of his own conduct, displays a lack of that which is termed a sense of shame.

104. True ambition (p. 358). " An ambitious man can decline a realm with a thousand chariots of war; but if he is not the man to do this, he declares it in the colour of his countenance in the matter of a dish of rice or a plate of soup " (and p. 296). True ambition arises from benevolence and righteousness. The ambitious are elevated above many vices. Here a yet higher ambition of virtue is suggested, which considers even the possession of a crown as a trifle. But it depends not upon external objects. A plate of soup is something of no account in comparison with a kingdom; it is only the predilection of the heart which imparts to things their positive moral value.

105. Supreme virtue (p. 371). " To let all the emotions and activities be thoroughly proper—that is supreme, is genuine virtue. Lamentation for the dead and sorrow should not be (merely) on account of the living. Let there be no deviating from the path of virtue, and this

not for the sake of gain. Let word and speech be sincere,
and this not merely for the sake of acting correctly."
According to Mencius, virtue consists also, not in the
external labour, but in the state of mind proper to the
same. Where the external corresponds to the internal,
and equally to all reasonable claims on the part of others,
there is indeed attained that which is possible to man;
but the acme of virtue is only then accomplished, when
the internal in all its emotions and activities corresponds
to the heaven-implanted idea—the Divine will.

(*d.*) *The Effect or Consequence of Virtue.*

106. The virtuous are able to help the age and lead the
people (p. 89). (Cf. Art. 317 *et seq.*) "There are three
dignities recognised in the Empire. Nobility is one, age
is another, and virtue is another. At the court nothing is
superior to rank; in rural society nothing is superior to
age; in helping the age and leading the people nothing is
superior to virtue" (*i.e.*, virtue is the best political factor).
Unhappily we often see virtue remaining in obscurity,
but even there she ought to be both salt and light.

107. He who improves himself obtains the realm (p.
171). "All that which one obtains not by conduct one
seeks by introspection in oneself. If one's own self is
made right the whole Empire rushes towards him." This
is said chiefly of princes. Every failure should afford an
opportunity for self-examination. This is true of all
actions, especially of works of charity, the carrying on
of government, and propriety of behaviour. It is to be
regretted that the good teaching here given is not generally followed; there would then be less bitterness in the
world, and much more true greatness achieved.

108. Virtue subdues men's hearts. (Cf. Art. 34 *ante.*)

109. And that indeed because it is inborn in the people.
(Cf. Art. 19 *ante.*)

110. "She spreads far and wide more quickly than an

imperial decree by couriers" (p. 60). Virtue touches a kindred chord in the human breast. Equally the majority feels that every higher virtue has been acquired by trouble and sorrow. One also involuntarily admires the perfected work in morals and religion (as is also the case in other departments) as long as he is not hindered by envy.

CHAPTER II.

VIRTUE IN SPEECH.

(a.) The Importance of this.

111. THE words reveal the heart (p. 67). "What is the meaning of understanding words?" so asked a disciple. Mencius answered, "From one-sided expressions I know how they (the speakers) are darkened; by extravagant sort of talk I know they are degraded; by vulgar expressions I know how they deviate (err); by prevaricating speech I know wherein they are defective." It is worthy of remark that Mencius here only treats of bad expressions. Bad language may with certainty disclose something kindred in the heart, but it is not the same with good words.

112. Speech and the eye (p. 182). Mencius says, "Nothing in the whole body is more honourable than the eye; it cannot conceal its evil.[1] If all is right in the breast, the eye beams brightly; if there is wrong in the breast, then the eye is dull. Hear his words and consider his eyes, how can a man conceal himself?" Although, therefore, Mencius did not despise the speech as the medium of communication by which the human heart is disclosed, he is yet far from placing too much confidence in words. He demands something more authentic, but finds that, not as does Confucius in the conduct, but, strikingly deviating from him, in the eye. In every case Confucius has chosen

[1] Cf. Boston Monday Lectures, by Rev. Joseph Cook, "On Solar Self-Culture."

the most certain proof. It is worthy of note that both means of proof were also used as such by Christ. But as a sure sign for judging in the case of others, only the fruits were to be regarded, or, as Confucius without a figure says, the conduct (Matt. vi. 22, vii. 20).

(b.) *What is to be Avoided (Negative).*

113. Presumptuous words (p. 260). "To speak of high matters when in an inferior position is sin." According to the context, one ought only to think about the fulfilment of those duties which lie nearest. But even to the present time much mischief is brought about by people who talk about matters which are too high for their comprehension. In doing this they neglect their own vocation. " Do not be curious about what is not your business " is an ancient golden rule.

114. " Words lacking reality are ominous of mischief. But the tenor (essence) of mischief-making words is to obscure men of excellence " (p. 200). At all events, this is said in relation to slanders. It is allowed by all that these are prolific of mischief. The reasons are correctly given by Mencius. Speech, which is untrue even when it is not meant to be direct slander, awakens mistrust and arouses prejudice : that is to say, it hinders many from forming an independent and unprejudiced judgment. The result of this is that the goodness or excellence of many men does not meet with proper recognition, and is often, so to speak, trodden in the dust.

115. But Mencius himself permitted himself to be guilty of untruths of so-called courtesy (pp. 86, 133).

116. We are warned also against uncharitable suggestions (p. 197). "They who are always blaming what is not good in others ought (to know) how great subsequent evils they must meet with." Consequently see to it that thou dost not thyself that which thou condemnest in another. It is every way a more obvious reflection to think

of the evil one draws upon himself in the shape of the enmity of the person he calumniates. This enmity is often so much the greater the truer and more striking has been the charge brought against him. It would be much better for acquaintances, especially those of the fairer sex, if conversation about others were absolutely forbidden beyond what duty calls for.

117. The cause is disclosed (p. 187). "Men begin talking lightly just because they meet with no reproof." There would be much less foolish talking and prating going on in the world if those who are profound in their judgments did but speak more often in the way of earnest, faithful reproof. It is indeed-evil when frivolous men set themselves up for critics and pronounce judgment upon things which are too deep for their shallowness and too high for their pigmy minds.

118. In contrast to this we have another evil (p. 187). Mencius said, "The evil of men is that they fondly wish to be teachers of others." He who teaches others should before all things teach himself, *i.e.*, to be a practical example of his doctrine. There are indeed many epicureans we grant. He who teaches should consequently always fully appropriate that which serves to improve and deepen the good and noble within us, and set it before others in his own case.

119. With uncharitable men it is impossible to converse (p. 174). " How is it possible to converse with the cruel ? They hold their danger to be security, their evil for gain ; they rejoice in that which casts them to the ground. If one could speak with these cruel men, how could there be fallen states and ruined families ? " Good words are ineffectual where they do not meet with a good reception. The wise listens to the counsels of others, not in order to follow the opinion of every one, but to find that which is right and eternally good. By the use of this is obtained safety and true profit.

120. Mencius speaks also of another hopeless race of

men (p. 177). He says, "One can discuss nothing with those who ruin themselves; one can do nothing with those who throw themselves away. To converse without propriety and righteousness is called doing violence to one's self; if I myself cannot continue in benevolence and act in righteousness, it is termed self-destruction." (Cf. Art. 145.) Men who turn a deaf ear to expostulation have generally already broken with themselves, and stand in opposition to the requirements of their inmost purest humanity. With such there is not only no desire for truth, but a determined enmity thereto, either open or concealed. What good, then, is conversation with such? They have no wish to improve themselves, but simply desire to hear that which is in harmony with their degraded nature.

(c.) What we Ought to Strive for (Positive).

121. To hear good words (p. 202). Yu (an ancient emperor, 2000 B.C.) abhorred generous wine and loved good words (conversation) (p. 81). "He made obeisance when he heard good words." People like Yu are not only rare amongst princes, but are as a rule not often to be met with in the world. Many hold it for a point of honour to take nothing from others, i.e., not from inferiors or so-called subordinates. True humility straightway submits itself to truth without regard to the position of him who may happen to be its medium.

122. That word and speech be sincere has been already mentioned (Art. 105 ante).

123. To be intelligible and profound. Mencius said (p. 370), "To speak of the near and signify the distant is good speech; a narrow principle with a wide application is good management (Tao). The words of the superior man do not go below the girdle, yet they contain Tao." According to the commentary, the near relates to the improvement of the heart, the distant to the service of

Heaven (God). The narrow is benevolence and righteousness; the wide is the propagation of virtue throughout
the realm. All teaching must invariably come back to
the renewing of the heart (cultivation of the heart) as the
foundation of every moral, legal, or political edifice. Where
that is not the case we only find castles in the air, Utopias
which can never be realised, but which rather make the
evil worse. Many socialistic schemes are of this kind.
On the other hand, we ought not to forget that the state,
or, in the highest sense, the kingdom of God (*i.e.*, the revelation of perfected humanity in its entirety), is over the
heart. In this respect the doctrine of Jesus is unequalled.

124. Brevity in our expressions. Mencius said (p. 199),
"One learns comprehensively and puts it down diffusively
in detail, in order then to give it to others in a brief com-
pendium." We must remember that on the part of the
Confucianists solid knowledge was of old always insisted
upon. Unfortunately this only consists now in scholastic
learning without any vivifying energy for the heart or the
state. We find many words in modern Chinese writings,
especially in the commentaries, and very little sense. A
purifying criticism is very much wanted, which, like a
fresh breeze, may drive away the chaff.[1] It is and will
be the mark of a master-mind to possess well-grounded
information, embracing all details of a subject, and yet to
be able to present it in a condensed and vigorous statement.

[1] Many noble - minded positive
theologians might cure themselves
of their extreme anxiety in the face
of modern negative criticism by a
glance at the rigidity of China or of
the Papacy. Scientific opposition
serves to fertilise knowledge; frivolity and animosity alone injure the
truth.

CHAPTER III.

THE FOUR CARDINAL VIRTUES.

THESE form the fourfold manifestations of the moral nature of individuals, and are thence the essence of all isolated virtues. For the origin of these, *vide* Art. 21 *ante*.

1. WISDOM.

(a.) *Characteristics of Wisdom.*

125. It is not subtilty. Mencius said (p. 207), "That which is to be abhorred in the worldly-wise is their subtilty. Were the wise such as Yu, who led away the water, wisdom would be blameless. Yu led away the water so that the process caused no inconvenience. Were the wise to take the lead without causing inconvenience, their wisdom would be great." Mencius keeps in view the chief point : great wisdom is not in a multiplicity of things, the not occasioning of difficult circumstances, but in avoiding these whilst quietly progressing.

126. Natural and independent knowledge (p. 332). "That which men are capable of without learning, it is their best capacity; what they know without pondering over it, is their best knowledge. Little children, without exception, know how to love their parents; when they are older they without exception honour their elder brother. Attachment to parents is love ; respect to seniors is righteousness. It is not otherwise; they are (known and) recognised throughout the world." Moral knowledge is not something learned, but has its roots in the proper nature of

men, which, generally speaking, only comes to clear consciousness by degrees. This consciousness is the knowledge in a peculiar sense (Plato's " Memory ").

127. Wisdom recognises, consequently, "the realisation of benevolence and righteousness " (p. 188).

128. It is directed towards important objects. Mencius said (p. 352), "Nothing is unknown to the wise, yet they ought to strive after those things which are most important. Nothing is unlovable to the benevolent, yet their energy is directed towards (loving) their parents and the excellent. The very wisdom of Yaou and Shun did not embrace all things, but apprehended before everything that which is chiefly to be striven for."

Multiplicity of knowledge often leads to indecision in judgment and uncertainty in action. The truly wise lay hold firmly of the question immediately before them, and, spite of a multitude of events and claims around them, keep it steadily in view.

129. It consists also in seeking the lost heart. (Cf. sec. 26.)

(*b.*) *Practical Application of Wisdom.*

130. It enables us to recognise what is holy (the holy man), (p. 71). This point is illustrated in the three disciples of Confucius. The right explanation is as follows :—These three men, although sufficiently intelligent to recognise in Confucius the holy man, yet did not come up to him. On the other hand, their inferiority to him did not arise from anything vulgar or ignoble. Knowledge was to them the conviction that in the holy is realised the holy and the true. This wisdom is moral nature. A single example may serve for explanation. He who recognises the ideal in the plays of Shakespeare or the music of Beethoven does not readily praise bad composition, nor is he drawn away by lighter works, which may in themselves be good, but are not perfected in a masterly style. These disciples of Confucius recognised

G

in their master their ethical ideal. This should much more be the case with Christians, who recognise in Christ the highest, most complete realisation of the human ideal. But this recognition is only by way of preparation. Its object is to bring about a complete resemblance to the ethical ideal. Only after sincere struggles can one understand the nature of sin and the depths of divine grace in the incarnation. The Chinese enter not into the inner realm of holiness. There are, alas! not a few of such Chinese in Christendom.

131. It is both to originate and skilfully to carry out (p. 248). "To commence a particular thing is the work of wisdom, to complete it is the work of holiness. Wisdom may be likened to skill, holiness to power. To shoot with the bow a distance of more than a hundred paces is the attainment of thy power; to hit the mark is not of thy power." According to the context, Confucius is treating of harmony of sound; therefore beginning and ending combine wisdom and holiness in one. One requires both, just as archery requires power and skill. The Chinese think, alas! that everything comes from one's own power without divine assistance, and have carried it farther, even to cases of mercy.

132. It chooses a benevolent neighbourhood (p. 80), in order to be able to practise benevolence.

133. Imparts prudence to counsel (p. 243), so that one gives no advice where there is nothing to be advised. This kind belongs to prudence, and consequently indicates that in China also the word "wisdom" contains both ideas. But prudence is here to be taken ethically.

134. It makes use of an advantageous policy (p. 31). "Only the wise are able with a small (state) to serve a large (one)," namely, in view of the whole empire. Here wisdom stands in opposition to delusion and obstinacy. Only by means of wise compliance did the ruler named in the text escape total annihilation, and obtain in after time more, so to speak, than he had beforehand lost. But

for the effecting of this there is required a clear appre-
hension of the situation at the moment, hope for the
future, and courage to meet everything in the way of
opposition.

135. It never lets the opportunity slip by (p. 59). "The
people of Ts'e have a saying, 'Although one has wisdom,
that is not like seizing the opportunity; although one has
the implements of husbandry, that is not the same as
waiting for the proper season.'" Here we have shown us
the difference between real wisdom and mere learning or
knowledge, which are often called wisdom. Genuine
wisdom is practical in its nature, and it is characterised,
generally speaking, neither by irresolution, which misses
its object, nor by precipitation, which rushes to its ruin.

2. BENEVOLENCE.

(a.) *The Idea Considered Subjectively.*

136. It is of man's heart. (Cf. Art. 26 *ante.*[1])

137. "It is manhood" (p. 361). (Cf. Art. 75.)

138. It is universal both in disposition and in practice
(p. 369). "All men have something that they cannot
endure; if carried on to that which they can endure, it is
benevolence. All men have something that they do not
do; extended to that which they do, it is righteousness.
If men could carry out (completely) the feeling of not
injuring others, there would be more benevolence than is
necessary. If men could (fully) carry out the feeling of
not breaking through and not climbing over (walls) [pre-
scribed bounds], there would be more righteousness than
is necessary." In these passages it is clearly laid down
that benevolence is not accidental, but is worked out from
man's veritable nature, and that not in a developed form,
but in the disposition which shows itself in all men. How
the disconnected indications should be turned to account
is the moral problem which we have to solve.

[1] Digest of Confucius, p. 66.

139. It is approached in the exercise of reciprocity (p. 327). "In seeking after benevolence, nothing brings one nearer to it than skilfully to exercise reciprocity." It is to be considered that according to this place reciprocity does not thoroughly exhaust the idea of benevolence, but only exhibits a sort of approach to it. But reciprocity is that step in advance towards benevolence whose practical importance must be immediately evident to every one. We will here add the social aspect of this virtue in order to obtain a well-balanced picture of the same; its political bearings will be dwelt upon subsequently.

(b.) The Idea Socially.

140. Its realisation is the "service of parents" (p. 189), and this is termed "attachment to parents" (p. 332). For "there never was a benevolent man who left his kindred in the lurch" (p. 3).

141. The "admonishing" of one's parents (p. 303). It is very singular to find this classed under the idea of benevolence, and not under that of filial affection; but this serves to show the difference as well as the close affinity which exists between the two virtues.

142. Care of the aged is also termed benevolence (p. 337).

(c.) Hindrances to the Personal Exercise of Benevolence.

143. Want of success therein is one's own fault (p. 81). "The benevolent man is like the archer who assumes the proper position and then shoots. If he does not excel, he is not indignant with those who surpass him; he returns and seeks the cause in himself." He does so (p. 209) even when he endeavours to hold a most friendly interview with any one and meets with a rude repulse. "The superior man is distinguished from other men in this whereby he guards his heart; the superior man guards his heart by benevolence and preserves it by propriety. The

benevolent loves men, the man of propriety honours them.
He who loves men is straightway beloved by them; he
who honours men is forthwith honoured by them.   Is
there a man who treats me discourteously ?   The superior
man will look into his conduct : " Surely I am not benevolent; surely I am lacking in propriety.   Has this thing
been deserved by me ?"   He considers himself and is benevolent; he considers and he has propriety.   If the obstinacy
of the other still remain, the superior man will again yield
to reflection : " Certainly I am not sincere (true)."   He
considers himself and is sincere.   If the obstinate opponent
remains the same, the superior man declares, " That is none
other than a lost man.   Such a man!   What choice is
there to be made between him and a brute ?   What good
is it to get oneself into difficulties with a brute ? "   The
demeanour of others towards us is in a great measure
dependent upon our own conduct, therefore the adjust-
ment of an unhappy state of relations with any one is to
be commenced in our own demeanour.   If the other party
is of the same benevolent disposition, a friendly state of
affairs is immediately established.   Unfortunately one
finds far too many people of another spirit, who never
permit themselves to be persuaded in the course of a
friendly interview, but whose mistrust and enmity are
only thereby increased.   The term " brute " is not altogether suitable for such men, for all kinds of brutes, even
the wild beasts, suffer themselves to be more or less
tamed by friendly treatment, and, so to speak, show
attachment in response.

144. The evil results of hindering benevolence by false
doctrine show themselves in Sensualism and Socialism
(p. 158).   With Sensualism everything turns to " I," and
there no other lord is recognised (no authority).   With
Socialism there is " universal love ; " there distinctions are
given up, even those of nature.   " To be without father or
sovereign, that is brutal," said Mencius very cuttingly.
From a benevolent standpoint one must employ contro-

versy, which unveils and battles with false doctrine; but
in order to make plain the way for truth, there must be
something besides that negative criticism which pulls
down but knows not how to build up.

145. He, however, who does not continue benevolent
actually casts himself away (p. 177). " Can I not continue
in benevolence and do I wander from righteousness? This
is termed casting one's self away. Benevolence is the
peaceful habitation of men; righteousness is the direct
path of men. For the peaceful habitation to remain
empty and uninhabited, to abandon the right path and not
to walk in it—Oh, how deplorable!" (Cf. Art. 120 *ante.*)
Such men in this way make themselves more miserable
than others, for they discard that by which their inmost
being acquires its satisfaction. But the ultimate source
of soul-happiness is God, from whom, as the First Cause,
proceed all genuine love and righteousness.

146. Immature benevolence is, however, not good (p.
297). "The five kinds of grain are the finest among
seeds, yet if they be not ripe, they are not equal to ripe
weeds. Benevolence also is only of value in its maturity."
A very important truth is here set forth. We speak
indeed of "unripe products," without thinking it our
business to dwell farther on them. Besides, in the present
day, one seldom finds time for perfect ripening. Many
things are left in an immature state. Even in the
exercise of works of charity there is often partial injury
effected through immaturity, that is, by well-meant but
unintelligent zeal.

147. It is more powerful when in due proportion than
wrong-doing (p. 297). "Benevolence overcomes wrong-
doing (its opposite) as water overcomes fire. Those who
now exercise benevolence are, however, as if they went
to extinguish the fire of a cartload of wood with a pitcher
of water; it does not go out; so they say, 'Water cannot
extinguish fire.' This confirms those who are the reverse
of benevolent. The result is nothing but destruction."

The same reproach one can hear even to the present day, and it will be heard even until the world's end. He who cannot overcome opposition with his faith, his love, &c., should before all things look to it whether there does not exist a state of affairs such as that described by Mencius.

(d.) *The Kind of Exercise.*

148. One's earthly vocation makes no difference (p. 80). Mencius said, "Is the fletcher in some way less benevolent than the armourer? The fletcher fears lest men should not be wounded, and the armourer's only fear is lest they should be wounded. Just so is it with the exorcist and the coffinmaker. Thence it is that a man should not be other than circumspect in his vocation." The Commentary says, "From of old until the present time have the exorcists before all healed by beat of drum." That this superstition should have prevailed universally in China even to our own time, is no good omen for Chinese civilisation. Similar in one respect, it yet differs essentially from the ethico-religious method of healing peculiar to Christendom by means of prayer, laying on of hands, &c. In the former the effect is ascribed to the trumpet or the formula of the prayers of the exorcist; in the latter, to the power of faith as the most intense force of the soul, which affects not only the formation of the organism but its renovation also. The calling of an exorcist consequently stands in no sense upon the same level of civilisation with that of the coffinmaker. It is requisite in the choice of a calling to weigh accurately its aim and moral value. One may find his livelihood and much besides in any department of professional industry. The man who, unconstrained by necessity, makes choice of a calling, indicates his character by that very choice.

149. Wealth is not benevolent, benevolence is not wealthy (p. 116). "Yang Hoo said, 'He to whom wealth is the object of action will not be benevolent; he to whom

benevolence is the object of action will not be rich.'" This is much like the declaration, "How hardly shall they that have riches enter into the kingdom of God." There, however, the acquisition of earthly goods is placed in opposition to that of heavenly.

150. It is to be exercised from an inner motive (p. 201). "Mencius said, 'That whereby man differs from the beasts is but a trifle: the people generally cast it away, the superior man preserves it. Shun was full of intelligence in reference to the multitude of things, and experienced in human relations, he wrought *out* benevolence and righteousness, and not merely *according* to benevolence and righteousness.'" The difference between man and beast is often treated of nowadays, and frequently the decision is not to the honour of men. That after more than a thousand years' development of civilisation, theories are current which throw ridicule upon humanity, proves most incontrovertibly that civilisation and humanity are not necessarily co-ordinately developed; indeed they may, so to speak, proceed in opposition to each other. "That which is requisite for the spirit of man is to measure the extent of its desires," says a modern sage.

151. Propriety and righteousness are the results (p. 81). "Malevolent and unwise, indecorous and unrighteous— that is human bondage. To be the slave of men and to be ashamed. of being a slave, is like being a bower and ashamed of making bows, or being a fletcher and ashamed of making arrows. If one is ashamed of that (his bondage to men), there is nothing better for him than to practise benevolence." "Blessed are the meek," &c. In the region of morals knowledge is not its own object, and propriety, like righteousness, is subordinated to benevolence, which answers to love. (*Vide* the next Article.)

152. Reputation for benevolence is better than talk about it (p. 331). "Mencius said that benevolent words do not impress men so deeply as a reputation for benevolence." A man's reputation declares the nature of his

everyday conduct; fine words any babbler can employ. The word (preached) proceeds from one's own mouth; the reputation is the verdict of many tongues. But that one ought not to trust too much to a good reputation Confucius at least recognised in Analect xv. 27, and Mencius also. (Cf. Arts. 112 and 100.)

153. It extends itself specially and chiefly to the people (p. 352). "Mencius said the superior man in his position with regard to creatures loves them, but is not benevolent to them;[1] towards the people he exercises benevolence, but is not confiding; he is confiding towards those who are to be relied upon (*i.e.*, parents), and benevolent towards the people; benevolent towards the people and charitable towards things." Christianity also permits gradations in love. Universal love without any gradations is, generally speaking, a matter of impossibility. Benevolence has ever something of grace and mercy in it, and is, therefore, not practicable from the inferior to the superior.

154. Begins with that which is near and extends to the remote[2] (p. 353). "Mencius said, 'Veritably the reverse of benevolent is King Hwuy of Leang!' The benevolent, commencing with that which he loves, goes on to that which he does not love. Those who are the reverse, commencing with that which they do not love, reach that which they do love." The next paragraph explains this. The king deprived his subjects of their estates and sacrificed them in his wars. After a great defeat he would yet make another attempt; and because he was dubious about gaining the victory, he urged on his beloved young son, and sacrificed him with them. "That is termed commencing with that which is not loved (death), one reaches that which is beloved (a son)." So it is that there exists a certain necessity in good things as well as in bad for the consecutive carrying out of an undertaking which is

---

[1] *i.e.*, Does not treat them as fellow-creatures. *Benevolence* is to be understood all through this as the thorough observing of all our duties to our fellow-men. Mr. Faber uses *Humanität humane*, &c.

[2] "Charity begins at home."

once begun. One very rarely succeeds in escaping the consequences. Therein lies already a judgment. (For benevolence in relation to the realm, see Arts. 327–329, &c.)

3. RIGHTEOUSNESS.[1]

The idea of righteousness is different from that of right. This indicates external claims upon us, that the inner motive. Hence it is possible for them both to be in opposition, *e.g.*, an action can be right without being righteous; more rarely is the reverse the case, the being righteous without being right.

(*a.*) *Righteousness belongs to the Original or Essential Nature of Men.*

155. Hence it is common to all hearts. (Cf. Art. 6.)

156. Consequently it is not learnt from without. (Cf. Art. 13.)

157. It is the correct path for men. (Cf. Art. 152.)

158. It is consequently not so much the condition as the proper conduct of man. (Cf. Art. 13.)

159. It is more than life (p. 287). "Mencius said, I like fish, and I also like bear's paws; if the two are not to be had together, I let the fish go and take the bear's paws. I like life and I also like righteousness; if the two are not to be retained together, I let go life and hold to righteousness. Life also appertains to the things which I desire, but if amongst the things which I desire there is something greater than life, I will not on this account retain it (life) by baseness of conduct. Death, again, appertains to the things which I hate; but if amongst the things which I hate there is something greater than death, therefore there are calamities which I do not avoid. Let it be granted that of those things which men desire there is nothing greater than life, should not man employ every

---

[1] See Digest of Confucius, p. 76.

means by which life may be retained? Supposing that amongst the things hated by men there is nothing greater than death, why should not man do everything by which calamities might be avoided? After this fashion one might live, and yet ofttimes one does not adopt it: after that one might avoid calamities, and yet ofttimes one does not adopt it. The cause of this happening is that what man desires is greater than life, and what man hates is greater than death. It is not distinguished men only who are of this mind; every one is of the same way of thinking. It is the distinguished, however, who succeed in never losing it."[1] That life is not the chiefest amongst good things, men often involuntarily prove in opposition to the inrooted, materialistic convictions of their hearts. But in this fact lies another, viz., that this inner sense of righteousness reaches out beyond this life, so that thereby man attains to a higher destiny. Concerning this, however, the Chinese know nothing of themselves. The gospel of the kingdom, with its righteousness, is the only satisfying complement of man's intuitive idea. Apart from this it would be simple folly to throw away one's best good, his life, for an empty idea.

160. In its nature it yields respect (p. 275). "Righteousness embodies in action our (inclination to) honour (others), therefore it is said to be internal" (see pp. 255 and 332). "Respect from inferiors to superiors," and *vice versa,* and "respect for elders," are righteousness. With the recognition (of honour due), however, Mencius refers righteousness to the same foundation as propriety.

161. It permits nothing improper. (Cf. Art. 138 *ante.*) Righteousness is realised by a practical recognition of the rights of others. If this took place in all state relations, life would, generally speaking, be easy. In spite, however, of oppositions, the idea of righteousness

---

[1] An idea glorified by Christianity into St. Augustine's "Thou hast made us for Thyself, and our restless hearts disquiet themselves until they find rest in Thee."

proves itself to be categorically imperative in man's inner being.

162. Its opposite is gain (p. 305). Mencius meets with a diplomatist who would fain make peace between two states which are at war with one another. Mencius asks how he will set about it; he replies that "he will show them that the war is not profitable. On the contrary, said Mencius, if these kings disband their armies for the sake of profit, the officers of their armies will rejoice at the disbanding, and find their delight in profit. Subordinates will be smitten with the love of gain in the service of their rulers, sons will conduct themselves in the same way towards their fathers, and brothers towards brethren; so at last ruler and minister, father and son, elder and younger brother, will cast away from them benevolence and righteousness, and in their mutual intercourse will strive after profit; but this has never yet happened without ruin following. On the contrary, it is the other way with benevolence and righteousness." In modern politics much is thought to have been attained when the unprofitable nature of any undertaking has been proved. Profit in the shape of gold and gear is palpable and evident. The advantages of benevolence and righteousness are far too mystical for the politics of most diplomatists.

163. The subjective result is contentment or self-satisfaction (p. 329). "He who prizes virtue and rejoices in righteousness may well be cheerful. Therefore in destitution the scholar does not lose righteousness, in prosperity he departs not from the *Tao*. It is because in poverty he loses not righteousness that the scholar finds himself; it is because in prosperity he leaves not the *Tao* (way) that the people do not lose hope." Man can only find satisfaction in that which he seeks. The obtaining of this always proceeds in the direction of an ideal which is very rarely realised. A definite object satisfies only so far as it corresponds to our ideal, which is never fully the case. He, therefore, who seeks the idea itself, and devotes him-

self entirely to that, becomes thereby independent of external matters as regards the inner emotions of his spiritual life.

(b.) *Righteousness as Exercised towards our Fellow-Men.*

164. The declining of a kingdom is only negative (p. 345). "All people believe that if one offered the kingdom of Ts'e to the (capricious) Chung-tsze in an unrighteous manner, he would not accept it. That is (merely) righteousness which will not have a bowl of rice or a plate of soup. There is nothing greater than man [in his social relations]. On account of his holding aloof from these, this man has no relatives, sovereign, minister, superiors or inferiors. How can one believe in his greatness?" It is indeed far easier to withdraw one's self altogether from the business of daily life than whilst living and energising in the world to keep one's self unspotted therefrom. Man has duties which he is called upon to fulfil towards other men, and every one has his special gift which has been conferred upon him. He who misanthropically despairs of his fellow-men is unjust to them. Regarding this point the Confucianists as well as evangelic Christianity are right in contradistinction to all monkish quietism.

165. Its nearest exhibition is the service of brethren. (See Art. 127.)

166. Wrong is straightway abolished (p. 154). (Cf. Art. 441.) "The minister of the state of Sung said, 'I cannot this year give up the duties at the passes and in the markets and receive a tenth instead, but permit me to lighten these duties until next year, and then give them up, how would that do?' Mencius answered, 'That is just like a man who every day purloins fowls from his neighbours. Some one says to him, That is not the way of the superior man. He replies, Permit me to give up somewhat of my doings, and till next year to take only

one fowl a month and then give it up entirely. When one is convinced of unrighteousness, it ought to be at once abandoned. Why wait till next year?'"[1] Delay in the matter of self-improvement or in the putting down of social and political wrongs is always evil. In the case adduced it would at all events have been said, "The deficiency in the treasury must first be provided for some other way." It is possible that Mencius, with his preference for the old system of government, went too far. But if there exist an abuse, there ought to be straightway a search made after the proper means for removing it, and indeed of uprooting it; half measures only make the evil worse.

167. Is not to be carried too far in yielding to scruples (p. 255). "A disciple said to Mencius, 'I venture to ask what kind of feeling is signified in making presents?' Mencius answered, 'Respect.' 'Under what circumstances is the persistent declining (of a present) disrespectful?' He replied, 'When an honourable man presents anything, to say did he obtain this rightly or wrongly? and then to decline it; this is disrespectful, therefore one does not refuse (a present).' Thereupon the disciple said, 'Supposing that one does not refuse by word of mouth but in his heart, saying, He took it unrighteously from the people; may it not then be declined under some pretext?' He replied, 'If it were offered seasonably and tendered with propriety, Confucius would have received it.' The disciple upon this said, 'There is one, for instance, who plunders people beyond the boundaries: ought the fruit of such robbery, when offered seasonably and tendered with propriety, to be accepted?' He answered, 'It ought not. In the .Announcement to the Prince of Káng (Shoo King, p. 392), it is said, He who violently attacks men,

[1] Wise were Christian English-men if they would only act on the principle here enunciated by the ancient heathen in reference to opium and the Imperial traffic in that drug in India.

desiring their goods, reckless and fearless of the punishment of death, is abhorred by all. Such are to be
executed without previous warning. . . . How can the
presents of such be accepted?' He (the disciple) said,
'Our princes nowadays take from their subjects like
robbers, but if they make a present with propriety, the
superior man accepts it. I venture to ask how can this
be justified?' Mencius replied, 'Reflect, sir, whether if
an emperor should arise, he would gather together all the
present princes and execute them severally (as robbers),
or would he first give them warning, and if they did not
change their ways then first execute them? For if we
call every one that takes what does not belong to him a
robber, we begin to press the analogy (resemblance) and
push righteousness to extremes. When Confucius held
office in Loo, the people of Loo strove together for the
game, and Confucius strove also for it. If the striving
after game was proper, how much more the reception of
a present of the same?'" These presents refer, consequently, not to such as friends make to each other, but to
those from persons in high position to scholars to attach
them to their interests. Mencius skilfully rejects moral
puritanism and takes up a legal standpoint. The purely
ethical conception, however, is not unimportant. It is
this: the holding of one's self firmly to fixed principles,
yet without losing moral freedom. This is certainly a
difficult matter, of which very little can be said generally.
It relates principally to actions which, although morally
harmless in themselves, become of a doubtful character
through a peculiar connection with blameworthy matters.
In any case, one has to take care, in entering into any
connection of that kind, that with the final results all
that it presupposes be also accepted. St. Paul exhibits
the right view, 1 Corinthians x. 27, 28.

168. Position also influences it (p. 275). The villager
who is older than the elder brother is more honoured
because of his position, and the younger brother when

sacrificing to ancestors is more honoured than one's uncle, for the same reason. (Cf. Arts. 3 and 13.)

169. It is to be preserved even when adverse to our parents (p. 345). "Some one asked, 'When Shun was emperor and Kaou-yaou chief-justice, how would it have been if Koosow (the emperor's father) had murdered any one?' Mencius answered, 'He would simply have apprehended him.' 'But would not Shun have forbidden it?' 'How could Shun have forbidden it?' 'For he had received the office (of chief-justice to care for righteousness).' 'What then would Shun have done?' 'Why, he would have regarded his abandoning the empire in the same light as the throwing away of an old shoe. Privately he would have fled with his father on his back to the seashore, beside which he would have lived retired his whole life long, cheerful and happy, and forgetting the empire.'" This solution of the conflict between legal and natural duty is, indeed, somewhat singular, but is agreeable to our moral sentiments. Righteousness would have been recognised in the arrest of the criminal, and partially appeased by the voluntary self-exile of the imperial son. It is a correct opinion which is here advocated, that the bonds of natural affection should not be sundered even by crime itself. But it is quite another thing to give to such crime one's inward consent or even assistance. Each one who is capable of judging is responsible for his individual moral standpoint, without reference to the example of nearest relatives, superiors, &c. Shun also sighed over his wicked father, and succeeded afterwards in reforming him by his own steadfastness in good.

170. The same idea of righteousness often underlies several different external appearances (p. 237). "Confucius said, 'In the case of Tang and Yu, the succession to the crown was indirect; in the case of Hea Hau, Yin, and Chow, it was direct; their righteousness was the same.' The first-named passed over their own sons and chose worthy ministers as their successors; the last three had

worthy sons. Consequently in both cases the people who were in a position to fulfil their duty to the realm gave their support to the throne. Each ruler consequently acted wrongly either towards his own son or towards the empire.

171. Artisans have to submit to those who labour with their minds (p. 125). "One labours either with his heart (mind) or with his strength; those who labour with their minds rule men; those who labour with their strength are ruled by men. That those who are ruled should support the rulers, and the rulers be supported by them, is a general principle which holds everywhere." This general principle cannot be upset so long as mental labour is necessary amongst men. It cannot in any way be altered by any democratic or communistic experiments, which only set up some modern form of the same principle in the place of the earlier.

172. There is no danger of the ruler being neglected thereby [1] (p. 3). "There was never yet righteousness which made the ruler an afterthought." (Cf. sec. 148.)

4. PROPRIETY.

(a.) *Its Source and Signification.*

173. It takes its origin from the excellent amongst men (p. 53). "Propriety and righteousness arise amongst the excellent." We are not to understand that these were the discoverers thereof; the idea and rudiments of these, it is plainly maintained by Mencius, exist in all men, but the peculiar form in which they find expression is determined by the leading men of each age.

174. The essential characteristic of it is respect (p. 209). "He who observes propriety respects others." (Cf. Art. 150.) Propriety has consequently the same root as righteousness, but these assume separate forms, as is shown in the next paragraph. Earlier we have seen

[1] Cardinal Wolsey's "Ego et rex meus" affords a striking instance of the truth of this section.

(Arts. 5 and 21) that propriety is traced back to the sense of reverence and delicacy in the heart, whilst righteousness, on the other hand, is ascribed to the sense of shame, which we usually call conscience: the sense of right is also a usual term, but it is more of a paraphrase than a definition.

175. Its realisation is "the ordering, and adorning, in the first place, of parental and fraternal affection" (p. 190). (Cf. Art. 127.) The relationship to his parents and brothers and sisters is the first in which man finds himself placed in this life. The family is, so to speak, the laboratory in which man is quietly prepared for his work at large.

176. Propriety is more than mere natural motives, yet there are circumstances in which it has to give way to these (p. 298). "A man of Yin once asked a disciple of Mencius, 'Which is the more important, propriety or eating?' He answered, 'Propriety.' 'Which is more important, propriety or marriage?' He answered, 'Propriety.' 'If eating according to propriety brings hunger and death, whilst, on the contrary, eating in spite of propriety obtains food, must propriety still be observed?' 'If one cannot obtain a wife by going in person to receive her, but can obtain a wife without going in person, is a personal reception indispensable?' The disciple could not reply. The next day he went to Mencius to discuss it with him. Mencius said, 'Oh, what difficulty is there in answering that? If you do not consider the beginning, but simply compare the ends, you may make a cubic inch of wood higher than a lofty mountain. Gold is heavier than feathers, but is it so said with regard to a gold clasp and a cartload of feathers? If you compare that which is most important in eating with that which is of smallest account in propriety, wherefore stop at eating being more important? If you compare that which is most important in marriage (the sexual desire) with that which is of smallest account in propriety, why simply make marriage more important? Go and reply to him:

If you by wrenching your elder brother's arms and snatching away his food can get nourishment, but without such violence can obtain nothing to eat, ought you to wrench his arm? If you can obtain a wife by climbing over a neighbour's wall and abducting his daughter, but cannot obtain a wife without abduction, ought you then to commit abduction?'" This extract displays far too great subtilty. In actual life such cases are far more rarely met with than in theories or fiction. And even according to Chinese teaching, propriety should never be divorced from nature and become unnatural, but should exhibit that which is really good in nature in its most beauteous form. Therefore it is impossible to provide definitely, rules which shall apply to all times and cases. The natural is living and manifold, rules are dead and rigid. We may express the idea of propriety thus: Nobility of mind in a graceful exterior.

177. External position alters its observance (p. 346). "Mencius came from Fan to Ts'e; as he saw from far the son of the king of Ts'e, he said, sighing deeply, ' Position alters the demeanour, nourishment the body. Oh, how great is the importance of position! for are we not all children of men?'" Everyday experience shows that the consciousness of worth or power, of mental or some other superiority, exercises the greatest influence upon the external demeanour of men. Where this happens naturally, it makes a good impression, but where a lofty bearing is assumed without any ground for it, it is repulsive. The Christian ought ever to remain conscious of his high calling, such consciousness serving better to elevate his demeanour than a host of compendiums of Christian morality.

178. No impropriety (p. 196). Mencius said, "A great man does not use propriety which is improper, or righteousness which is unrighteous." Alas! there are many such proprieties which are improper, much justice which is injustice; but more than ordinary wisdom is needed to distinguish clearly one from the other, and higher prin-

ciples than ordinarily prevail to put oneself in opposition to the customary line of action.

179. If one meets with no responsive propriety, he retires into himself and seeks self-improvement. (Cf. Art. 150 *ante.*)

180. "By observing the customs (of the people) we understand the government" (p. 71). The customs of a country and the nature of its government must be in harmony; at least a difference cannot long continue. But the government should always in every relation occupy a higher position than the customs which obtain amongst the masses of its subjects. It is only by its elevating tendency that a government secures the loyalty of its people and secures their esteem.

181. Hunger makes it impossible for the people to observe propriety (p. 24). "Now provision is made for the sustenance of the people in such a way that when they look after their betters they have not enough for their parents; and regarding their inferiors, they lack sufficiency for the support of wife and children. In good years their life is incessantly embittered; in bad years they cannot escape death and destruction. Thus their only thought is how to escape death, and they dread not being able to accomplish it. How can they have leisure to cultivate propriety and righteousness?" It is well known that hunger overleaps all barriers. Where one does not confine one's self simply to individual cases but takes a wider range, it will be perceived that there are ever political and likewise moral evils lying in the background.[1]

(b.) *Special Requirements of Propriety for the Defunct.*

182. Coffins seven inches thick (p. 97).

183. Simple burial to be given up.

184. Three years' mourning (p. 112).

---

[1] This is equally true of China, A.D. 1878, as the fearful famines prevalent during the past two years in the northern provinces sadly testify. It is computed that in the early part of 1878 nearly five millions perished, whilst human flesh was eaten, even that of kinsfolk.

185. Second mourning (p. 53).

186. Mourning of the disciples of Confucius. (Cf. Art. 461.)

187. Ministers on quitting office to put on mourning. (Cf. Art. 338.)

(*c.*) *For Various Occasions.*

188. Relationship makes a difference. (Cf. Art. 305.)

189. Scholars and teachers. (Cf. Art. 460.)

190. Prompt obedience of officials. (Cf. Arts. 190, 396, 423.)

Those special usages and requirements which Mencius mentions we pass over. The three years' mourning for deceased parents he regards as most important, and will permit of no relaxation in regard to this in any way.

191. It has nothing to do with useless questions (p. 353). " If the three years' mourning is an impossibility, and yet one is very particular about that of the three and five months; if one bolts his rice and gulps his soup, yet asks about making the meat small without using his teeth (to tear it), this is termed being ignorant of what one ought to do." People who " strain out a gnat and swallow a camel " are to be met with at all times everywhere. Such often trouble themselves vastly about trifles because they are ignorant of the true bearing of things. They either hold tenaciously to dead forms, of which the spirit has long since departed, or haggle over externals simply in order to keep up appearances. Unhappily this is not the case amongst the modern Chinese only. In reference to rites, Mencius on the whole is more liberal than Confucius, save that in the observance of funeral obsequies and the sacrifice for the defunct he is equally firm with his master. This point will be treated of more fully subsequently under the head of social relations. In general it strikes us as a peculiarity of the moral doctrines of Mencius that duties are not distinguished from their special virtues. This distinction is properly an artificial

one, and puts difficulties in the way of perfecting many modern text-books of morals. According to Mencius, virtue is not something learned, something acquired from without, but it is the intuitive noble nature of man in a concrete form for practical life. Separate virtues are only individual, regulated, recurring expressions of one and the same moral principle according to the definite direction imparted to it. This has been already discussed in our explanations concerning human nature and destiny, as they are inherent in man and are in various ways either developed or destroyed. It occurs also in our discussions concerning virtue, being treated of in connection with this very nature and destiny, only not judged of from within, but from without, and consequently in the activities of practical life. Therefore it is that virtue in itself is of great value, even when socially its value may not be highly estimated. It is this which makes Confucianism superior to all other Chinese systems. It generally results in this, that only in the autonomy of the state itself can be manifested the full importance of the moral culture of the individual. For Confucianism, alas! knows of no other commonweal, no kingdom of God where the virtue recognised by the state may be valued according to moral righteousness. Its strength is, therefore, likewise the weakness of the system. Chinese sensualism discovered this weakness, and demonstrated from it the worthlessness of virtue in general. Chinese socialism also separates itself at this point from proper humanitarianism, in that it recognises no individual virtue as of value in itself, but simply as of theoretic value, or in so far as it is a social or political virtue. We can thus better understand why Confucianism styles itself the happy medium. As opposed to both sensualism and socialism it has a right so to style itself. Both these systems represent the very opposite of Confucianism, as well as of certain special truths of which we treat more fully in another place.

Book II.

THE PRACTICAL EXHIBITION OF MORAL SCIENCE.

———o———

PART I.—IN THE INDIVIDUAL CHARACTER.

Mencius distinguished four varied gradations of the moral personality : (1.) The scholar, who at that time was likewise a candidate for the Government service and the lower official positions ; (2.) the great man, who generally occupied the higher positions ; (3.) the superior man or sage, who represented the highest grade of human official worthiness ; (4.) and the holy or perfected man, the ethical ideal.

————

CHAPTER I.

THE SCHOLAR.

192. "HE elevates his will" (p. 344). (Cf. Art. 352 and 18b.)

193. He requires no external inducement (p. 330). Mencius said, "They who wait for a King Wan and then rise are ordinary people. Distinguished scholars arise without a King Wan." That which goes no farther than it is urged is simply an inert mass. Where spirit and life rule there must be indications of internal energy and productivity.

194. Has pleasure in Tao (principle), not in force (p. 328). Mencius said, "The (excellent) monarchs of antiquity loved goodness and forgot power ; how then could the excellent scholars of antiquity act otherwise ?

They took delight in their Tao (principle) and forgot the power of men. If kings and dukes did not come to visit them with all respect and propriety, they did not often go to see them, how much less could these obtain them for ministers (court officials)?" On account of this, which is peculiarly higher culture, the learned and the unlearned are, even to this very day, disunited. Anyway, the ancient Chinese culture was moral in ˙its nature, and so different from most modern. For this reason, however, such culture is an unsaleable commodity, yielding no external profit to the genuine scholar. He accepts no position of influence which places him in opposition to his views or convictions.

195. Therefore he receives no revenue (salary) without office, but simply assistance (p. 260). "A disciple asked, ' Why does not a scholar depend upon princes ?' Mencius answered, ' He does not venture to do so. That a prince, after he has lost his territory, should depend upon princes is proper ; for a scholar to depend upon princes is improper.' The disciple said, ' Would he then receive a present of corn from his sovereign ?' He answered, ' He would.' ' On what principle ?' He replied, ' The sovereign has to afford help to his subjects.' ' Why may he receive assistance yet not take salary ?' Answered, ' He dare not venture it.' ' Permit me to ask why is it so ?' Answered, ' The watchmen at the door with the staff have an appointed office, whereby their support comes to them from the prince. He who, without a properly appointed office, receives salary from his prince makes himself despicable.' " In this it is signified that the scholar does not put himself at the disposal of his superior, for his own selfish interests, as " Counsellor So-and-so." His actions should be well defined on account of his office. " Clear views as to justice and duty make true men."

196. It does not cast itself away in order to please the people (p. 364). " When there was famine in Ts'e, some one said to Mencius, ' The people all expect that your

worship will again cause the granary of Tang to be opened; but this will scarcely occur a second time.' Mencius said, 'That would be like Fung-foo. There lived amongst the people of Tsin one Fung-foo; he was skilled in tiger-hunting, but afterwards became a famous scholar. As such he went to the wild district, where the people were hunting a tiger. The tiger turned at bay in an angle of the hill, where no one ventured to approach it. Seeing Fung-foo at a distance, they ran to meet him. He rolled up his sleeves and descended from his carriage.' The whole crowd were delighted, but the scholars laughed at him.'" To capture a tiger was beneath the dignity of a scholar, as not ordinarily pertaining to his vocation. The tiger also could not otherwise possibly escape his destiny. Famine and the tiger's tooth are not, generally speaking, analogous. It would have been a work of mercy to intercede with the prince for his people. Mencius appears, however, to have felt that he would obtain nothing but a refusal and the making of himself ridiculous; besides which, he held no official position. Confucius acted otherwise (Analect. xiv. 21), but he held office at the time, and so fulfilled his duty.

197. The judgment of the masses is no criterion for him (p. 362). The best of people (in the text, Confucius and King Wan) are often the most hated and worst slandered. This is an indisputable proof of the moral degradation existing amongst men. It is often not so much the result of an evil intention as of the bewilderment occasioned by some passion.

198. For "the masses are very thoughtless" (p. 327).

199. The scholar is a singular being.

CHAPTER II.

THE GREAT MAN.

200. "HE cultivates the greatness of his nature," the moral and not the sensual motives (pp. 292, 293). (See Art. 14.)

201. He strives in word and deed after righteousness (p. 198). "The words of great men do not necessarily tend to sincerity nor their conduct to reality, but they consist simply in righteousness." He who offends not in word is a perfect man. Theoretically he takes up a firm position as to what he ought and ought not to say. His ruling principle is truth. Where one cannot or dare not say the truth by reason of compulsion, one should have the courage to declare that. It is continually a matter of experience that every purpose should not be stubbornly carried out into action. Only it is difficult to attain to the true practical view, so as not to let oneself be discouraged just there where resolution is required. Much is often lost through blind zeal. The same occurs also in political life, where the laws are carried out with thorough strictness, which results in many things not previously reckoned upon. Even in this our own day there are amongst officials far more perversely obstinate little men than really great ones. (See Analect. xiii. 20.)

202. He removes injustice from the heart of his sovereign (p. 186). "Mencius said, 'It avails not to censure men or to lay the blame of anything upon the government, the great man alone is able to sever injustice from the heart of his sovereign. If the ruler is benevolent,

every one is benevolent; is the ruler righteous, every one will be righteous; is the ruler correct, every one will be correct and the state will be established.'" It is often impossible to remedy mistakes from without. But in order to effect an external reformation from within, it is necessary that influence be brought to bear on the heart, which is more often the result of a life than of words alone. True greatness of character is demanded for this, which shall make this its object.

203. He does not repel the people from him.

204. The summing up of the character of the great man[1] is given us (p. 141) when Mencius says, " He dwells in the wide dwelling under the sky; he takes up the right position under heaven; he walks in the great Tao (principle) under heaven; if he attains his desire (of office), he identifies himself with the good of the people; if he cannot obtain his desire, he goes on his way (Tao) alone. Wealth and honours cannot make him arrogant; poverty and neglect cannot pervert him; power and force of arms cannot bind him. Such a man is called truly great and courageous." Genuine manhood is also defined morally; it pursues a noble aim and is steadfast in its prosecution. (Cf. Art. 376.)

---

[1] The object which our philosopher has in view here seems to be that indicated by the poet—

> " Lives of great men all remind us
> We may make our lives sublime."
> —*Psalm of Life* (*Longfellow*).

CHAPTER III.

THE SUPERIOR MAN OR SAGE.[1]

(a.) His Individuality.

205. Is generally different from other men (p. 333). "Mencius said, 'When Shun was dwelling under trees and rocks in the depths of the mountains, with deer and swine around him, that wherein he differed from the savages of the mountain fastnesses was very trifling. Yet, if he happened to hear a good word or to see a good action, he was like the swollen torrent of the Yangtze or Yellow river, which overflows and cannot be restrained.'" Mencius here indicates very skilfully the characteristics of the superior man. It is not any outer mark, it is no obtrusive external manifestation, but it is the direction towards goodness, and the energising of all that is good in the soul extending thence into the conduct generally. But alas! in these days one is more likely to find such truly superior men in the depths of the forests than in magnificent palaces.

206. His equality with other men (p. 81). "The greatness of the great Shun consisted in this, that he had what was good in him in common with mankind; he gave up his own and sought other men's; he rejoiced to receive (to learn) from others, and thus to do good. . . . To learn from other men how to practise what is good is to do good with men. The superior man, therefore, has nothing greater than his doing good with other men." Where there is actual superiority, a course of action like that of

[1] See Digest of Confucius, 90–96.

Shun is the only right one. He gave up his own way not so as to violate his principles, but only in reference to that which agreed with them, allowing himself in this to be guided by the people. These had, therefore, a feeling of partnership in goodness with him.

207. He preserves that which distinguishes man from the brutes. (Cf. Art. 143.)

208. His will is directed towards Tao (Art. 80).

209. By means of Tao (principle) he acquires depth, and thereby masters himself (p. 198). "Mencius said, ' The superior man makes deep research with Tao (principle), because he wishes to get possession of himself. Having gained himself, he abides in peace; abiding in peace, he commits himself to what is profound; committing himself to the profound, he receives from the right and the left, and arrives at his origin. On this account the superior man desires to get possession of himself.' " Of what advantage is it to know much of external things if we know not ourselves ? Man never finds peace externally; it is only inward, and only then when he is in harmony with himself, that is, with his prototype. When this is the case, one stands far above the contradictory opinions of men, and can let everything act on him without danger of injury, because he lets himself be led back to his own proper origin, whence springs the true nobility of all men. Then is attained that personal conviction which is not grounded upon external authority, and which does not fade away into subjective uncertainty. It is conviction arising from predetermined goodness and its source—the supreme good—God.

210. His aspirations tend only towards benevolence (Art. 72).

211. He has sympathy with the brute creation (p. 15).

212. He has faults also.

213. He reforms his failings and does not palliate them (p. 101). "The superior men of antiquity reformed their faults; the superior men of our day persist in their

errors. The faults of the former were like the eclipses of the sun and moon; every one saw them, but after their renovation every one admired them. Do the superior men nowadays simply persist in their faults? (No); they come afterwards, so to speak, with apologies for them." At the present time both superior men and the masses are guilty of new and worse faults in order to palliate their former failings. To recognise a fault is often no disgrace, but is always humiliating. Manifest improvement takes place actually only in the case of the well-meaning, but anything apparently tending to this re-establishes confidence. Unhappily, however, many acrimonious individuals seek their triumph in the faults of others, magnifying these, and taking advantage of a confession in their own sense (of its meaning). This snatching after opportunities for maliciously or imperiously subjugating our fellow-men, which often results in their moral destruction, is a great obstacle to the reformation of those faults of which one is frequently sensible.

214. His grief is that he cannot come up to his ideal.

215. He strives after certainty.

216. His delight (p. 335). Mencius said, " The superior man delights himself in three things, the imperial dignity not included : 1. That his father and mother are both alive and his brothers cause no anxiety. 2. That looking upward he has nothing of which to be ashamed before Heaven, and looking down has no cause to blush before men. 3. That he obtains those most conspicuous for talent throughout the empire in order to instruct and educate them." This delight actually consists in the noblest aspirations which man can have upon earth. The first point is the expression of natural moral feeling, the second of the religious feeling and sense of justice, the third the desire for work which shall be reproductive and imperishable. Qualified fellow-labourers and successors ! how can he who finds such be other than joyous ?

217. He is ashamed of not being equal to his renown.

218. He remains true to himself whether he be neglected or an emperor.

219. His judgment differs from that of the world (p. 218). "From the point of view which the superior man takes of the manner in which men strive after wealth, honour, gain, and preferment, it is seldom otherwise than that it should cause their wives and concubines to be ashamed and need to weep." It is well known that the proper nobility of man is terribly weakened, and, indeed, trodden under foot, in the strenuous effort to acquire these four things. On this account there are very many tears shed in this our own day.

(b.) *His Conduct.*

220. He is an example in word and deed (p. 371). "That which the superior man keeps in view is the cultivation of himself, whereby the whole realm attains to peace. The infirmity of men is that they neglect their own fields and weed those of other people ; what they require from others is difficult, and what they impose upon themselves is easy." He who wishes to effect anything in the world must exhibit his idea in his own personality. Thereby one works upon another imperceptibly, that is, so far as there is any susceptibility on the part of others.

221. He clings to the standard (p. 377). "He simply reverts to the standard (Holy Scripture). If the standard is correct the mass of the people is elevated ; if the masses are elevated we find no vice or depravity." Well is it for him who has a rule to which he can cling. He will then rest on certainty. Yet better is it, verily, if his conscience is so enlightened concerning his proper original disposition as to enable him to act normally. The thought becomes Christian when brought into apposition with the Bible and with the unction, the teaching which is of God. In another place it is said, "The superior man fulfils the law simply and only in order to await that which is pre-

destined." The superior man, consequently, does not permit himself to be influenced by external considerations and influences, but follows the natural law of his ideal, the will of God. Thus he proceeds steadily and surely, preserving his peace of mind, and finally obtaining more than the world can, with all its feverish restlessness and haste in the struggle for happiness. Yet it is no stoical resignation which is here recommended. The inborn moral law must be fulfilled; this the superior man acts 'out voluntarily as the problem of life; everything else is but secondary. This is actually in a slightly different form a fundamental doctrine of Christian truth. But to how few Christians, alas! has this become the law of their daily ₁lives! The minding of the world rules in many who profess and call themselves Christians.

222. In this way he works transformingly (p. 331). "Wherever the superior man passes by, transformation is effected; where he remains, it is as a spirit; towards the upper and lower he flows forth with heaven and earth; is this termed helping it forward only a little?" No man remains entirely without influence over his surroundings. It is everywhere logically correct that the superior man works in such a manner, in proportion to his capacity, but in reality it is seldom the case. The cause lies in the contrariety and opposition which approach on every side and exert their baneful influences.

223. He does not fight from choice (p. 86). "The superior man does not contend from choice, when he to whom the whole realm voluntarily submits attacks him against whom even relations are in rebellion; but if he has to fight, he conquers." This virtue alone ought to subdue all hearts to him, and so secure dominion for him. Confucianists have learnt, alas! and that not only from Chinese history, which affords numberless examples, that the evil are far more agreeable to the passions of their supporters, and that sin and vice obtain authority more easily than virtue; for men are more easily governed

through their appetites than through their affection for the ideal.

224. He does not injure men to obtain land.

225. His virtue is like the wind.

226. He is inflexible.

227. He exhibits neither narrowness nor insolence.

228. His affection is graduated, embracing things, people, and relations.

229. His influence extends to the fifth generation.

230. He guides his sovereign aright.

231. Is not niggardly.

232. Does not vex his children.

233. Employs various methods of education.

234. Holds no intercourse with the haughty.

235. His forbearance has limits.

(c.) *The Treatment which he Experiences.*

236. This, unhappily, does not correspond to his work, but is altogether discouraging. "He is deceived," even by his subordinates (p. 224).

237. "The masses do not comprehend him" (p. 311).

238. He is sometimes in "great distress externally" (p. 362).

239. He receives support from those in power (p. 92).

240. Sustenance afforded by the state for his counsel is "criticised but justified" (p. 344).

241. Yet this assistance is to be rendered in an honourable manner (p. 262).

242. He ought not to be paid off.

243. He will not permit himself to be either entrapped or allured by vain forms. Mencius said (p. 347), "Support without affection is termed being reckoned with the swine. Affection without reverence is the same as rearing a pet animal. Honour and respect are there before silkstuffs are presented. Honour and respect without reality cannot constrain the superior man without some-

I

thing further." Words and deeds corresponding remove as far as possible all doubt as to the sentiment which superiors actually entertain towards us. One knows then whereabouts he is.

244. Corresponding treatment on the part of princes.

245. Why he is not himself the Emperor. (Cf. Arts. 270–1.

CHAPTER IV.

THE HOLY OR IDEAL MAN.[1]

(a.) *His Individuality.*

246. "INFLUENCE which is great and transforming is
termed holiness" (p. 366). Holiness which one cannot
comprehend is termed spiritual (godlike). (Cf. Art. 56
ante.) Consequently holiness has its sphere of operation
within the limits of human comprehension, yet the next
step in advance lands us in the region of the incomprehensible, which is the marvellous.

247. The work of holiness is to make perfect.

248. Benevolence and wisdom are his distinguishing
characteristics.

249. Filial affection and brotherhood.

250. Holiness is the efficient of human relations (p. 168).
Mencius said, "The square and compass are the efficients
of curves and quadrangles. The holy man is the efficient
of human relations." In holiness, therefore, is exhibited
the highest human perfection, that which is gifted for
everything, but specially on the side of morals ; for the
ethical is with Mencius the specifically human. It is also
to be considered that holiness does not consist in separa-
tion from other men, but in the fulfilment of our normal
social relations to them.

251. "He has attained before others to that which is
common to all men." (Cf. Art. 6 *ante.*) That is to say,
the holy man is fully conscious of possessing in subjection

[1] See Digest of Confucius, p. 43.

to the power of his will that which is innate in all men as the norm of human faculties.

252. Holy men tend towards the same moral end, although they arrive at it by different paths (p. 192). " Shun was a man of the Eastern barbarians, King Wan of the Western. The places of their births and deaths are more than a thousand miles distant from each other; they were separated from each other in time by more than a thousand years. If their tendency had been throughly worked out in the middle kingdom (China), they would have been in entire correspondence, like the two halves of a seal. The manner in which the former holy men and those of later days acted was one and the same." Inquiry is much more generally directed to the origin of any one than to that to which his energies are directed. In view of the true end of humanity, this alone is of importance ; that of almost none, or at best of merely subordinate importance. These heralds of the revelation of what is human corresponded to each other in essentials; so did the heralds of divine revelation, but only in their tendency and aim. All individualities demand a teleologic consideration in the above sense, in order to be understood.

253. He offers to men that chief good which nothing else can supply.

254. The holy men are the same in kind as ourselves, but are simply perfected individuals (p. 71). (Cf. Arts. 6 and 302.) " What the unicorn is amongst quadrupeds, the phoenix amongst birds, the T'ae mountain amongst hills, rivers and oceans amongst rainpools in regard to kind, that the holy are amongst people generally; they are of the same kind, but standing out from those of like kind, they tower above their contemporaries." The passage quoted in Art. 6 ante brings out the equality very sharply ; in this we have simply the difference noted, but it is one of degree, not one arising from a diversity of nature.

255. This difference, however, depends upon action and practice, as it is with physical strength (p. 301). " One

does not exert himself to do impossibilities; but to walk slowly behind one of his elders is called fraternal; to hasten quickly in front of him is contrary to the duty of a brother. Is a man any way unable to walk slowly? It is simply not done." Holiness is consequently the result of habit. Every one can attain to this if he constantly seeks to do so, but here it is that the majority of men come short. Besides which, the matter is not always quite so simple as slowly following after others. Mencius elsewhere clearly states that many have also from birth somewhat of advantage.

256. Imitation of the ancient models brings it about (p. 110). "They (the holy men) were men. I am also a man; why should I stand in awe of them? Yen Yuen said, 'What kind of man was Shun? What sort of man am I? He who exerts himself becomes the same.'" One may well say that the difference between the holy and other men consists chiefly in this, that they are less unmanly. They represent manhood in its integrity. On this ground every one can take them as examples of the attainable.

(b.) *The Holy Man's Manner of Acting.*

257. He aims at preserving the purity of his own individuality (p. 240). "I have never heard of one who made himself crooked making others straight; how much less could one who disgraced himself rectify the empire? The actions of the holy men were not thus. Whether they were remote or near, whether resigning or not, these (the actions) referred simply to the preservation of their personal purity." The man who wishes to be an exponent of his theories must first identify himself with his ideal. Such would then be an entire man. The keeping of the person pure from all inconsistent actions becomes thus intelligible. The aim of moral working consists, indeed, in nothing else but the transference to others of that

which has already found individual expression in one's self. The individual is the result and goal of human development.

258. His actions are directed to securing the commonweal (p. 166). "After the holy men had exercised to the utmost the thoughts of their hearts, they caused a sympathising government to follow, and benevolence overspread the realm." Hence arises a series of causes and results similar to that formulated by the Apostle Paul, faith and works. First that which is internal and individual, then follows the perfected good as the natural outcome of the same, and at the same time the test or touchstone of the internal.

259. The holy man cares for the nourishment of the people (p. 338); that is, "he makes pulse and grain as abundant as water and fire." This is naturally only when the holy man finds himself in a corresponding position in the state, especially as prince or prime minister.

260. He appoints teachers for the people (p. 127). "The holy man (i.e., Shun) was anxious about the rudeness of the people, on which account he appointed an officer to instruct them in the five duties." (Cf. Art. 76.) We shall treat at length of these five duties, which in Chinese opinion embrace the whole of social life. Here we simply remark that to the ancient Chinese the material side of civilisation was never the most important; this was rather only a preliminary step to the moral problem of human life.

261. He is himself the teacher of many generations, and exerts a yet more powerful influence over his own time (p. 360). Mencius said, "The holy man is the teacher of a hundred generations; hence if they hear the fame of Pih-e, the impure become modest, and the timid resolute. If they hear the fame of Hwuy of Lew-hea, the mean become generous, the narrow-minded liberal. These acquired such fame a hundred generations since, that after a hundred generations every one who hears of it without

exception feels aroused by it. Could this take place
except in the case of the holy? and how much more did
they influence those with whom they were personally in
contact?" It is a well-known fact that genius often
develops its full influence for the first time after many
generations. Nevertheless it often escapes notice that
this is only possible through an intensive influence upon
one's contemporaries, which also is chiefly confined to the
circle of one's friends and disciples. (For Pih-e see Art.
272, and for Hwuy of Lew-hea see Art. 273.)

262. Mencius holds himself to be a holy man like
Yaou and Shun.

263. Gifted holy men follow his words.

264. The holy man does not change his teaching.

(*c.*) *Those who were Recognised by Mencius as Holy Men.*

We pause here and combine the various judgments
which Mencius has passed upon these several holy men.
This will be all the more interesting, because many of
these passages are only to be found in his pages. These
extracts are also valuable in other respects in a digest of
Mencius.

1. *Yaou and Shun* (2356–2206 B.C.)

265. Holiness was not learned by these, but was
essential. Therefore Mencius appealed to these when
he discoursed concerning the goodness of our essential
nature. Their principles consisted in benevolence and
righteousness, in filial affection, and also in fraternal.
The imitation of these their principles on the part of
rulers without benevolent government would indeed be
useless trouble. Yaou's chief attention was directed to
the regulation of floods, and Shun carried this out. Both
turned their attention to the discovery of fit men for
official positions. Notwithstanding which, there was

during the time of Yaou a (rascal) Seang. Their wisdom did not comprehend all things, but applied itself to the most necessary. Their benevolence was not indiscriminating love, but manifested itself towards relatives and the excellent. In their times a prince who should ruthlessly plunge his people into war would not have been tolerated. Their taxes were tithes; Yaou was an exemplary ruler and Shun the model of a minister. Confucius spoke of them in terms of high praise. (Cf. Anal. 8, 19, and 18, although there are slight variations in the text.) Mencius, it appears, with Tsae-go, held Confucius to be more excellent than both Yaou and Shun. Concerning Shun alone, Mencius is more full of detail, so that we may well assume him to have been the moral ideal of our philosopher. Shun was an Eastern barbarian, the places of whose birth and death are told us. He was the son of a bad father, one Koo-sow. Whilst Shun lived in the recesses of the mountains amongst the wild beasts, there was but little difference between him and the savages, but he was deeply moved whenever he heard a good word or saw a good action. His greatness consisted in this, that he constantly practised well-doing to men, giving himself up to it and loving it, and took hints from others also as to how to do good. He rose to his high position from the pasture. There was nothing extravagant in his receiving the empire from Yaou; it was simply conformable to Tao (principle). Although Yaou gave him his nine sons as attendants, his two daughters as wives, and placed all officials, together with the oxen, sheep, and storehouses, at his command for his sustenance, Shun yet dwelt amongst the pastures. Then Yaou raised him to the highest post in the empire. Shun was the son-in-law of the Emperor, and often also his host; consequently there existed friendship between the Emperor and his subject. He ate his simple fare as if it were to be thus all his life; he comported himself in his imperial majesty as if he had been born to it. He rose at cock-

crow and zealously strove to do good. He was clear as
to his relations to his surroundings, punctilious in the
observance of his duties; starting from benevolence and
righteousness, he did nothing except in accordance with
these. He gave attention to the education of his people.
Shun married without previously informing his parents,
but his intention sanctified the deed. His filial love was
nevertheless extreme. At the age of fifty he had intense
longings after his parents. He wept for his parents
under the open sky without entertaining any grudge
against them. He valued not the affection of the realm
so long as he could not overcome the aversion of his
parents; he accomplished this at last by the scrupulous
fulfilment of his duties towards them. He honoured and
supported his father with his best, and served him as he
did the Emperor. As Emperor, in case of the necessity
arising, he would not have maintained the righteousness
of his course against his own father, but abandoning the
empire, he would have fled with him into the retirement
of private life. Shun showed himself an excellent brother
in the case of his stepbrother Seang, who wished to
murder him. Yaou appointed him to preside over the
sacrifice before the people, and both Heaven and the
people accepted him. Afterwards Shun likewise did not
appoint his own son, but his regent Yu, to whom the
realm then came. From these extracts we perceive that
the virtue of Shun displayed itself in all the moral and
social relations, whether as son or brother, husband,
father, friend, minister or emperor, upon the throne as
in the wilderness, amongst men as when alone. We
have no exceptions to make save in the case of the double
marriage, even with two sisters, and that this took place
against the will of his parents.[1]

[1] To prevent disfiguring the pages by frequent numerals, I have omitted the references to the various parts of Mencius from which the sentences are collected composing this and following Articles.

2. *Yu the Great, Founder of the Hea Dynasty* (2205–2197 B.C.)

266. He abhorred old wine and loved good (speech) words; when he heard these he made obeisance. He led away the water of the great flood in such a way that it caused no inconvenience elsewhere. He diverted the course of nine rivers, in doing which he was eight years absent from his home, which he three times passed by without entering. He felt that if any one had been drowned in that region, it would have been as if he himself had drowned them. Finally, he took Yeh as his coadjutor in the government and presented him before Heaven (as his successor). In this case we have self-sacrificing activity for the good of the realm placed in the foreground.

3. *T'ang, Founder of the Yin or Shang Dynasty* (1766–1754 B.C.)

267. Was nine feet in height. He made that his own which Yaou and Shun had by nature. He held fast the mean and appointed the skilful without restriction. Three times he sent messengers to E-yun to call him to office. E-yun went five times to T'ang and five times to Kee. T'ang first learned from E-yun and then made him his minister; thus he became emperor without trouble.[1] Kee helped T'ang in that he inclined the people towards him. They would rather have died with Kee than have lived under him. T'ang's territory was only seventy Chinese miles in extent. He manifested his great benevolence in that with a great territory he served the small state of Ko. However, Ko murdered a boy, so it came to a war of extermination; then T'ang destroyed eleven princes. He

---

[1] Kee was a tyrant hated by the people. Ch. Cl, vol. ii. p. 4, note.

punished the ruler and comforted the people, hence he was everywhere welcomed as seasonable rain. He banished Kee, but slew him not. Amongst his successors were skilful monarchs, until Woo Ting ascended the throne (T'ang to Woo Ting, 1765–1323). The downfall of the dynasty followed not long after (in 1153 B.C.) It is said a prince cannot be made to become a T'ang or Woo. T'ang came to be regarded as the deliverer from the trouble which had been caused by a tyrant. It mattered nothing to Mencius that it was any way rebellion. For more details on this point see Sections 370–374, and 424–425. Excepting this, T'ang was one of the noblest characters in Chinese history, but he appears to have been forced on gradually by circumstances from one step to another, until Kee was finally dethroned.

4. *Kings Wan and Woo, Founders of the Chow Dynasty* (1150 B.C.)

268. King Wan was a Western barbarian, whose birthplace and place of death are told us. He was ten cubits high. He regarded the people as a sore (wound), and looked towards the right way as if he saw it not. His plan was munificent. He cared for the widows, widowers, childless, and orphans. He nourished well the aged, therefore they followed him. He cared for their being nourished (by their relations) in their several families. He urged on his people to build a tower and to lay out a pond, and his people rejoiced that he shared his pleasure with them. Grasscutters, wood-gatherers, hare and pheasant catchers were allowed in his park. From (motives of) humanity he rendered services to the barbarians of Kwan. His bravery was shown in his driving back an inroad of the barbarians, and saving the land. With one outburst of anger he gave the realm peace. He obtained dominion as sovereign, though possessing only one hundred miles (of territory). He renewed Chow, and made a new

partition of the land. Taxes and socage were tithes. His
example influenced his wife, his brother, his kindred, and
the neighbouring states. Under his rule the people loved
the good. Duke Chow took him for his example. Although
he was one hundred years old, still his virtue did not
penetrate the whole realm. He could not entirely do
away with men's aversion (to his plans), but again he did
not allow his reputation to fall to the ground. He did not
accept of the realm because the people were not in favour
of his doing so. He was the equal in capacity of the more
ancient holy man Shun. In the time of Mencius, the
people expected another King Wan, who should rouse
them up. King, or more rightly Duke Wan, was, according to these quotations, a philanthropic prince, who considered it very important to aim at the well-being of his
subjects and of the land generally. Confucius also thought
highly of him, because, besides the power and influence
which he possessed, he had also the fidelity of his vassals
(Anal. 8, 20). Any way he was conscious that he would
meet with much stubborn opposition, so that he would
frequently have very much at stake besides open rebellion.

5. *King Woo* (1122–1116 B.C.)

269. That which Yaou and Shun had naturally he made
his own. He neither overlooked the nearest nor forgot
that which is far off. Under him the people loved the
good. He and Duke Chow followed the virtue of their
father Wan, so that it permeated the empire. He carried
out well Wan's plans. He felt ashamed that one man
(the Emperor Chow [1]) was misconducting himself in the
realm; that was his bravery. With one outburst of
anger he gave peace to the empire. He saved the people
as if from water and fire. The tyrant Chow helped him
so far as to drive the people to him. When he marched
against Yen he had only 300 chariots of war and 3000

[1] Dr. Legge says Kĕĕ, p. 33.

bodyguards. He overthrew the tyrant Chow, but did not murder the sovereign. He took the government because the people wished it. But the giving the realm a mighty bath of blood so little suited the theory of Mencius, that he doubted the report. The personal character of Woo is not plain from these passages, but the fact that the people under him loved the good indicates that his good example shone before them. The main point appears to be the deliverance of the people from a tyrannical sovereign. Of him, as of T'ang, it is well said with reference to their rebellion, that his was not the nature of a holy man.

6. *Duke Chow.*

270. He took his father Wan as his teacher, that is, for his example. He sought to unite in himself the virtues of Yu, T'ang, Wan, and Woo, and to exercise them. If he found anything that was unsuited to his time, he thought it over day and night; when he found the solution, he waited for the morning to carry it out. With Woo he brought the virtue of Wan into general recognition throughout the empire. He assisted Woo to destroy the tyrant Chow. He fought against Yen, and slew its ruler three years later. He drove the Feileen to the sea and slew it, destroyed fifty states, drove away the wild beasts, and so greatly benefited the realm. He came twice against the barbarians of the West and North. He would have struck down the heretics (Yang and Mih, &c.) as if barbarians. (Bear in mind the much-be-praised tolerance of the Chinese for opposing doctrines.) He made his elder brother, Kwanshuh, protector over the state of Yen, which thereon rebelled. It was impossible for Duke Chow to know this beforehand, but the error lay on the side of right; he also rectified his fault. He was invested with the state of Loo, that was not more than one hundred li in extent. He did not become emperor because no tyrant (Kee or Chow) occupied the

throne. His teaching was placed on a level with that
of Confucius (Chung Ni). Duke Chow was at all events
a talented statesman, who imparted stability to the war-
like acquisitions of Woo. His talent was not merely of
an intellectual, but of a moral nature also.

(d.) Comparison of Four Kinds of Holy Men.

1. E-Yin, the Official Holy Man.

271. He was a farmer of the land of Sin, and took
delight in the principles of Yaou and Shun. That which
opposed their justice and principles he would not have
esteemed even for the reward of an empire. Were it accompanied by one thousand teams he would not have regarded
it; he would neither have given nor have received a single
straw of that which was not according to their justice and
principles. T'ang had to invite him thrice ere he decided
to leave his fields with the idea of making T'ang a ruler
like Yaou and Shun and his people like theirs. Therefore
it does not appear right to assert that he took office in both
peaceful and troublous times, and that he went five times
to T'ang and five times to Kĕĕ (it is explained as a media-
tor). He held himself to be one who recognised the
supremacy of the right, and therefore to be called from
heaven to teach the same to the people. He thought that
if he did not make them sharers in the beneficence of
Yaou and Shun, it would be the same as if he cast them
into a roadside ditch. So he took upon himself the heavy
burden of the government, and went on that account to
T'ang and advised him by attacking Hea to save his people.
T'ang first learned from him and then made him his
minister, and so became Emperor without trouble. Like
Duke Chow, and for the same cause, he would not become
Emperor. He sent T'ang's successor into exile for three
years. He said, "I cannot lower myself to the level of
those who are inconsistent;" he also banished T'ae Kĕa

to T'ung (to the grave of T'ang). This pleased the people greatly. When T'ae Këa became virtuous he brought him back, and this greatly delighted the people. E-Yin was a man of great energy, and he it was, according to all appearances, who chiefly induced T'ang to take the steps he did against Këě; for T'ang, according to the story in the Shoo King, seems never entirely to have overcome the scruples of conscience. But that E-Yin, under T'ae Këa, made no effort to place himself upon the throne is greatly to his honour, and shows that he was a loyal and upright character.

2. *The Pure Pih-e with the Name Hwan.*

272. He was a son of the king of Uchung ; Shootsze was his younger brother. He served no ruler who was not to his mind, and had no friend who was not like himself. He would not appear at the court of a bad man nor converse with an evil man, both being to him like sitting amidst coals or filth in one's festal attire. It is said that he thought the same when he found himself with a villager. He carried his hatred to wrong so far that he thought it necessary, if he stood near a villager whose cap was not properly adjusted, to move away with a lofty mien as if in danger of infection. On this account also he received nothing from princes, even when it was offered with good words and commands. His non-reception arose from this, that nothing should induce him to approach them. On this account Mencius calls him narrow-minded, and decides that neither he nor E-Yin can be regarded as the equals of Confucius. Pih-e remained in an inferior position simply that he might not serve a degenerate (prince) with his talents. To avoid Chow he dwelt on the coast of the North Sea, yet joined himself to King Wan on hearing of his undertakings, because he took good care of the aged. As a holy man and as a teacher of a hundred generations he is ranked with Hwuy of Lew Hea. On

hearing the fame of Pih-e the profligate became modest
and cowards brave. Pih-e was a singular specimen of a
holy man, yet such people are undoubtedly of great use
in the courts of princes, a kind of court conscience. His
end was very sad. Desiring to know nothing of the
rebellion of Woo, he withdrew with his brother to the
mountains and perished of hunger.

3. *The Obliging Hwuy of Lew Hea.*

273. He was a contemporary of Confucius (?), a native
of Loo, by name Chin Wo and the surname Kim. He
was not ashamed of a profligate prince, nor did he find an
inferior office too low for him. When elevated he did not
conceal his talent ; it must work according to his principles. If neglected he murmured not; in misery and
want he grieved not. Therefore he said, " Thou art thyself,
I am myself ; although thou shouldst stand by me with your
breast and arms or thy whole body naked, how could that
defile me ? " Hence he transacted business indifferently
with people without prejudice to himself. When pressed
to remain he remained, thus giving proof that going away
was not of importance to him. Yet he was by no means
fickle, and would not have changed his purpose for the
throne of the Duke. He was likewise a teacher of one
hundred generations. If they hear of him, the mean
become generous, and the narrow-minded liberal. This is
any way nearer to the Christian ideal than the former.
To preserve oneself unspotted amidst corrupted surroundings is to manifest a rare force of character.

4. *The Man Suited to his Age—Confucius.*

274. He asserted that he was no holy man. He so
subdued men's hearts by his virtue, that seventy disciples
were devoted to him. He repudiated his former scholar,
Kew, who laid double imposts upon the people without

advantaging his prince, and generally rejected all who
lacked humanity. He was not indignant at the self-con-
ceited passing him by. He contented himself with disciples of mediocre talent and position, as he could not
obtain better. He hated all imitation which might be
confounded with the reality. The general corruption of
morals filled him with fear, and led him to compose the
Chronicle of Loo. He esteemed highly water which had
a source. He esteemed Yin Yun as a worthy on account
of his contentment. He praised the forester who would
not come when summoned (by his prince) in an improper
manner. He held closely to etiquette. He would not
put up at an unsuitable hostel in Wei or Ts'e, as report
went, but journeyed to and fro in accordance with propriety
and correctness. He accepted that which was offered on
principle (Tao), and might be received with propriety;
therefore he even received game, because he was an
official in Loo. He sought to carry out his teaching; if
unsuccessful, he went away; on this account it was that he
never stayed three full years in any state. He accepted
appointments under three several princes in their respec-
tive states. As accountant, his care was to be accurate in
his calculations. As steward of the fields, he sought to
make the oxen and sheep fat, strong, and of good size.
As minister of justice in Loo, because his counsel was not
followed, he waited for the next opportunity which offered
itself at the time of sacrifice and departed. When he left
Loo he went slowly, because it was his fatherland; when
he left Ts'e, he took with him the rice which should have
been prepared for his meal, uncooked. He remained in
office as long as it was possible to do so, and, when obliged
to, departed quickly. He felt uncomfortable if he remained
three months without a prince. Hwan, the master of the
horse in Sung, wished to kill him. His heart was dis-
tracted by grief at finding himself unloved by the crowd
of nobodies. The mourning of his disciples lasted for three
years after his death, as if for a father. From the begin-

K

ning of men there never was another Confucius. Mencius
sought to conform himself to Confucius. In the words of
Confucius Mencius also finds confirmation of his views
concerning the goodness of human nature. We here learn
very little about the proper personal character of Confucius; it is only his peculiar excellency as a teacher
which is mentioned, and specially as a servant of the state.
It is this which constitutes its importance. The political
economy of Confucius has preserved itself during thousands
of years, notwithstanding it has suffered much modification in the course of time. It is worthy of remark that
the holy men of most ancient times were emperors; in
later times the ministers took possession of the higher
rank; and that Confucius, who is now honoured as the
greatest of the holy, was never able to become minister of
state. In a certain degree, therefore, holiness stands in an
inverse ratio to worth in the eyes of men.

(e.) The Spiritual Stands Higher than the Holy Man.

275. Here man again comes in contact with Heaven
(God). (Cf. Arts. 8, 51, 53.) The highest ethical development fulfils the destiny of the creature, the idea of Heaven
(of God). Thus man walks in fullest intercourse with the
highest Being, and is able to co-operate in accomplishing
in the world the yet unexecuted purposes of God. We
perceive how closely this conception approaches to that
of the God-man. The high significance of individuality
is set forth in these extracts from Mencius in a way that
deserves our attention. Indeed, we find that universal
history keeps the same lesson before us. The theoretical
manuals of political economy very rarely, or with a lack
of firmness, uphold this important position. Throughout
the modern world there is a lack of individuality in the
state, the church, in science, and even in art. This is a
well-known and indisputable fact. But that it is in our
power to form this·individuality, yea, to cause ourselves

to approach to it, is a fact which seems very little known, and which is opposed by nearly all characterless individuals. Men seek to transfer the blame from themselves to their time and circumstances. Even under the most difficult circumstances the character develops itself, only thus it becomes more marked. But what is required is that a thoroughly formed character be kept before young people, and all capable of receiving instruction. The weakness of our times is caused by the mind being occupied by heroes of romance of a hazy or dubious virtue. The moral energy so sadly lacking in our contemporaries can never develop itself from these. The capacity is there, but its exercise and the motive for the same are both lacking. We must gaze upon men with a nature like ourselves, but who have brought that nature to the highest development to which man can attain, and this not in fiction, but in reality. We must look at the difficulties with which these heroes had to strive, and recognise that these were of the same nature as those which surround us. Such considerations arouse confidence in one's own high destiny to a sublime vocation; they witness to the possibility of overcoming difficulties, and awaken courage to wrestle with the same. But it is necessary to consider also the means through the faithful use of which the aim is to be attained. Mencius only knew of a rigid morality, a purifying of the heart and nourishment of every germ of good, and the exercise of wisdom, humanity, righteousness, and propriety. In one word, the subjugation of the appetites and passions by means of the ideal of human nature, and the gradual perfection and final sovereignty of this latter. The great evil of the modern world is the undue excitement of the nerves by the habitual use of all kinds of narcotics, both in a real and metaphorical sense. Hence the sensual appetites become more powerful than would be the case in their normal condition.. But the moral sense not being able to obtain the mastery over the senses, man rectifies his condition as well as he can, yet is ever restless

under the enervation that follows upon moral intoxication.
The very philosophical systems by which the world-pain
is soothed are not calculated to restore its normal rest.
Their nature is disunion and therefore disquiet. Vigorous
characters are an impossibility under such circumstances;
at the best there obtains a kind of geniality, but mostly a
gloomy restlessness. We require in both men and women
characters in which the moral ideal shall reign supreme,
in which consequently a kindly contentment and harmony
of soul shall prevail. Such can then with more full and
complete individuality grasp the problem which their
God sets before them in external life. Position, whether
high or low, is a matter of indifference to the individual
governed by Christian morality. That attained in one's
self remains for eternity, and first manifests its full worth
when the heavenly kingdom, wherein governs perfect
moral righteousness, shines forth in its majesty. But
such a character will seek fully to master whatever it lays
hold of in its earthly vocation. Perfection even in trifles
is the earnest endeavour of the moral character. This
endeavour arises not from the desire of external reward,
although it rightly allows the reception of that to which
it is entitled, but from the motive within, from delight in
the perfect. The man photographs himself even in his
acts. Any way Mencius offers much in this section which
is worthy of consideration. This ancient Chinese character ought to supply us with a motive to simulate as
Christians the ancient heathen in that which is good.
Every higher step in civilisation ought and can prove
itself an advance only as it exhibits the lower steps more
fully perfected in itself. Therefore it is we do not place
ourselves upon the same standpoint of virtue as the
heathen. The Christian, on account of his standpoint of
faith, and gifted by the Holy Spirit with a new and
renovating life, must be ashamed if the heathen can excel
him in goodness. That would be no fault of the gospel,
but a failure in appropriating the grace of God which

meets us there in its fulness, not as of old in intuitive illumination. The Chinese in their everyday life are still farther removed from the doctrine of their teacher Mencius than of old; but on this account his doctrine can be made use of as a corrective. It represents the conscience of China. That conscience is the knowledge of an original law of good, which is the standard of the difference between it and the actual attainment of the individual; thereby a feeling of guilt is conceived, and a desire for the reconciliation of defective practice with the beautiful ideal is aroused and kept alive.

PART II.

THE ETHICO-SOCIAL RELATIONS.

———o———

CHAPTER I.

FATHER AND SON.

(a.) *The Father.*

276. INFLUENCE of affection (p. 218). "When father and mother love their son, he rejoices and does not forget them." The nature of the love of parents is unfortunately not defined, though that is important in order to distinguish the purely natural (instinctive) love from its ethical conformation and transformation. This passage is closely connected with that in which only the duty of sons is inculcated to win the love of their parents, and not the duty of parents to love their children.

277. "Exhortations on arriving at maturity" (p. 140). These are referred to, but not described.

278. "The father does not instruct the son himself" (p. 184). "A disciple asked, 'Why does not the superior man teach his own son?' Mencius answered, 'It comports not with his authority. Instruction must be accompanied by correction. If there be not correction (of habits, &c.), there will follow passion (severity); if severity ensues there will be perverse ill-temper. (The son says), "My honoured sire instructs me in what is correct, yet does not

tend towards what is right" (does not himself act rightly)
So there is discord between father and son; when that is
the case it is bad. The ancients exchanged sons and so
instructed them. Between father and son there should
be no censure compelling one to be good. If there
be, alienation will result: nothing is so injurious as
alienation.'" Rightly to unite severity with affection is
one of the most difficult problems in education. How
many failures are made on both sides is proved by the
number of spoilt young people. In the present day there
are far more owing to the prevalent overlooking of small
faults. We must also make a difference between instruction and education. The parent is seldom practically in
a position to instruct his child, but education should be
chiefly the work of the parents; these also should by
proper preparation put themselves in a position to effect
this. In the above passages we have nearly all that
Mencius has to say about the position of parents towards
their children. The duties of parents are not thought of.
How entirely different to this is the teaching of Christianity! The chief reason for this is that to the Chinese
children are the absolute possession of the father, and
that he may use them at his pleasure just as any other
of his belongings. So it has been with all heathen people,
and is now always the case with modern heathen. The
Bible presents quite another view of the case, viz., that
children are the possession of God, and the parents only
for a time the representatives of God; hence the parental
authority is naturally limited and modified even within
those just limits.

(b.) *The Son.*

279. Must avoid all unfilial conduct, as laziness, fond-
ness for play and drink, selfishness, profligacy, quarrel-
someness (pp. 212–214). A disciple said, "K'wang Chang
is called unfilial by the whole empire; how comes it, sire,

that you keep company with him, and, so to say, treat him
with courtesy ? " Mencius replied, " There are five things
which public opinion treats as unfilial : (1.) laziness in
the four limbs, and not paying attention to the nourishment of one's parents; (2.) play and an inclination to drink,
and not paying attention to the nourishment of one's
parents ; (3.) seeking to amass gold and goods, and not
paying attention to the nourishment of one's parents ; (4.)
following the desires of one's eyes and ears so that one's
parents come under judicial correction ; (5.) delight in
bravery and fighting, which brings the parents into
danger. Has Chang any one of these ? Yet Chang, as a
son, urged his father to that which is good, so that they
avoided one another. To urge one to good is the manner
between friends ; between father and son the urging to
good is the greatest violence to mutual good feeling.' Then
did not Chang at all desire the possession of wife and
child ? But because he had transgressed against his
father and dared not approach him, he sent away his
wife and cast out his son, so that he all his life received
no nourishment. He was convinced in his heart that if
he did not so act his sin would be exceeding great. Such
and no other is Chang." From another old work we learn
that Chang's mother was slain by his father on account
of a crime, and then simply buried. Chang became a
general, yet ventured not to give his mother a proper
burial without the consent of his father in spite of the
command of his prince. Hence came alienation between
father and son. The Christian reader can only call this a
sorrowful story, and perceive with grief how perverted is
the morality of the best of the Chinese in so important a
case. Mencius was of course not to blame in his intercourse with Chang, and Chang also certainly not for
urging his father to give an honourable interment to his
own mother, especially when the prince himself gave
occasion for it. That this Chang, because of the pain
caused by his disagreement with his father, should have

deprived himself of his own children, them of their father, and his wife of her husband, transcends our Christian notions. Similar things are happening in the China of our day.

280. Endeavours to have offspring (p. 189). Mencius said, "Three things are unfilial, and to lack posterity the most so. Shun married without informing (his parents); on account of having no posterity, the superior man regards this as informing them." (Cf. Art. 307.) The ancient custom of China required for marriage the informing of one's parents and their consent. In the present day it is yet more rigorous; sons as well as daughters are absolutely betrothed by their parents. The happy pair meet for the first time after the celebration of the marriage. On account of the hatred of his parents, Shun could not look for their approval, so decided of himself to do that which Mencius justifies out of a consideration for posterity, which here has attributed to it the highest moral worth. This decision has already caused great mischief in China. On it is based divorce because of childlessness, and polygamy for the sake of male posterity or for the obtaining of a greater number. Thus has been brought about all the mischief of a harem in the household as a matter of duty, of which China has been forced abundantly to taste the bitter fruits. But apart from that to which it has served as a foundation, the case before us is decidedly a corruption of morals. It never appears to have entered the Chinese mind that Shun by waiting would have attained to a much higher position morally. Yet this would be the simple result from the Chinese position of the absolute authority of the father. The son would have been obliged to wait until his father's view changed. This was the only course morally. According to Mencius's own showing, the son must properly be declared answerable for himself at the appointed time, *i.e.*, his majority, which the Chinese till now have never allowed. Thereby the absolute authority of the parents would be broken. Mencius also properly

places another principle above this ; but not the right o
men as individuals, nor the moral principle that marriage
is a universal duty .which special circumstances may
hinder but never ought to make impossible. The son
marries not for himself, but only in order to provide his
parents with posterity ; it is thus the interest of his
parents which guides him. We must not think that the
Chinaman by marriage establishes his own household.
The woman has to obey unconditionally her mother-in-
law just as the man his father. (See Art. 304.) For the
bringing into action of a higher principle there is lacking
in China the idea of a personal God, and yet more so of
the Heavenly Father of the New Testament, as well as the
moral filial relationship in which we stand to Him. On
this alone can be based a higher authority than that of
the human father.

281. "The preservation of one's self presupposes the
service of one's parents" (p. 185). This is evident,
but may easily be perverted. All sacrifice for king and
country is simply impossible during the lifetime of one's
parents. There are few officials in China who have not,
in time of danger, an old father or mother far away at
home, who urgently require the immediate return of their
son. The passage is right as regards the self - willed
putting of one's self in danger.

282. The service of parents as long as they live is a
fruit of humanity (p. 189).

283. This should not be external service, but " correspond to the wishes of the parents " (p. 186). (Cf.
sec. 140.)

284. Only submission to one's parents can satisfy the
heart ; there was a yearning after this even amongst the
ancients (pp. 218–221). "A disciple asked Mencius, 'Shun
went out in the fields crying and weeping to merciful
Heaven ; why did he weep and cry ? ' Mencius answered,
' Because of an unsatisfied yearning.' The scholar replied,
' If the parents love him, the son rejoices and forgets them

not; if they hate him, he vexes himself yet murmurs not; did Shun then murmur?' He answered, . . . 'You understand nothing. The heart of the filial son is not so devoid of feeling that he can say, "I exert my strength to cultivate the field; that is the duty of a son and nothing more; what is it to me that my father and mother do not love me?" The Emperor (Yaou) caused his children, nine sons and two daughters, the various officials, the cattle, sheep, and magazines to be made ready to serve Shun amidst the fields. Many of the scholars of the realm betook themselves to him, the emperor wished to have him as co-regent in the realm, and to make it all over to him; but because he was not in accord with his father and mother, he was as a forsaken man with no place of refuge. To be beloved by the scholars of the realm is what men covet, yet it was insufficient to assuage his sorrow. Great beauty is what men covet; he was married to both the daughters of the emperor, yet that was insufficient to assuage his grief. Wealth is what men covet; he possessed as wealth the whole realm, yet that was insufficient to assuage his grief. Honour is what men covet; he was honoured as emperor, yet that was insufficient to assuage his grief. To be beloved by men, to have great beauty, wealth, and honour, were insufficient to assuage his grief; only being brought into perfect accord with his father and mother could assuage it. In youth man yearns after his parents; when he perceives the desire of beauty he yearns after a young maiden; when he has wife and child he yearns after wife and child; in office he yearns after his sovereign; if he does not get on with his sovereign he has a burning within. But great filial affection has a lifelong yearning; at fifty years old to experience a yearning after father and mother, that have I seen in Shun.'" In this extract we have a beautiful proof that external fortune cannot satisfy the heart, but only the consciousness of duty fulfilled, and not that only, but a corresponding interchange of affection.

To patiently experience hatred where one brings love, and where there would naturally be love in return, that can only be in a mind satiated with love of God. Still Shun attained all that a filial mind could do from his standpoint.

285. Great filial piety consists in changing the mind of his parents. In continuation of the history of Shun (p. 190) Mencius said, "When the whole realm had great delight in him, and wished even to submit to him ; to consider this delight and the submission of the realm as a bundle of grass—that was Shun alone. Without winning his parents he believed he could not be a man ; without being in accord with his parents he could not be a son. Shun fulfilled the duty of serving his parents, and his father was reconciled ; with the reconciliation of his father the realm was transformed. By this reconciliation was established what father and son ought to be. This is great filial piety." This greatness consists also, according to Mencius, in one not following the caprices and mistakes of one's parents, and through such compliance strengthening them therein, but in one as a son, by conduct both with and without words, setting the truth before his parents in all filial love but with resolution.

286. Causes the parents to be honoured (pp. 226–230). It is here related that Shun as emperor was in an unnatural position in regard to his father, who became his subject. To this Mencius replies : " The father received the highest honour and the best care through the honour and position of his son. Yet Shun always remained a son." Nevertheless, Shun also had not anxiously aspired to high position on account of his father, but found himself on the throne as the result of his personal worth and decision of character. This was not at all furthered by the serious position he occupied in opposition to his parents and sisters and to their evil lives. In this Shun may even now serve as an example. To renounce nothing of the divine claims upon us, in opposition to one's nearest

relations and to those to whom the highest respect is due, and yet not to elevate oneself above those whom nature has made our superiors, this is ever an aim to be attained to with difficulty, but is an ethical problem.

288. Parents are not only to be served in life but "also after death by burial and sacrifices as propriety requires" (p. 112). (Cf. Arts. 183, 184.) For the burial the Confucianists as well as Mencius insist most strongly upon a coffin seven inches thick, and also upon two coffins one inside the other. The Socialists, on the other hand, will have only a single one, three inches thick, and avoid all parade, and that rightly. To honour the dead with a becoming burial corresponds to man's feelings; the opposite is a proof of brutal insensibility. The Confucian requirement of two seven-inch coffins is a ridiculous exaggeration; besides which, with a few exceptions, it is a matter of impossibility. The sacrifices required imply the continued existence of the departed, but make this dependent also upon the living.[1] This Chinese mourning, so pleaded for by Mencius and Confucius, is especially a proof of their hopelessness and ignorance concerning everlasting life. It is Christianity alone which sheds abroad light and offers security concerning that which lies beyond the grave: hence it is and remains for all time the only heart-satisfying religion. Reason reaches only to the grave; beyond it strikes out into unbelief, which is unreasoning, or into superstition, which is perverted reasoning. The humanitarian doctrines of Confucius and Mencius here degenerate into a mere torture of our hearts.

289. Service to the dead is accounted as more satisfactory than that to the living (p. 198). Mencius said, "Care for the living is not enough to be accounted a great thing (but merely natural), only the ceremonies for the dead can be accounted a great matter." We must observe in addition, that the funeral obsequies serve far

[1] See Digest of Confucius, p. 58, &c.

more for the satisfying of the feelings of the survivors.
The care of living parents, on the other hand, is itself
good. He who is not lacking in this will always feel it
necessary to provide proper burial for them.

290. Three years' mourning (p. 348) intimately connected with the former, is firmly insisted on by Confucianists, and indeed obtains to the present day. (See
Art. 191.) (Concerning blood-revenge, see Art. 347.)

(c.) *Reciprocal Relations between Father and Son.*

291. Concerning these Mencius only mentions "good-
will" (p. 88).

292. And "mutual attachment" (p. 127), as those that
should rule—first, of course, on the side of the father,
and then from the son.

293. From both there should be "no bitterness in
urging to do good" (pp. 184, 213), no cause of offence.
(Cf. Art. 284.) This is the teaching of Mencius on the
fundamental idea of Chinese social life. We may say
that we too possess the peculiar characteristic of the
same. We see the same idea recurring in all the other
social relations, specially, however, developed in those
of the sovereign and his officials (court servants). We
find this idea in absolute authority on one side and strict
subordination on the other. In case of immoral conduct
on the part of the father, the son should offer passive
resistance, so as to preserve the moral standpoint. The
great essential is unconditioned authority, which yet
ought to obtain recognition in an ethical manner.

CHAPTER II.

BRETHREN, ELDER AND YOUNGER.

By this is signified the brotherly relation, and chiefly the subordination of the younger to the elder brother.

294. Brotherhood is "the fruit of righteousness" (p. 189).[1] In the house amongst brothers and sisters commences the carrying out of right opinions. It is, however, to be well considered that the essential of this is not equality of position, but the direct recognition of diversity of rank, both with Confucius and Mencius. That so long as both are children, the younger brother should give way to the older, is based upon the very nature of things; this is here extended to the whole life.

295. Works educationally.

296. Strengthens the state.

297. Causes mutual confidence (p. 101). This is justified by Mencius even in cases of deception, as with Duke Chow. Notwithstanding that confidence is too often misplaced in one's nearest relatives, Mencius certainly seized the right point of view morally. So long as there exists any moral connection amongst those concerned, confidences will establish themselves, whilst frequent deceptions set friendship in flames and destroy the last atom of confidence.

298. Makes itself known as sympathy, attachment, and foresight (p. 223). "A disciple asked Mencius, 'His parents set Shun to work to complete the threshing-

[1] See Digest of Confucius, p. 75.

floor; when the ladder had been taken away his father
burnt the threshing-floor. They set him to clean out a well;
scarcely was he out of it than they came to bury him
in it. His brother Seang said, "The plan of covering in
the city-founding prince (in the well) is all of my weaving.
Oxen and sheep shall be my parents', the threshing-floor
my parents', the harp mine, the bow mine, my two sisters-
in-law will I require to serve me." He went and entered
into Shun's palace. Shun played upon the harp on the
couch. His brother said, "I think with anxious care upon
the government," and blushed. Shun answered, "This
whole crowd of officials do thou govern for me." Do we
know whether or not Shun perceived that his brother
wished to kill him?' Mencius answered, 'How should
he not have known it? Was his brother sorrowful? so
was Shun also sorrowful. Did he rejoice? then Shun also
rejoiced.'" In p. 224 we find a supplement to this. There
the same disciple said to Mencius, "'The brother (Seang)
made it his daily business to kill Shun. When Shun
became emperor, he only banished him. How is this?'
Mencius answered, 'He rewardèd him. Some think it to
be banishment.' The scholar said, 'Shun banished the
superintendent of works and one other official, slew the
prince of San Meaou, and imprisoned K'wanhin; these
four delinquents, the inhuman, were. removed, and the
realm acquiesced. Seang was the most inhuman, and
Shun rewarded him with Yeupé. Had then the people of
Yeupé sinned? Does a humane man really act thus, that
he removes other people but rewards his younger brother?'
He answered, 'A humane man does not retain his anger,
cherishes no ill-will against his brother, but loves him
heartily, and that is enough. Hearty affection for him
wishes him honoured, love for him wishes him wealthy.
Rewarding him with Yeupé made him both honoured and
wealthy. On the other hand, being himself emperor, could
hearty affection and love be named whilst his brother
remained a commoner?' 'Permit me to ask' (continued

the disciple), 'why some thought it to have been banishment?' Answered, 'Seang had nothing to do in his state; the emperor sent a plenipotentiary who should govern the state and render the revenues of it: therefore it is called banishment. Could it be permitted that he should oppress any subjects? But nevertheless Shun wished to be able to see him constantly, so he came continually to the court. He received Yeupé without tribute or government—that is plainly implied.'" In the foregoing is indicated an ideal relation between brother and brother, according to the view of Mencius and his followers. But we find a great deficiency in the complete absence of indignation against the brother's sin; of moral abhorrence of the criminal intention which might well be united with the greatest individual affection. This deficiency continues to adhere to the ethics of Mencius, even though we must regard the history on which it is founded as a fiction. Shun was already co-regent, and yet he was to have repaired the threshing-floor and cleaned out the well single-handed. Further, his brother goes to the palace to take both of Shun's wives, the daughters of the reigning emperor, for himself, and to appropriate to himself or to give to his parents the property which had been lent by Yaou to Shun. This is all ridiculous. We have in the foregoing all that Mencius teaches concerning the relation of one brother to another. The weakness of his ethics thus comes more plainly to the light. Not only is the far too great consideration given to procuring honours and riches a marked error; it leads in the end to nepotism, which has caused nothing but evil. Even reigning princes do not thereby strengthen their position, viz., by raising many of their nearest relatives to high offices, except when these are also individuals of great ability. So it is in every department of life. That brothers should mutually act in a brotherly way is moral; but it is also an element of morality that they be placed only in positions correspond-

L

ing to their abilities. Mencius here stands in opposition to his former theory, that only the worthy should become officials : that the unworthy should receive the dignity and revenues whilst others do the work is neither ethical nor politic.

CHAPTER III.

FRIENDS.[1]

299. ALL who are like-minded are friends by nature (p. 267). " Mencius said to a disciple, 'The well-educated of one locality makes friends with the well-educated of every place; the well-educated of a state with those of the state; he of the whole realm with those of the whole realm. If he finds the friendship of the scholars of the whole realm unsatisfying, he takes into consideration the foremost people of earlier days, recites their poems, reads their books. If he knows nothing of the people, he studies the history of their times. That is elevating friendship.' " " Birds of a feather flock together" is an old and a true saying. Friendship, to be enduring, requires a similarity in mind, or at least of endeavour. Ideal natures seldom find a perfect satisfying friendship in their immediate neighbourhood, often not in more distant acquaintance. Then literature generally steps in as a complement. Unhappily men now read too much, and that not to their instruction, but to their destruction; so it is that one seldom makes a friend of any one author, but having only a superficial acquaintance with him, never sounds his depths. But this is yet more important in the study of literature than in personal intercourse. The author presents his concentrated self in his books, and the whole contents of the mind-life are to be found together in very few pages. One should become absorbed in these, and

---

[1] Cf. Digest of Confucius, p. 74.

return to them again and again, as one naturally renews one's intercourse with an intimate friend. From the individual we may then proceed to the character of an entire period of history. Unhappily, owing to the present desire for novels and romances, sound taste is destroyed and one's mind ruined, so that one is rendered incapable of an intense friendship with the living, much less with the departed. This is true likewise in the department of religion. How few are there who let their Bible become their friend! However, the advice of Mencius is far more closely followed by European scholars than has been the case in China for years past. The Chinese, indeed, read the ancient works diligently and learn them by heart, yet one rarely meets with one thoroughly familiar with an old author, much less with the history of his time.

300. Friendship is only founded upon virtue and on no other consideration (p. 252). "A disciple said to Mencius, ' Permit me to ask concerning friendship.' Mencius replied, ' One does not form a friendship upon any consideration of age, or appearances, or relationship; friendship agrees with virtue and admits of no secondary consideration.' " This kind of friendship is purely ethical, and therefore of great value in culture; this, again, proves the ideal nature of Mencius.

301. The business of friendship is " mutual provocation to good " (p. 213). (Cf. Art. 279.) Of what use is friendship if we do not allow ourselves to be helped by it in doing good ? It affords the opportunity for overcoming a false sensitiveness and feeling of shame. It is one thing to have one's attention rightly directed in a friendly and gentle manner by a friend of either sex, and quite another when this is done in a contentious or even inimical and bitterly scornful way.

302. Mencius adduces an example to show that " the friendships of princes should be princely " (p. 255).

303. The ruler should honour as a teacher, not treat as merely a friend, him who is his superior in virtue and in

other respects (p. 265). " Duke Muh often took counsel
with Tsze-sze (grandson of Confucius), and said to him on
one occasion, ' Of old, lords over states with one thousand
war chariots made *friends* of scholars. How was that?'
Tsze-sze, being displeased, answered, ' The people of former days had a saying, Let him be served! but where did
they say let him be befriended?'" Mencius continues:
" Is it nothing that Tsze-sze was displeased ? ' According
to our positions, you, sir, are ruler and I am a servant of
the state; how could I venture to form a friendship with
the ruler (my sovereign)? According to virtue, you, sir,
ought to serve me; how, then, can friendship be formed
with me ?' If a ruler with one thousand war chariots desired friendship with him and could not obtain it, how
much less could he have done so if he had summoned him
to his presence ? " This quotation appears to contradict
the foregoing, but the same truth underlies it. The inner
equality fails here on account of external inequality. The
difference of external rank can only be let go with im-
punity when true intercommunication of heart takes
place. Where this is lacking, it is necessary to hold most
closely to these external forms as the only way of avoiding misunderstanding, offence, discontent, and hatred.
Mencius has only these few remarks to offer on the relations of friendship, yet these are both sound and striking.
The opportunity presents itself here for the evangelical
doctrine of the communion of faith. Moral and religious
culture is naturally furthered in such a sphere. The
circle of the family is too limited, and because it rests
upon a purely natural basis, although morally elevated,
seldom offers to each of its members that standpoint for
advancement, ethically and religiously, which is required.
The greater Church communities are again too extended ;
the individual relations of one to another are too much
wanting in them. Still this is not the place in which to
treat more at large the question of Christian communities.
Only let us add this reflection, that an ethical religious

friendship both is and must be above all, in the best sense of the word, the characteristic of the Church as of the Churches. Heathen religions know nothing of this, or have but a caricature of it in the mysteries of the initiated in the cloisters and the priesthood. In this we perceive the special excellency of Evangelical Christendom, the noblest and most perfect friendship which the world has ever seen. This is clearly evidenced by the history of the Christian Church.

CHAPTER IV.

MAN AND WIFE.[1]

304. As the basis of these relations, the various duties of the sexes are briefly and concisely stated (p. 128). "Man and wife are different," says the text literally; we might also translate it "separate." The sense is clear; it expresses the very opposite of that which, in the present day, is understood by "Emancipation."[2] Wherever social order prevails, this inequality will obtain in consequence of the difference, which has its basis in nature, although amongst all peoples who practise polygamy it is carried to extremes in the subjugation of the woman and her exclusion from social intercourse. Only when social intercourse between the sexes is pure and moral can it result in the elevation of both.

305. Men and women should not come into contact in giving and receiving, although there are exceptions (p. 183). "Some one asked, 'Does propriety require that men and women should not touch one another in giving and receiving?' Mencius replied, 'That is propriety.' He said again, 'If one's sister-in-law is sinking, ought she then to be drawn out with the hand?' He replied, 'It is wolfish not to draw out the sinking sister-in-law. The avoiding of contact between men and women in giving and receiving is propriety; the drawing out of the sinking sister-in-law with one's hand is praiseworthy.'" It is not easy to take into account the circumstances, because it is impossible to

---

[1] Cf. Digest of Confucius, p. 73.

[2] The "Rights of Women" are meant by this term.

frame rules to meet them, on which account much error occurs in practice. The exceptions to a universal rule should never be justified upon either merely subjective or objective grounds, but should also admit of proof as both necessary and humane.

306. Wedlock is the greatest of human relations (p. 221). "The uniting of man and wife is the greatest of human relationships." This is so because the regular propagation of mankind is thereby conditioned. Besides which, the well ordering of the political life of the state depends upon the same.

307. The consent of parents is necessary (p. 221). "A disciple asked, 'In the Book of Odes it is said—

"How oughtest thou to take a wife?
Father and mother must be asked."

If one believes these words, then no one more than Shun should have exemplified them; but why did Shun marry without so asking?' Mencius replied, 'Had he asked, he could never have married. For man and wife to be united is the greatest of human relationships; had he asked, he would have had to give up the greatest of human relationships because of the dissatisfaction of his parents, therefore he asked not.'" We must here grasp firmly the teaching of Moses on this point, "A man shall leave his father and his mother and cling to his wife." Yet there is an essential difference to be noted. According to the Mosaic position, the relationship of the married, as man to his wife, is closer than a son to his parents, but this is in the case of a marriage already concluded. The conclusion itself is made in the Bible dependent above all on the will of the parents. This remains ethically just, spite of the modern sentimental fashion of our times which plunges many young people in misery.

308. A go-between is necessary in making the choice (p. 144). "If a man-child be born, one desires for him a wife; if a female-child, a husband. This parental heart

all people have. If one waits not for the commands of parents and the arrangements of a go-between, but makes holes through walls in order to see another secretly, or gets over a wall to follow another, the parents and neighbours will despise such." For young people it is naturally more suitable to let the parents choose and make the necessary arrangements. It is indeed the case in China that unhappy marriages are proportionably fewer (excepting those which are disturbed by polygamy and the authority of the mother-in-law) than in lands where the young people, following their momentary inclinations, plunge into matrimony without rational reflection. To bring the inclination and the judgment into accordance with what is right is the moral way of proceeding. The consent of the parent or guardians should be obtained, but yet this is not an absolute condition in all cases; for a forced marriage against the inclination or where aversion exists is decidedly objectionable. Also an irrational affection, so long as it proves itself in a proper way to be really a true love, should, all considerations to the contrary notwithstanding, find recognition. The necessity of go-betweens is occasioned in China by the exclusion of the female sex from all free social intercourse.

309. Marriage is to be delayed only on account of the duty of nourishing parents.

310. Enforced marriage of a daughter to a barbarian.

311. Maternal admonition to the daughter bride (p. 141). "When a daughter is about to be married, her mother imparts instruction to her; whilst accompanying her to the door, she says by way of warning, ' When you come into your household, be respectful, be circumspect, do not oppose your husband. The vocation of wives and concubines is to act rightly in resignation.' " This admonition is to the point. Reverence is above all things necessary for a sound marriage relation; not merely the affection of the wife for the husband. Wives should be watchful in this respect if they wish to preserve the love

of their husbands. Holy Scripture also directs this. "Let
the wife see that she reverence her husband."

312. Purity of the marriage relation (p. 39). "The
king of T'se said, 'Your humble servant has a weakness ;
my weakness is to be addicted to the fair sex.' Mencius
answered, 'Of old the king of T'ae was addicted to the
fair sex, he loved his wife.'" It says of him in the Book
of Odes :—

> " The Duke Tan-foo of old came in the morning on
> A swift horse by the margin of the Western water ;
> He came twice to the foot of the K'e mountain.
> Having arrived with the Lady Kiang, they
> Chose together their dwelling-place (B.C. 1400).
> In those days there were at home no dissatisfied
> Maids, and abroad no unsettled men."

According to the ancient Book of Odes, the intercourse of
the sexes in China was quite unconstrained; the relation
of the two princely personages named was both exemplary
and monogamic, though we cannot prove this latter statement. Besides this, it is distinctly stated concerning the
most important woman in the ancient history of China that
the chief of her virtues was her treating the inferior wives
without either envy or·jealousy. It is sad to find so very
few passages in Chinese literature which can be adduced
in condemnation of the immorality of polygamy. I know
of very few which go as far as those of Mencius, and they
leave it an open question.

313. Divorce depends upon the will of the husband (p.
214). "An official cast out his wife and child because he
had injured his own father." (Cf. Art. 279.) This is the
only reference Mencius makes to the subject. Of him it
is recorded that he would have put away his own wife
because she nourished their child before his eyes, which
to him was contrary to all propriety. But the mother of
Mencius said to her holy son that the impropriety was
upon his side, for he ought to have knocked before he
entered the apartment of the women.

314. Remarriage.

315. Polygamy was then very ancient (p. 222). " Yaou, the ancient emperor, gave both his daughters to Shun to wife." Many Chinese now seek to explain away the fact that both sisters were given to be the wives of one man. But little is gained thereby, because it is contrary to natural feeling that one sister should be concubine and servant to the other as the lawful wife (Lev. xviii. 18).

316. Concubines are often mentioned by Mencius. See p. 216, where a wife and a concubine are conversing; p. 289, the service of concubines is mentioned, not only of one but of several, as was formerly and is now customary with officials; p. 372, "many hundred concubines;" and p. 313, according to which, following an ancient decree of the princes, a concubine might not be made a lawful wife. That polygamy is a political evil, Mencius might have deduced very plainly from the history of former times. The chronicle of the state of Loo is full of adultery arising from this very cause. We see that the teaching of Mencius as to the relation of man and wife is essentially conditioned by the idea of polygamy. On this account the wife is not permitted to have any kind of independence. It is Christianity alone which gives the wife her rightful place. The wife is religiously, morally, and legally the equal of her husband, yet socially her position is one of subordination to her husband. This is not only a biblical requirement, but is equally postulated on moral and natural grounds. Government by the wife is not only degrading to the husband, but is also a perversion of order, natural and divine.[1] Emancipation (the rights of woman) is dangerous to the state because destructive of the family. Marriage is made an impossibility to many men by reason of the ambitious pretensions of women, following the notions peculiar to our modern civilisation. Hence arises much of the evil

[1] See Shoo King, p. 302.

so prevalent in foreign lands where European merchants and officials frequently live in concubinage with natives. Hence also arises much of the modern form of prostitution and its accompanying evils. Women who advocate the rights of women can never take delight in the modest relations of the home; their joys are abroad in the great business of the world or in the saloons of society. Thus family life is disorganised and the training of children neglected. The best school education can only partially remedy this defect. In the family and the home should the soul of the child be cultivated and that of the adult find contentment. In this lies the problem for woman to solve. From a Christian standpoint, it is the vocation of woman to care for goodness of heart in the fullest sense of the word. I may be permitted to hint at yet another view. We condemn, and that rightly, polygamy; but what would the Chinese say of the many illegitimate births in Christian lands? We see thus what responsibilities are incurred in seeking to substitute one religion by another. The evil in human nature only takes another form. To meet this, the evangelical renovation of the heart by the divine power is an absolute necessity for securing moral purity.

· CHAPTER V.

THE SOVEREIGN AND MINISTERS.

Section I.—The Sovereign Individually.

THE relation between the sovereign and his ministers is, according to Mencius, not accidental but moral'; and so it really is. As soon as the moral bond is loosened between these, the constitution begins to suffer, and each fresh rupture hastens its dissolution. Each relation between these is conditioned from both sides. Not only are duties ethically imposed upon the minister, others corresponding belong to the sovereign. This arises from the moral individuality, which declares itself as ethical in their social positions. Mencius insists upon the principle that every man in regard to all the five social relations is a member of his immediate family and of the great human family also; and he retains his position therein by knowing how to realise his character as man according to the ideal already delineated. This same moral development is insisted upon for princes; for with Mencius there is no other morality for those in high authority than obtains for universal humanity [1] and which concerns every man. Hence we have but few hints for the inner development of the typical sovereign, yet these are enough to afford proof of the above assertion.

317. What is "born in the heart has its outcome in the government" (p. 68). (Cf. Arts. 33 and 106.),

---

[1] How far superior is the old Chinese philosopher in this respect to the teachings of a corrupt Christianity as formulated by the Jesuit casuists !

318. Hence the need of first thoroughly exercising the heart (spirit) previous to the work of governing (p. 166). (Cf. Art. 31.)

319. In case of failure the fault must be sought in one's self (p. 170). (Cf. Art. 107.) Therefore it is said, "If one rules men without attaining to the well-ordering (of the state), one must revert to one's own wisdom." (Cf. Art. 143.) We may boldly affirm that in all misgovernment, the administration, or in absolute monarchies the ruler, is alone to blame. The defect in wisdom usually shows itself in a mistaken judgment of the relations of things; frequently, too, in the choice of wrong means for the removal of what is injurious. Inefficient means may be classed with the wrong, and frequently do more injury. Mencius strikes the right nail on the head.

320. Such a sovereign "is willing to receive advice" (p. 90). To receive advice, for which he himself asks, after the pattern of the old ideal emperor, is a virtue which only proceeds from self-knowledge and the humility arising therefrom.

321. In constant practice of humanity. In times of quiet he ought to study the art of governing and of administering justice (p. 73). Mencius says, "Humanity brings glory, the opposite disgrace. Now to hate disgrace and continue in inhumanity is like hating damp and dwelling in a marsh (low ground). If one hates disgrace, there is nothing to surpass the esteeming of virtue and showing honour to scholars. The excellent should be in posts of honour, the able in official positions, noble houses in peace and quiet. When the times are thus, political economy and the administration of justice are manifested openly. Even great states will respect such (a ruler)." "L'état c'est moi" has some truth in it, only its meaning must be understood rather according to Mencius than Louis XIV. That meaning is, according to Mencius, that all the virtues of government are embodied in the sovereign, or that he exhibits as he unites them in himself. The

principal of all is benevolent nobility of mind. Yet this
ought not to degenerate into a good-natured negligence.
The ruler should ever keep in mind the requirements of the
realm. Being conscious of the insufficient power and perception of his own, as of the best minds, he should be anxious
to obtain gifted servants of the state, whilst especially
studious to be himself making progress in knowledge,
i.e., to acquire in its fulness, as far as man can, what is
necessary to the art of government. This takes place
best when the ruler develops actively the right which
subsists inwardly, and at the same time gives proper
attention to the labours of others. It ought to be the
problem which every ruler should propose to himself, how
to gain a standpoint above all parties; and this can only
happen when he examines without prejudice the various
positions of each, and holds to the best, yet without forgetting that a better is frequently possible.

322. Neglecting to progress in study causes misfortune.

323. "As is the monarch so are his subjects" (p. 186).
(Cf. Art. 212.) This truth obviously only holds good
generally; the exceptions are by no means rare.

324. He is merciful even to the brutes.

325. The example of the ancients is a mirror for princes
(p. 202). Mencius said, "Yu abhorred old wine and loved
good speech. T'ang held fast the mean and established
distinguished men after a bold manner. King Wan considered the people as an open wound; he looked to the
way (*Tao*) as if he scarcely saw it. King Woo despised
not the near and forgot not the remote. Duke Chow considered how to unite these three kings in himself, in order
to be able to display these four virtues. If anything would
not do, he looked at and considered it day and night; if
he happily solved it, he sat down and waited for the
morrow." This mirror for princes might serve for reflection in the present day. Verily, in constitutional states
it is very necessary that there be an able individual as

ruler, else he will soon come to nothing and government
be the plaything of parties.

SECT. II.—THE SOVEREIGN IN HIS DEMEANOUR TOWARDS
OTHERS.

(a.) *Towards the Realm.*

326. The ruler ever keeps in mind the government of
the whole, and therefore has no time for special endeavours
(p. 128). There were then Communists who proclaimed
absolute equality, saying that the prince ought himself to
plough, and also himself prepare his own food; and that
no man should be either the lord over or the servant to
another. Mencius first proves the impossibility of carrying out such doctrines in any human community, for
that is founded upon the division of labour; then he
explains this, especially dwelling on the difference between
mental and physical labour, and the work of government for the sake of the common weal. Thence he goes
on to moral and political considerations. Mencius said,
"Men have a principle (Tao): with plenty to eat, warm
clothing, and comfortable dwellings, without instruction
they approach the brutes. The sage (Yaou) grieved over
this, and appointed See as the minister of instruction, to
teach men their duties. Between father and son there
exists attachment; between sovereign and minister, righteousness; between husband and wife, discrimination;
between elder and younger brethren, the observance of
rank; between friends, fidelity." Then he reminds us
farther that the personal anxiety of holy kings was directed
to this, "the obtaining of capable ministers; he whose care
is, on the contrary, directed to the cultivation of his fields,
is a farmer and nothing more," says Mencius. The public
life of a monarch permits of no well-grounded knowledge,
still less of the personal development of particular forms
of labour. Nevertheless it remains that he should examine
into the relative importance of each branch of industry,

and according to that make provision in a special manner
for the elevation of each in like proportion. Especially
ought he rightly to grasp the relations of the various
branches to each other and to the whole. Here there is
work enough for the Government of a state (home politics).
As far as is possible all that is good should be encouraged,
and that in a way to make each render support to the other.

327. He is benevolent or humane (p. 168). "He who
rules not his subjects as did Yaou oppresses them. There
are properly only two ways, that of humanity and of
inhumanity. If the subjects are oppressed to the utter-
most, the sovereign himself is murdered and the state
destroyed ; if oppression is not so severe, his person is in
danger and the state is weakened. He receives those nick-
names of 'the Dark,' 'the Cruel,' which even pious sons
and affectionate nephews cannot alter in a hundred
generations." Benevolence (humanity) should underlie
all the personal activity of a sovereign, who thereby
serves both himself and the state. The result of the
opposite course is often displayed in history. The same
is true of every sort of authority. The assumption of an
air of authority is by no means that which really governs
subordinates ; on the contrary, it tends to excite opposition.

328. Mencius adds (p. 116), " The excellent sovereign is
gracious, politic, and courtly towards inferiors ; what he
takes from the people is according to law" (*i.e.*, legal taxes).
Elsewhere (p. 180) he explains this : " A gracious sovereign does not despise other men ; the politic never take
by force from the people" (because he knows how to
make his lawful revenues suffice). "The ruler who does
both, who despises and plunders, only fears ; none obey
him. How can such a one be gracious and politic ? Have
graciousness and frugality ever been brought about by the
tone of the voice and a smiling countenance ? " For every
Government, as well as for the ruler himself, authority
is the fundamental condition of existence. When this
authority rests upon a firm foundation, upon essential

M

superiority, moral power, and sanctified right, the pompous assertions of external power are unnecessary and injurious. We should never seek dignity where it is not to be found, nor think it lessened by things which only remotely affect it. Frugality will be considered farther on. Courtesy towards inferiors might be studied with advantage by many who are in authority. As to legality, many Governments know how, in spite of legal restraints, to satisfy their illegal desires in a legal manner. This knowledge is the property of no one party. It is probable that the ruling diplomats of the modern world are no less distinguished than their classic predecessors for dulcet tones and smiling faces.

(*b.*) *The Demeanour of the Sovereign towards Officials.*

329. He only advances the benevolent to high positions (p. 166). "The holy men, after they had fully developed the thoughts of their hearts, let sympathetic (merciful) government follow as an institution, and benevolence overspread the realm. Hence it is said, in order to build high, one ought to avail oneself of elevations; to dig deep, one must use streams and lowlands. He who has to do with government and does not avail himself of the acts of former kings, how can he rightly be termed wise? Therefore it is only the benevolent who are rightly put in high positions. If the inhuman is found in a high position, he disseminates his wickedness amongst the masses." Many points of importance are here brought forward. First we have the embodiment in the outer actions of the inward preparation. It is not enough that good plans be formed; there is no lack of these in our more modern times. Those whom we mean to guide must be impressed by the fact that amid all our measures we only aim at bettering their condition. He alone is sympathetic who allows himself to be influenced by the requirements of others. Again, we must look around us for points of

support in a common-sense study of history and by
making the experiences of others of use to ourselves.
This is not to be done by being able to enumerate a mass
of dates and events, but by comprehending the heights
and depths of man's nature, and by taking up a position
corresponding to one's own moral aim. Thus we raise
ourselves above the merely personal standpoint, which
always gives an impression of self-will, and approach, by
means of our connection with the noblest spirits of antiquity, the feeling of universal humanity. Only it is one
thing to place oneself upon the height, and thereby obtain
for oneself a higher view and perception, and another to
stand below the height of the ancients, to admire, and
possibly at best imitate them. Besides, it is important
to observe and make use of every advantage our own
times offer, *i.e.*, to employ in the service of the state all
the finer intellects of the day.

330. The selection of officials should be with a view to
the progress of the realm (p. 129). (Cf. Art. 321.) " To find
a man for the realm," says Mencius, " is called humanity ;
therefore it is easy to hand over the realm to a man, but
difficult to find a man for the realm." He is treating
here of the succession, which naturally is generally a
simple and easy matter. On the other hand, the selection of a capable co-regent and successor is very difficult,
and supposes great penetration on the part of the selector.
In history the choice of the ruler has generally proved
evil, because the choice has mostly been governed by
selfish considerations.

331. Only men of capacity should be summoned to
office (p. 73). (Cf. Art. 321.) " Let the excellent be in
posts of honour, the able hold office." The nomination of
officials is in the power of the ruler, or at least is conditioned by his influence. The well-being of the commonwealth is dependent upon this, just as the health of the
human body is dependent upon the state of the several
members. It is therefore of importance that the choice

should not be made dependent upon merely subjective
grounds, but in the interests of the welfare of the realm.
. 332. The ruler should in this trust more to experience
than to common report (p. 41). "Mencius saw the king
of Ts'e and said to him, 'What we call an old-established
state is not said of high trees, but of hereditary states-.
men. The king has no attached officials. Those appointed yesterday are lost to-day without knowing why.'
The king said, 'How can I discover their incapacity and
so avoid them?' He answered, 'If the ruler promotes
an excellent man for one of the states, as if he had not
received sufficient consideration, he will place commoners
above nobles and strangers before relatives; how dare he
do this incautiously? If all around take him to be an
excellent man, he is not therefore one on that account; if
all dignitaries hold him to be an excellent man, it is not
to be taken for granted; but if this happens on the part
of all the people of a state, one may look into it, and finding him to be an excellent man, forthwith employ him.
If all one's surroundings or all the dignitaries declare
any one to be unsuitable, one does not pay attention to
this; but if it happens on the part of all the people of a
state, one examines into it: if he is proved to be unsuitable we must remove him. If the whole of one's surroundings or all the dignitaries pronounce him worthy of
death, one does not listen to them; but if all the people say
so, we inquire into it: if he is shown to be so, he must
then be put to death. Thus it is said the inhabitants of
the country put him to death. By such conduct, therefore,
may one. become as the father and mother of one's people.'"
The above naturally refers to the higher state officials.
The appointment of these is always one of the most important of the duties of a sovereign. To make the be-
stowal of the higher positions the result of examination,
as is the case with the lower, would be destructive. As a
rule, it is every way to be desired that those already exa-
mined, and also candidates for the service of the state,

should be advanced to such posts. But in any case it is important that in making the choice the decision should not depend upon mere business-like ability, for this may be possessed by any able secretary. Intellect and character are the essential requirements for high positions of trust. Another important consideration is also postulated. The ruler should neither incline to his own view before that of others, nor to the wishes of those in high positions, for these are generally coloured by self or party considerations, but to the wishes of those for whom the official is appointed. Only well-known and generally recognised individuals are adapted for such positions. But even then it is important that the ruler clearly understand the grounds of such popularity, and examine into them before deciding in the interests of the state. For the removal of such officials the foregoing considerations are equally applicable. A high state official should never be made the plaything of envy, malevolence, and other caprices, otherwise the sovereign will only be surrounded with weathercocks.

333. As is the lord so are his servants.

334. Proper respect to be paid to officials (p. 194). " Mencius discourses to the king of Ts'e : ' If a ruler regards his officials as hands and feet, they will regard him as the heart and stomach; if he regards his officials as dogs and horses, they will regard him as a farmer; and if he regards them as earth and grass, they will regard him as a thief and an enemy.' " If Mencius really said this to the face of the tyrant, it is worthy of all honour. Any way, the teaching of Mencius preserves a large measure of individual liberty to the higher officials. The passage contains a very bitter truth of universal application in all relations between rulers and dependants, employers and employed. Unhappily each seeks to throw the blame of unhappy relations upon the other side. There are faults on both sides, but Mencius is right in this, that the initiative rests with the superior.

335. No cold treatment (p. 337). (Cf. Art. 243.) Mencius said, " Support without affection is called reckoning one as a pig; to love and not respect is to treat one as a pet calf. There must be honour and respect before the presentation of silk stuffs. An empty show of honour .and respect can never attach the superior man [to you]. Something more is wanted." Rulers are extremely sensitive about high treason, and other persons of rank also about disrespectful conduct towards themselves; but how seldom is their treatment of dependants of that noble and manly character which is absolutely requisite in the interchange of courtesy by equals! The social questions of the present day arise in great part from these considerations.

336. The cause why so frequently able men are not to be obtained (p. 266). (Cf. Art. 244.) " If the prince desires to see a man distinguished (by his ability) but in an indirect way, it is as if he wished him to enter a room but shut the door against him. For righteousness is the way and propriety the door. But only the superior man can follow this way and go in and out of this door." What is good is often desired, but the intention is carried out in such a manner that any good result is frustrated. We act upon self-will, that is in most cases not according to objective right, and yet less according to reason, but in accordance with our subjective inclination. This is necessarily repugnant to any man of character.

337. True beneficence towards them (p. 262). " Cooked meat was often presented by Duke Muh to the grandson of Confucius, Tsze-sze. Tsze-sze was displeased at this. At last he motioned the messenger to the door, bowed twice with his head to the earth, turning his face to the north, and declined to receive it, saying, ' Henceforth I know the sovereign feeds me as a dog or a horse.' Since that time no servant brought him presents. He who takes delight in men of ability and can neither put them in office nor support them, how can he be said to take delight in ability? A disciple of Mencius said, ' I venture

to ask in what way should a ruler support a superior man so that that support may be received?' He replied, 'It is to be done by command of the ruler; the superior man then receives it with a twofold motion of the hands and bowing of the head. On this follows the keeper of the stores with grain and the head of the kitchen with flesh, without mentioning the command of the ruler. Tsze-sze regarded it as sacrificial flesh, which caused him the annoyance of (paying) continual compliments; and this is not the right way of affording support to the superior man. There was Yaou (in his action) towards Shun. He made his nine sons serve him, gave him his two daughters in marriage, and made ready all the officials, oxen, sheep, stores, and magazines of grain to support Shun (labouring) amongst the cultivated fields; thence he raised him and appointed him to the highest position. Thence it is said, A king or duke publicly honouring a man of ability.'" Tsze-sze was so prominent amongst his contemporaries, that one of the higher official positions was his due. If the prince, for some reason or other, was unwilling to elevate him to this, he should still have offered him support in a more delicate manner. This is a universal principle. Many great people think that their assistance is in itself so surpassingly great a favour as to forget that very much depends upon the manner in which a gift is offered. A small present given with heartfelt delicacy, does more good than a rich gift which makes one feel continually the sensation of accepting alms. A so-called beneficence is often harder to bear than misery. The foregoing also shows that in ancient China delicacy of feeling was as highly developed as is the reverse now-a-days.

338. In cases of resignation a threefold courtesy is to be observed (p. 195), and on taking their final departure the officials will put on mourning attire. "The king of T'se said, 'Propriety requires mourning attire to be put on for the old ruler; what must take place in order that the

officials put on mourning?' He replied, 'Their admonitions must have had results, their advice have been listened to, and blessings have flowed down to the people. If the official has reasons for departing, the ruler will permit him an escort over the boundaries, and will send also in advance to the place to which he betakes himself. If he remain away three years without returning, then first he takes back the fields and residences. This is called observing threefold propriety. If this be so, then will mourning be put on for him. Now, on the contrary (continues Mencius), one is a minister and his exhortations have no result; his advice is not listened to, and no blessings flow down to the people. If one has reasons for departure, the ruler seeks to detain him by force, and carries it to extremities in the place to which he goes. On the day of departure he takes back the fields and residences. This is called robbery and enmity; why should one put on mourning apparel for a robber and an enemy?'" The threefold propriety consists first, therefore, in the counsel of officials being rightly estimated; that will give confidence and happiness in their service, especially when with this there is brought about a real improvement in the condition of the people. It is taken for granted that the proposals have reference to the welfare of the community. Secondly, in the departure from office without enmity of mistrust, but with every mark of honour, being escorted to the boundaries and recommended by a special message to a neighbouring court. Thirdly, in the anticipation of a friendly return, therefore at first only a furlough of three years; during this, the revenues of those public lands which form the income of the higher officials remain at his disposal. Whether this revenue would be permitted to cross the boundaries is not plain, and could hardly be supposed, but in case of his return, it would be given up to him. Only when the three years had expired would this possession be forfeited. There is here indicated a paternal relation between the sovereign and his officials which, even in ancient China, rarely existed.

339. The grounds of dismissal. (See Art.˙420.) Those of departure are, according to Art. 332, neither the displeasure of the dignitaries nor the surroundings of the sovereign, but that of the people, which the sovereign, after careful examination, finds well founded.

(c.) Towards the People.

340. Treats them gently (p. 202). (Cf. Art. 325.) "King Wan treated the people like a wound." All rough handling of a wound gives pain and increases the inflammation. On the other hand, we must not let ourselves be hindered by pain from cleansing and binding up a wound, necessarily also from cutting, burning, sewing up, and such like; but these only in order to bring about a healing of the same. All infliction of pain which does not contribute towards healing is objectionable, even in the slightest degree, and no physician claiming to be humane would permit himself to have recourse it. The human organisation, specially that of a sufferer, was never intended to furnish physicians with opportunities for experiments. Just so is it with the people. Unfortunately in this time of modern progress many various and injurious experiments have been tried in the departments of both social and political organisation. It is a pity that the pain of the patient's wounds is unfelt by the physician.

341. Preserves strict conformity with the laws of the ancients (p. 165). In the Book of Odes it is said—

> " Never transgressing and never forgetting,
> But following after the old ideal."

" It has never yet happened," says Mencius here, "that any one following the laws of the earlier monarchs has committed a fault." The Chinese are, indeed, evil spoken of as hyper-conservative, and it is not to be disputed that this is frequently the case in a very disagreeable manner. But the defender of conservatism after the Chinese way defends only that which is good in old times, and not everything that is ancient. Indeed, one often thinks that everything good may be found in antiquity, forgetting the progress of development, and likewise that possibly something better may be found in other directions.

342. Does not allow himself to be guided by his own private interests (p. 2). "Mencius had an audience of the king of Liang. The king said, 'Venerable sir, you thought a thousand miles (li) was not too far to come to see me, possibly being in possession of that which shall be profitable to my state.' Mencius replied, 'Why must the king say *profit*? There are humanity and righteousness, and therewith enough. If the king says, what is profitable to my state, the upper classes will say, what is profitable to our families, the scholars and the common people will say, what is profitable to ourselves. The upper and lower classes will emulate each other in gaining profit, and the state will be endangered. In a state with ten thousand chariots of war, the family with a thousand chariots will murder the ruler; and in a state of a thousand chariots, the same will be done by a family with a hundred. To take a hundred thousand from ten thousand thousand is yet not too little; if one places righteousness in the background and profit in the forefront, no one will be satisfied without deeds of robbery. Let the king say simply humanity and righteousness, and nothing farther; why must profit be spoken about?'" The private interests of princes and high officials have already brought many a state to the ground. When that is prevented by other circumstances, these still occasion much confusion, bloodshed, and destruction. The interest of the state is and remains the highest interest of the ruler. This is also well known by most masters. We only deceive ourselves concerning our real interests. Is it not too much the thought of the present day that these

consist exclusively in material profit? Mencius, more
than 2200 years since, condemned the much-vaunted
utilitarianism of our day. Humanity and righteousness
conjoined are, for him, the only true polestar of good
government.

343. Observes his duty towards those suffering need
(p. 261). "The ruler must afford help to his subjects in
their need." (Cf. Art. 195.) This passage refers firstly
to scholars, but admits also of a universal application,
like the foregoing. The ruler is held answerable for the
welfare of his people, and endeavours himself to make
atonement in famine (p. 8). "Dogs and swine consume
the food of men (says Mencius to the king of Liang), and
yet one knows no frugality; on the roads lie those perishing of hunger, yet one perceives no opening (of the
storehouses). Men die, and it is said, 'Not I, but the
year is in fault.' What difference is there here between
killing any one and saying, Not I, the weapon is in fault?
If the king ceases to lay the blame upon the year, he will
make the people of the realm draw round him.'" That is,
when they find help from the king, they will rally round
him from all sides, the more so in bad years.

344. He cares for the physical well-being of his people,
because that conditions their moral welfare (p. 338).
"The people cannot live without fire and water. If any
one knocks in the darkness of night at the door of one of
the people and asks for water or fire, there is no one who
would refuse it, that is sufficiently plain. If a holy man
rules the realm, he will make pulse and grain like water
and fire. If these, the chief staples of food, are as abundant
as water and fire, how can inhumanity obtain amongst
the people?" (P. 24.) "A judicious ruler will therefore
take measures to provide for the vital requirements of his
people. He will manage so that they, looking upward,
have a sufficiency to serve their fathers and mothers, and,
looking downward, have a sufficiency for the support of
wife and children, that in good years they may be able

to eat their fill, and in bad years to avoid starvation; then they may be urged onward to what is good, because it will be easy for the people to follow after it." With Mencius man's material needs are to be supplied equally with and by means of the moral. (Cf. Arts. 326, 444 and ff.) Neglected poverty always brings with it great dangers to morality, and in consequence to the welfare of the state. Still abundance of provision by itself will never make people moral.[1] We see far too often that the wealthy are the most morally degraded. The well-to-do too frequently think more of the gratification of the sensual desires than of the cultivation of their higher nature. It must ever be the aim of a truly benevolent administration to take such measures as that every, even the poorest, subject may be able to find his proper support in a right way. This is best brought about by means of universal industry, which generally invigorates the people; by frugality even in the higher circles; specially by thrift and temperance amongst the working classes. To this end the greatest possible extension of agriculture and of all kinds of industry is requisite, so that he who will work may be able to find work by which he may support himself and his family.

345*a*. He is gentle in awarding punishment (p. 23). "The possession of a well-balanced mind, without any certain means of existence, is only possible for the cultivated. With the people, on the contrary, uncertainty as to the means of existence draws after it indecision of mind. Where there are no fixed principles, there is to be found every possible kind of idleness, vulgarity, evil, and debauchery. When crime follows, then to visit it with punishment is called ensnaring the people; but how can the people be ensnared if a humane ruler is on the throne?" A purely external application of justice or the law, in which no consideration is given to the circumstances which occasioned the deed, is terrible injustice. Justice

[1] In sacred writ the story of Sodom is a proof of this.

ought always to be perfected by equity, or, according to Mencius, to be corrected by humanity.

345*b.* The relatives of criminals should not be held answerable (p. 38). "Criminals were never punished in wife and child." This was under King Wan (cf. Art. 442). That which is said in the Commentary throws a pleasing light upon the humanity of the ancient Chinese civilisation. But it appears, nevertheless, that, with very few exceptions, the custom of to-day of holding families responsible even then prevailed, as the very intimation which Mencius here gives indicates clearly. In the present day the whole clan is responsible for the individual, which gives rise to much injustice. Slavery is quite customary, but in a very mild form.

346. Preachers of humanity and righteousness ought to be supported by the state (p. 145). "Some one said to Mencius, 'It is not right that students should be fed without rendering service.' Mencius replied, 'Were there, sir, no universal exchange for labour, in order to supply deficiency by superfluity, the farmer would retain his superfluous corn, the woman keep all superfluous material for clothes. Were this exchange the same, the joiner as well as the wheelwright would receive their support from you, sir. Now, if there be a man who is filial at home and brotherly without, who holds the doctrine of the earlier kings, and by it so assists later monarchs that they learn it, he receives no support from you, sir. But why do you honour joiners and wheelwrights and esteem that mean which urges to humanity and righteousness?' He answered, the object of joiners and wheelwrights is directed to the seeking of support; is the object of the superior man who urges on the doctrine (Tao) also that, viz., the seeking for support?' He replied, 'Why do you, sir, seize upon his object? He who makes himself of service to you ought to be, and is to be, supported. Which, then, do you recompense, his object or his service?' He replied, 'His object.' Mencius answered,

'There is a man who disfigures the roof and smears the walls; his object is to obtain support by his work; do you support him?' 'No!' was the answer. Mencius said, 'Then, sir, you recompense the service and not the intention.'" The vocation of the preacher may thus, on the principle of the division of labour, demand recognition for itself in the state as a kind of industrial occupation. Humanity and righteousness, we dare also add to these the religion of Christ, are necessities for the life of the state, as the satisfaction of many requirements of the lower physical as of the higher spiritual life. The noble yearning of man's heart for the eternal, concealed though it be in many cases, demands its satisfaction. The present ruling passion of the human heart is simply the sensual and selfish. Unless that which is higher be persistently aroused and nourished in him, it will infallibly perish. China in her present condition is an eloquent instance. People like Mencius are, alas! great rarities in China.

347. He leaves blood-revenge to the people (p. 357). (Art. 184.) "Mencius said, 'From henceforward I recognise the seriousness of murdering any one's relation. He who kills a man's father, his own father will be killed by another. He who kills a man's brother, his own brother will be killed by another. Thus indeed he does not kill them himself, but it lacks very little of being the same thing.'" Blood-revenge is a miserable makeshift, in times when the power of the executive is not sufficiently far-reaching. The matter in dispute generally excites the spirit of family revenge, until it comes to be a lingering and murderous feud. Each execution is not a murder, and passion belongs not to impartial judges. In the Mosaic law a limit was assigned to unjust revenge by the cities of refuge and the investigation to be made by appointed judges. The basis for the administration of justice must ever be the Christian requirement, "Revenge not yourselves." The avenger listens to God and His representative upon earth, the Government which upholds

right and justice. If, on the one hand, there are many imperfections to be deplored, on the other, it is much better than when every one takes the law into his own hand, which leads to lynch law. This state of things can, however, only become general when there is actually no justice to be had from the Government. Where, on the other hand, sentence is passed fearlessly and impartially, and yet in accord with strict justice, there the desire for private revenge lessens and at last disappears. Private wrongs will then be punished lawfully. We see in the foregoing teaching about blood-revenge an error full of danger to the state, which bears evil fruit in China even to our own day.

SECT. III.—THE RULER AS FEUDAL PRINCE OR EMPEROR.

(a.) Feudal Princes.

348. A fief, like an office, depends upon the emperor (p. 98). " A dignitary asked privately, ' May Yen (a state) be attacked ? ' Mencius answered, ' It may. Tse-kwai (a former ruler) ought properly not to have given away Yen, and Tse-shi (a former minister, now ruler) ought not to have received Yen from any one (without the imperial permission). Were there here an official whom your reverence liked, and to whom, without informing the emperor, you gave on your own authority rank and revenues, and this official received these also of his own will, without any order from the emperor, how then ? What difference would there be between this proceeding and that ? ' " " The people of Ts'e attacked Yen. Some one asked, ' Was that a direction to Ts'e to attack Yen ? ' He answered, ' In no way. Some dignitary asked whether Yen might be attacked, and I answered, It might. He understood it thus, and attacked Yen. Had he asked, Who may attack it ? the answer would have been, He who is commanded by Heaven, he may attack it. Were a murder

committed, and any one asked, May the murderer be killed? the answer would be, He may. Were any one to inquire, Who may kill him? the reply would be, He who is the criminal judge may kill him. But for Yen to be attacked by Yen, what kind of injunction would that be?" Tse-kwai ascended the throne of Yen in B.C. 319. The king of Ts'e sent Sootai, an able diplomatist, who, being bribed by Tsi-shi, the minister of Yen (with a hundred pieces of gold), counselled Tse-kwai to transfer the province to his minister, which he did, so that the minister became ruler. He who is commanded by Heaven is naturally the emperor, whose authority and power were in those times greatly in abeyance. The princes did pretty much as they liked. Now it is even worse in China, for the villages carry on a kind of war against each other. It is clear that an empire must one day be ruined in this way. It is dubious from the quotation what was the opinion of Mencius, as the intention of his questioner could hardly have been concealed from him. Possibly he gave this answer because he was only asked privately and not officially.

349. Feudal princes are rewarded and punished by the emperor (p. 311). Mencius said, "The five chieftains sinned against the three (model) kings; the present princes sin against the five chieftains. The governors of to-day sin against the princes. The visit of the emperor to the princes is called a hunting excursion; the attendance at court of the princes is called an official report. In early years, the tilling of the fields was proved, and the deficiency of the crops in harvest supplied, so as to meet the necessities of the case. If the emperor explored the boundaries and found the cultivated area augmented, the farms in order, the old people supported, the skilful honoured, rising men in the offices of state, then he gave a reward, a reward of land. If he explored a region and found the ground uncultivated, the old neglected, the excellent forgotten, and parasites in the offices of state, then he

administered rebuke. The first occasion of neglecting to appear at court brought a degradation of rank (to the prince); the second, loss of territory; if it happened a third time, the forces of the realm marched against him. The emperor pronounced sentence but did not execute it; the princes executed it but did not pronounce it. The five chieftains, on the contrary, required princes to carry out sentence on princes. Therefore it is said, The five chieftains sin against the (model) kings." Formerly the princes had not only the desire to govern, and that well, as is frequent in later days, but also to work out the problem of civilisation. Just so the emperor. By means of the regulated appearance at court the vassals were kept in dependence upon the emperor, the central power of the realm. The emperor witnessed for himself the kind of authority exercised in the various states, and could not in those days be deceived by false reports, as is the case in China in the present day. There was also a great advantage in the clear distinction made between the administration of justice and the execution of the sentence. The emperor pronounced judgment on the princes, but the carrying out of the same was by means of the princes. In the case of particular states, the execution of justice was committed to the prince of the neighbouring state. This would all have worked very well if the emperors had not very soon become dissolute. As they gave themselves up to pleasure, their power declined, and that of the princes increased. In the time of Mencius the emperor had less territory to govern than the Germany of the seventeenth century.

350. A confederation of princes, B.C. 650 (p. 313). "Duke Wan was the most accomplished of the five chieftains. He assembled the princes in K'wei Ke'w. He bound the sacrificial animals with the document upon them, but spilt no blood. The first enactment ran thus : ' The extermination of the unfilial ; no exchange of the entail ; no concubine to become lawful wife.' The second

N

enactment, 'The excellent to be honoured; the talented to be searched out, in order to distinguish those of ability.' The third, 'Respect to be paid to the aged; compassion to be shown to the young; guests and strangers not to be forgotten.' The fourth, 'The lower officials not to hold hereditary offices; the business of one office not to be of various kinds; the reception of subordinates to be circumspect; no premeditated putting to death of a governor.' The fifth, 'No deceptive coast embankments; no suppression of the sales of grain; no investiture (with rank) without proclamation.' It is said all the four contracting parties returned after the completion of the compact with mutual farewells. The princes of to-day, continues Mencius, repudiate all these five requirements, hence it is said they sin against the five chieftains." This agreement is in every way a most interesting document, and gives us at a glance a view of the social and political life of those early days, B.C. 700. We see that the emperor had then almost no authority, being only slightly recognised in the fifth clause as lord over the feudal princes.

(*b.*) *Feudal Princes may aspire to Imperial Dignity.*

351. "Unity is strength" (p. 12). This is of force against that division of interests by which every state and every little town only thinks upon the things which concern itself.

352. No wrong ought to be perpetrated on this account, still less should any innocent person be punished (pp. 70 and 344). "The son of the king asked, 'What is the business of a scholar?' 'The improvement of the will.' 'What is the improvement of the will?' 'Nothing but humanity and righteousness. To slay an innocent man is inhuman; to take what is not proper is unrighteous.' 'What is the habitation?' (sphere of action). 'It is humanity.' 'What is the way?' 'It is righteousness. With this the problem of the great man is solved.'" The will (cf. Art. 186) gives to man's life its direction,

and from this it chiefly proceeds. He who slays an innocent man has as yet taken no direction towards what is good. In a legal sense also the idea of crime is, of course, much weakened. Already many innocent people have been legally sentenced to death. In China there is much in criminal cases that excites our repugnance. For instance, a wealthy criminal can purchase a substitute. Villages often force poor wretches to give themselves up as guilty, and to confess to crimes which they have never committed. In such ways one thinks to satisfy appearances with the law or the magistrates. It is now as of old with regard to extortion under every conceivable pretext. How lightly human life was esteemed in the time of Mencius is shown by p. 15 : "There is not one amongst the shepherds of men throughout the whole realm who does not take pleasure in executions. Were there any who did not take pleasure in executions, the people throughout the empire would lift up their heads and look to him; verily it would be so. The people would stream towards him as water pours downwards irresistibly; who can restrain it ? "

353. The people are the political foundation for the emperor (p. 360). "He who wins the people becomes emperor; he who wins the emperor becomes prince; he who wins the prince becomes a governor." We must, however, bear in mind that Mencius does not set the imperial dignity in prospect before every one, but only for one of the reigning feudal princes, who formerly frequently became emperors. It is characteristic that the highest dignity is made dependent not upon the will of the princes, but upon that of the lowest foundation of society, the people ; and this is worthy of reflection. The consciousness of this dependence upon the people universally ought to have been a wholesome corrective to the emperor against autocratic despotism. But we must, at the same time, remark that this idea of Mencius has never been worked out in China.

354. The people gather round him who protects them (p. 14). "The king of Ts'e asked, ' What virtue appertains to the obtaining of the highest authority?' He replied, ' Protecting the people, and then no one can hinder from the supreme authority.'" (Cf. Art. 55.) That this king was the man to do so, Mencius inferred from the fact that he pitied an ox which he saw led to sacrifice, "which resisted like an innocent man who approached the place of execution." It is too often the case that the nobility know how to treat well their dogs and horses, and even their cattle, but not their domestics and dependants. There is no objection to the prescribed expedient, the obtaining of the supreme authority by the spread of such sentiments amongst the people that they establish their own protection; but the history of the world nowhere shows that the many-headed hydra can be brought into subjection without bloodshed.

355. Humane government is the only way (p. 359). Mencius said, "There are inhuman (princes) who have gained a state, but no inhuman (prince) has obtained the whole realm." The meaning is, that no inhuman prince has ever founded a new dynasty. A military despotism can establish itself without any other virtue than bravery, but with the victory the power begins to crumble away. Humanity conquers slowly, but its victories remain.

356. Inhumanity loses what humanity gains (p. 170). Mencius said, "The three dynasties (Hea, Yen, Chow) obtained the realm by humanity, and they lost it through inhumanity. This is in every case that whereby a state falls or rises, is established or decays. If the emperor is inhuman, he will not guard the four seas (the empire); if the princes are inhuman, they will not guard the spirits of the fields; if the higher and lower officials are inhuman, they will not guard the ancestral temples; if the scholars and people are inhuman, they will not guard the four limits of the body. If any one now has pleasure in in-humanity and yet hates death and destruction, this is

like hating drunkenness, yet putting oneself in the power of wine." We think, and with reason, that Mencius ascribes to humanity and its opposite a much greater effect upon the life of the state than to almost any other factor. Monarchs especially, and small authorities also, should remember that inhuman or unloving conduct forfeits the confidence of subordinates. Then it is that every one soon thinks how he may best protect himself against the same. What is really good in the superior will then only be accepted so far as it corresponds to the private interests of those under him. Thus social bonds are loosened, and revolution breaks out and spreads at the slightest inducement. One ought to distinguish clearly between the causes and the occasion of such a crisis.

357a. Humanity wins the heart of men (p. 175). Mencius said, "Kee and Chow (ancient tyrants) lost the realm because they lost the people; they lost the people because they lost men's hearts. There is but one way to win the empire; to win the people is to win the realm. There is but one way to win the people; to win their hearts is to win the people. There is but one way to win their hearts : give them and lead them according to their desires, and offer them not what they abhor—that approaches it! The people betake themselves to the humane just as water hastens downwards or as game flees to the desert. Therefore it is the otter which drives the fishes together into deep water; the hawk which drives the birds together into the bushes; Kee and Chaou who drive the people together to T'ang and Woo (the founders of new dynasties). Were there a lover of humanity among the present rulers, the princes would collectively strive together for him; and even if he did not wish to become emperor, he could not avoid it. The present emperor would be as if one sought three-year [1] wormwood for a seven years' sickness; if that cannot even be drawn, it will not be obtained in a lifetime. If the

---

[1] The Chinese consider this the medicine for chronic complaints.

will is not directed to humanity, there will be lifelong
trouble and disgrace, with death and destruction as its
end." Evil treatment scatters the people, love draws
them in proportion as they are uncorrupted. But to
avoid oppression and cruelty, the people will willingly
put themselves under almost any power that will promise
them protection and good treatment.

357b. No enforcing of goodness, but continual education leading to it. (Cf. Art. 445.) Governments frequently fail in this respect. There is often too great
haste in reforms for which the people are not prepared.
Not that faint-heartedness is to be commended, but quiet
firmness, which ever progresses step by step. We must
beware of imitating the advance of a rope-dancer without
his balance.

358. Neither great family influence nor long time is requisite (p. 59). " Neither of the three dynasties had more
than a thousand li, and the state of Ts'e had just as much
land. Nor does the territory require to be extended nor
the people increased, in order to become drawn together.
By the carrying out of a humane government these
arrived at the imperial dignity, and no one could with-
stand that." It is generally true that an emperor, even
without imposing family influence, may obtain and retain
his influence over the vassal princes by means of his personal virtue, but it is seldom possible for his successors.
So it has been in China and in other lands.

359. The humane ruler has no enemy in the realm (p.
11). " When the king secures humane government for
the people, there is a diminution of imprisonment and
fines, duties and taxes are lightened, ploughing is heavy
and weeding light; so that adults have a quiet day in
which they may cultivate filial and brotherly affection,
truth, and faith, in order thereby to serve at home their
father and elder brother, and abroad their seniors and
superiors, so that one can use a staff to beat back the
hard coat of mail and sharp weapons of Tsin and Shu.

These rob their subjects of their time, so that they can neither weed nor plough to support their father and mother. The parents freezing and starving; brothers, wives, and children are scattered and destroyed. These crush their subjects to the ground. If the king sets up his tribunal over these, who then will oppose him? Therefore it is said the humane has no enemy." (Cf. Art. 440.) A humane government returns to works of peace, and seeks to avoid war and strife. A policy of peace abroad and paternal care for those at home generally does away with much enmity, but not with envy and wickedness. The armed selfishness of neighbouring states is often an evil enemy against whom one must necessarily be watchful. Men and their policy are now swayed by one of several lower passions, against which beautiful theories are of no use, although the keeping in view of the ideal is of great importance. For practical use we ought to give attention to their actual working out, so that the wavering springs of motives of popular life be not misunderstood. In spite of all her teaching about humanity, China has not had fewer wars than other countries.

360. To support his theory Mencius criticises the Shoo King, or Book of Documents, p. 355. "Better," says he, "no book than to believe the whole contents. . . . A humane ruler has no enemy throughout the realm. How can blood wash away the mortar-pestle if the greatest humanity is in conflict with the greatest inhumanity?" Mencius does not reflect that under a tyrant the lowest minds very often feel well off and live by the plunder and oppression of the good. It· is also interesting to see how a former beautiful and well-intentioned theory has called forth a so-called unprejudiced criticism. We must always discriminate between acts which are open to criticism (*i.e.,* the testimony for and against which is to be impartially weighed) and the interpretation of those acts. In this our subjectivity has ample room for speculation. The min-

gling of the objective acts with their subjective explanation
has already caused much error and misunderstanding.
Many modern Bible criticisms are strangely like this of
Mencius, which is 2300 years old. But in the department
of natural science it is not better. Hypotheses are often
put in the place of fact, *i.e.*, facts are explained by them,
until finally a large number of other facts are discovered
by which the neck of the theory is broken. Then as usual
the old song goes on from the beginning.

361. No military operations are required (p. 355).
Mencius said, " There are people who say, I can place the
battle in array well, I can lead the fight well—that is a
great sin. If the ruler of the state loves humanity, he has
no enemy throughout the realm." No enemy except the
enemies of humanity, likewise all egotists.

362. The virtue of humanity in rulers is characterised
by its effects (p. 22). " Now the king displays a government which makes humanity widely known, so that the
officials throughout the realm wish for a place at court ;
all husbandmen wish to be appointed to the royal de-
mesnes ; all merchants and traders wish to have stores in
the royal markets ; all travellers wish to journey over the
king's highway ; all throughout the empire who have to
complain of their rulers wish to complain before the king.
If these all continue thus, who can restrain them ? "
Mencius only considers in all these quotations the power
of goodness ; he leaves out the might of evil. The good
conquers not without a struggle. This is true in the
department of politics as in every other. But there is and
remains a great difference when the struggle is loved and
sought, or whether it is forced on from the other side,
because of noblest striving for the good of humanity. The
State of the political power has in this case to wage her
warfare decidedly. But it is otherwise in the department
of religion. Christ has forbidden the use of external
power for His religion ; it is only to be extended and protected by means of the power of truth and by free testimony.

The so-called religious wars have all remarkably little to
do with religion proper. Mencius naturally places himself
upon a religious standpoint with this humanity. But
thereby he mingles the religious with the political, and
demands from the state what even a greater organised
religious society (the Church) can hardly carry out. The
case is worth reflection.

363. The example of T'ang and Woo (p. 147). "A
disciple asked, ' Sung is a small state; if now it be brought
under imperial government, and Ts'e and Ts'oo hate it and
seize upon it, how then?' Mencius answered, 'T'ang
dwelt in Po with Ko as a neighbouring state. The Count
of Ko was neglectful and did not sacrifice. T'ang sent to
ask him, "Why did he not sacrifice?" The answer was,
"There is a lack of victims." T'ang supplied him with
oxen and sheep. Count Ko ate them and did not sacrifice.
T'ang once more sent to him asking, "Why is the sacrifice
still not offered?" The answer was, "There is a lack of
grain." T'ang sent the people of Po to till the fields for
him; the aged and the weak carried food to them. The
Count of Ko led out his people; if he met any one
with wine, rice, millet, or corn, he took them from him;
if he would not give them up, he was killed. There was
a lad who was killed on account of millet and meat, and
plundered.'" This is what is said in the Shoo King,
" The Count of Ko was an enemy to those with supplies."
On account of the murder of this boy he was chastised,
and every one within the four seas (the empire) said, "It
is not that he may become rich by possessing the empire,
but to revenge a common man and woman." T'ang began
the work of executing justice with Ko, and went on to
eleven others, and yet he had no enemy in the empire.
When he brought the East into order, the barbarians of
the West were discontented; when he reduced the South
to order, the savages of the North were discontented and
said, " Why does he leave us to the last?" The people
longed for him as for rain in a great drought. Those who

went to the markets did not cease, the work in the fields experienced no change. He punished the rulers and comforted the people; he was like seasonable rain. The people had great joy. The Shoo King says, " We expected our ruler—he is here; he brings no punishment" (p. 149). " There remained still some (princes) not reduced to subjection. King Woo brought the East into order, and tranquillised the scholars and women; these brought baskets full of their black and yellow silk. United to our king of Chow, good shall befall us! They betook themselves as subjects to the great city of Chow. The principal men received their principal men with presents of black and yellow silk in baskets; the common people received their common people with baskets full of rice and dishes of soup. He saved the people as from water and fire, and only seized the tyrannical. In the great declaration, Shoo King, it is said, 'My forces are displayed; if they press forward into his territory they will lay hands on the tyrant. The punishment of death shall be inflicted on him, so that T'ang will be surpassed.' They do not work now to govern in an imperial way as is affirmed; if things were carried on in an imperial way, then every one within the four seas would lift up his head, and looking forth with the wish that (this prince) might become monarch. Although T'se and T'soo are great, what would there be to fear?" Both these princes, T'ang and Woo, were rebels against their emperor; according to Mencius, they were still morally justified in the act. Through their example Mencius wishes to incite the princes of his time to imitation; he preaches simply rebellion in every passage that treats of striving after the imperial dignity or of supremacy in the realm. The type which is put forward in the above passages consists in helping the oppressed and innocent by taking them under protection against tyranny, and in interceding for the people with all one's power.

364. At times a humane prince, even at the head of a

great state, may "for a time serve a small state" (p. 31).
(Cf. Arts. 134 and 52.) The humane prince has especially
the welfare of his people in his eye, and does not sacrifice
that so far as other matters are concerned, taxation, loss,
&c. Nowadays much capital is made of the honour of
the crown or of the nation, and it is important to consider this. The lives and the welfare of the subjects
must ever be a far higher consideration. The realm
which considers these has already arrived at victory. We
must consider the difference it makes in this case whether
it be a great or small feudal prince who behaves peace-
fully. The possession of the realm is conditioned by the
peaceful policy of the great states against the small ones.
On the other hand, the possession of the smaller states
depends upon their peaceful position with regard to the
great ones. This is good teaching, but it has never long
been followed.

365. Previously excepted imperial prerogative is no
hindrance (p. 37). "The king of Ts'e asked, 'All the
people advise me to pull down the Hall of Light; shall I
pull it down or abstain from so doing?' Mencius replied,
'The Hall of Light is a hall for the emperor; if the king
wishes to carry out an imperial government it must not
be pulled down.'" This hall was a place for the assembly
of the princes, with an altar on which sacrifice was offered
to the imperial ancestors. There is a great difference
between Mencius and Confucius in thus favouring such an
idea of a vassal overriding the imperial prerogative (cf.
Anal.) The empire in the days of Mencius was in process
of dissolution.

(c.) *The Ruler as Emperor.*

366*a.* "Inspection" of the feudal princes (p. 311).
(Cf. Art. 249.) The emperor himself was the chief con-
troller. It would be a good thing if this were also the
case in European states. Too much confidence cannot be
placed in officials even here without injury to the empire.

The press, where it recognises its duty, is of use as an argus-eyed guardian of the public weal, yet in spite of this we are ever and anon surprised by unexpected jobs or dangerous neglect in one or other department. 366*b*. Yet this inspection should never become a mere pleasure excursion at the cost of the country, as it had already become on the part of the vassal princes, and also once on the part of the emperor (p. 35). "Now it is not so ; an army marches and consumes the provisions. The hungry are not fed and the toilers are not rested. With blinded eyes they (the courtiers) intrigue amongst themselves. The people give themselves up to secret wickedness. The decrees of the emperor remain disregarded (by the princes), the people are oppressed. Food and drink are, so to say, washed away." Out of the ancient tours of inspection had been already formed parties of pleasure. It appears that the Chinese nobles held four of these annually. In the spring they went downwards to the sea-coast, in summer they streamed upwards towards the mountains, in harvest-time they followed the chase, in winter enjoyed their drinking-bouts,—a life which nobles and princes in Europe also have understood without the help of the Chinese. The perversion and degeneracy here implied are best treated when we go back to the original idea of an inspection resulting in readjustment. This is equally true of State Churches and other institutions. A form is never to be put in the place of reality.

367. The sole right "to determine upon a war as a punishment" (p. 99). (Cf. Art. 348.) No feudal prince has the right to make war upon another. The army only marches when commissioned by the emperor. Had this been firmly carried out, the history of China would naturally have been very different. The stipulations of Arts. 349, 366, 367, are far-reaching enough to establish the supremacy of the emperor. But the emperor must naturally have the power to assert his rights, and must not try to escape the incidental discomforts.

368. Rites and music are only to be determined by the emperor; so Confucius teaches most explicitly in the Analects and Doctrines of the Mean. But Mencius deviates from him in this important point (Art. 173). Generally he asserts that propriety comes from the excellent, and in Art. 180 that the Government, and therefore the vassals, determine the rites and music. Thus Mencius lets slip the most important means of securing uniformity in the empire. Confucius had a keener perception of the importance of lawful forms, although he also has not pronounced thereon with sufficient clearness. Any way it is erroneous and full of danger to the unity of the state organisation when the varying ritual of different states or provinces has developed itself independently. Certain fundamental outlines must be adhered to, but every free movement need not be restrained. The state should present an organisation whose individuality contributes to the unity of the whole. Only this unity ought not to become absolutism, for such would soon find itself unable to penetrate the inactive material of the masses. Confucius here stands upon this side—Mencius on that.

369a. Even the imperial power does not do away with ties of nature, especially the relation of the son to the father (p. 345). (Cf. Art. 169.) The emperor is, and remains, a man, and should know himself to be such. This view of himself will not lessen his true dignity, but preserve in him a spirit of real humility before God and man, whilst winning for him the respect of all true manly minds amongst his subjects. It is rarely that an emperor has a father such as Koosow; but it makes a good impression upon the people when excellent relations exist between the ruler and his family.

369b. Influence of a noble emperor on the people (p. 331). Mencius said, "The subjects of a chieftain are serene and contented; those of a monarch are animated. They murmur not if he slay them; they consider it not if he advantage them. They betake themselves daily to

good, and know not who causes this. Then wherever the
superior man passes through, transformation takes places ;
where he abides, wonders happen. He influences those
above and below like heaven and earth. Is this in any
sense a small improvement ?" The great influence of a
superior ruler upon his subjects is here somewhat exaggerated. This influence, results not merely from the
possession of justice and righteousness, but is the outcome of the full individuality in action. Teachers use
analogies which often exert great influence although they
neither possess depth of affinity nor striking superficial
resemblance. The results depend not only upon the
natural disposition, although that greatly assists towards
them, but are to be arrived at in a moral way. This
should be the special endeavour of every worker, according
to his department of labour, for the highest ideal can very
seldom be attained to.

(d.) The Results of Evil Government.

370. The state is weakened (p. 169). (Cf. Art. 327.)
The passage defines what is called bad government, viz.,
when the aim of government is not the welfare of the
people, morally and materially, as was the aim of the
ideal emperors, Yaou and Shun. It is frequently asserted
that the state must be weakened by selfish government.
(Cf. Arts. 342, 352, &c.)

371. The person of the ruler is endangered (Art. 327).
The people will then look upon their ruler as their greatest
enemy, and will seek to protect themselves from him,
leaving him in his difficulties and assisting in his overthrow.

372. Rebellion by relatives (p. 85). " He who follows
the right track (Tao) has much help ; he who loses it has
little. If it comes to extremes, with the least help his
relatives will rebel : if it comes to the extreme, with much
help all the realm betakes itself to him." The last explanation is by far the best. Many foolish actions of the

ruler and some scandal or other cause the falling away
of subjects, and even one's nearest surroundings; when
the mad whirl reaches its climax, there remains but
rebellion, in which all, even blood relatives, take part.
The history of the Roman Cæsars offers many examples.
It is worthy of note that Mencius never speaks of a
revolution of the people. The people never revolt in the
form of a popular uprising, but let themselves be guided
by revolutionary leaders, yielding themselves to those
by whom they believe their painfully felt hardships will
be mitigated. Mencius only recognises the established
princely houses as such leaders of the people; in this he
differs essentially from modern teachers of revolution.

373. Deposition of the sovereign (cf. Arts. 57 and
424, 425, p. 40). "Mencius said to the king of Ts'e, ' When
a court official intrusts wife and children to a friend and
travels to Ts'oo, but on his return finds wife and children
suffering from cold and hunger, what should he do with
him?' The king answered, 'Cast him off.' He said,
'What is to be done with the chief-justice who cannot
control his subordinates?' The king said, 'Dismiss him.'
Mencius said, 'What is to be done when within the four
boundaries no order prevails?' The king looked to the
right and left and spoke of other things." The analogies
are striking: no wonder that the king looked strangely.
But this doctrine of Mencius opens out some weighty
considerations. It may find application among feudal
princes, but who is to depose an emperor or other sovereign
prince? The answer would naturally be, the people.
That is unthinkable. The United States is a case in
point. There the President is chosen by the people, but
he can only be deposed by the sentence of the courts, not
by the people who chose him. For this are needed also
the requisite legal forms to bring about the impeachment
of the ruler, to procure a legal decision, and beyond this
the power necessary to the carrying of it out. Where
these conditions are lacking, to proclaim such a doctrine

is to teach sedition, and is not only morally wrong, but criminal also. Mencius is in these candid remarks very different from his master, Confucius, who never permitted himself to use such language. It is singular that the Socialism of that day did not propound anything on this subject. According to Mencius, there was no possibility of interfering with the emperor, but yet he might be overthrown by Heaven.

374. The murder of tyrants (cf. Art. 327, p. 43). "The king of Ts'e asked, 'Is it true that T'ang has banished Kee, and King Woo slain Chow?' Mencius answered, 'It is so stated in the records.' He said, 'Dare a minister put his sovereign to death? He who outrages humanity is called a robber; he who outrages righteousness is called a villain; a man who is a villain and a robber is called a subject (a common man). I have heard of the execution of a subject called Chow, but never of the murder of a sovereign." (Cf. p. 169, and Analects.) The commentator remarks here, "A king or duke lowers himself by evil deeds to the status of a subject." Mencius apparently regards the murder of a tyrant equally with the deposition of a sovereign as permissible. Any way he never speaks against them, although the history of his time offered ample opportunity. Amongst Christians, any way, he has the Jesuit Mariana on his side. Evangelical Christians, however, must reject all such doctrines with horror. The power of life and death ought not, even in the case of ordinary people, to be left to the will of any private person, much less in the case of princes, whose affairs are far more difficult of reformation. That tyrannical princes lower themselves to the level of their meanest subjects is a subterfuge which makes no difference to the principle here laid down. Even the worst of villains ought not to be slain by every one. That would be punishable murder. This Mencius himself teaches (Art. 348). Well-ordered trials and sentences in accordance with established law are alone permissible, both rightly and morally. If a

prince rages with bloodthirsty ferocity, many legal means are at the disposal of able ministers of state to restrain him within ever-narrowing bounds, and even at last within four empty walls. The murder of princes, as a horrible means of seeking advantage for the sovereign, is altogether bad. A tyrant can only rage as he finds corresponding scope and helpers for his crimes. If such be forthcoming in a State to any extent, then tyranny is nothing else but the punishment of God for long-standing moral corruption. The best means for helping to obviate such a state of things is universal moral reformation, repentance, and renovation.

Sect. IV.—Ministers.

1. Their Prerequisites, Duties, and Failures.

(a.) *Preparation.*

375. The preparation of a good minister takes place in adversity (p. 333). (Cf. Art. 49.) Mencius said, "Men in possession of ability, wisdom, counsel, and intelligence are generally formed by trouble. The deserted official and the illegitimate son strengthen their hearts circumspectly and reflect upon the difficulties they meet; thus they succeed." The struggle with difficulties is a better school for the formation of character than the ordinary high school where everything goes in its appointed groove. The mental as well as the physical powers require exercise to enable them to work out great problems. According to Art. 49, Heaven calls out its exceptional witnesses and labourers.

376. Continual self-improvement (p. 334). Mencius said, "There are servants of the prince who serve their ruler out of desire of doing eye-service. There are ministers who are peacemakers for the spirits of the land; they find their pleasure in procuring peace for the spirits of the land. These are subjects of Heaven; they grasp that which ought to be in the empire, and endeavour to carry that

o

out. These are great men ; they aim at self-improvement, and things then become reformed." Concerning great men see Arts. 200–204. The importance of these is here expressed as forming statesmen of decided character and beneficial influence upon the ruler and his realm.

377. Virtue is to them the highest honour (p. 89). " There are three things recognised as of worth throughout the empire—age, rank, and virtue. For helping on our times and directing the people, nothing transcends virtue." This is equally true of the ruler and of the state officials. It is singular that only ethical requirements and not intellectual are insisted upon by Mencius. These last are not excluded, but are presupposed ; still they are not esteemed the chief thing. There is great danger nowadays in the predominance given to what is intellectual. This is increasingly the case in all offices ; the intellectual is made the great characteristic of management. Especially is this to be noted as a great evil in the ecclesiastical department, where the religious element, which ought to be the chief standard, is entirely lost in the intellectual. Reform is clearly needed here. If one wishes really to help the Church, it is most important to distinguish rightly the worldly from the religious element. True religion can never become dangerous to the state, but a worldly Church may, whose ministers seek their highest honour, not in religious virtue as servants of Christ, but in the pomp, and dignity, and lordly authority of the Episcopate or other corresponding position.

378. Their character to appear both host and guest.

379. He only who makes himself ridiculous will be ridiculed.

380. Under certain circumstances he may receive alms.

(b.) Ministers Seeking Office.

381. Before being called, " a personal meeting " with the prince " is to be avoided " (pp. 152 and 137). Can-

didates should not press their services upon the prince or
try to ingratiate themselves with him, but wait to see if
he will freely recognise their worth. Only thus can a fair
field be secured for their influence.

382. The sovereign must first make search (p. 264).
" 'Why,' asked Mencius of an unemployed scholar, ' does
the sovereign make a visit ? ' He answered, ' On account
of (the scholar's) extensive information, or on account of
his great ability.' Mencius replied, ' If it is on account
of his extensive information, the emperor would never
call a teacher to himself ; how much less would a prince !
If it is on account of his great ability, I have never heard
that one wishing to see such a one, *calls* him to come ' "
(but *goes* to him first). It seems to us an extraordinary
idea that a prince should pay the first visit to a subject,
even if he be a man of great ability. But we must consider that the relations of those times were more simple,
and that even those princes very rarely corresponded to
the ideal of such teachers as Mencius.

383. " Righteousness is the way, propriety is the door
to the prince's presence " (p. 267). (Cf. Art. 336.) The
scholar does not cast himself away by these, but acquires
reputation. Only he must not think the time long before
this arrives. Candidates for office need more patience
than other people.

384. Light-mindedness is to be avoided in accepting
office.

385. Likewise over-scrupulousness.

386. Time and circumstances must be considered. The
first of these destroys either the official or his work; the
second lets slip favourable circumstances which offer an
opportunity of making use of one's acquirements. Both
time and circumstances need to be well considered.
Therefore the mind must be alive to what the necessity
of the case requires, neither abandoning principles nor
carrying these to absurd extremes. This calls for wisdom
from above.

387. An office is often necessary to preserve the means for the appointed sacrifices (p. 142). "Some one asked, 'Did the superior men of ancient times take office?' Mencius answered, 'They did take office.' Tradition says, Confucius, when he was three months without either office or sovereign, was quite put out. If he went over the boundary, he was sure to have the proper present packed up. Kung Ming E said, 'If the men of old were three months without a sovereign, people condoled with them. Was not this condolence after three months without a ruler precipitate?' Mencius said, 'The loss of office to a scholar is just what the loss of a state is to a prince. It says in the Book of Rites (Li Ke), The prince has tilled his field in order to obtain grain for the sacrificial vessels. His wife breeds silk-worms in order to make the garments. If the victims be not perfect, the grain, the vessels not pure, the garments not complete, he dare not sacrifice. But the scholar also does not sacrifice when he has no field. If the victims, the grain vessels, the garments, be not perfect, he dare not hold festival; is not that a sufficient cause for condolence? Why did Confucius pack up a present whenever he crossed the boundaries? Office is to the scholar what the plough is to the farmer. Does the farmer leave his plough behind when he removes over the boundaries? The ancients had no desire to avoid office, yet they hated what was irregular. To go to the prince in an irregular way is of a piece with breaking through walls'" (burglary). It is a good point in Confucianism that it makes binding upon scholars the duty of not withdrawing themselves from the public service, but of seeking in that their highest destiny. Taouists and Buddhists, on the other hand, naturally draw back selfishly. All monasticism has its root in selfishness, whether refined or gross. The followers of Confucius and Mencius, with but few exceptions, have gone over to its opposite form, the chase after power and splendour. But the blame of this must not be laid to the

account of Mencius, as is plain from his teaching in the passage above. We see also here the importance of sacrifice.

(c.) *The Minister Entering upon Office.*

388. Unfitness leads to destruction (p. 368). " One took office in Ts'e. Mencius said, ' That is death to him.' When he was put to death the disciples asked, ' How did you know, sire, that he would be put to death ? ' He replied, ' He was a man of some little talent, but he had never followed the mystery (Tao) of the superior man, so that he was simply fated to bring death upon himself.' " Through overweening vanity many a one has come to ruin. He who will not be advised cannot be helped. To pass a good examination is by no means a guarantee of practical ability.

389. Love of good is a sufficient guarantee (p. 319). " The state of Loo desired to confer its government upon Yo Ching Sze. Mencius said, ' When I heard it, I was so glad that I could not sleep.' A disciple asked, ' Is Yo a man of determination ? ' ' No ! ' ' Is he a man of judgment ? ' ' No ! ' ' Has he extensive information ? ' ' No ! ' ' Wherefore, then, was there this sleepless joy ? ' He answered, ' He is a man who loves what is good.' ' Is, then, the love of good all-sufficient ? ' ' Love of goodness is more than enough for the whole empire; how much more for the state of Loo ! For when there is love of goodness there, every one will come from within the four seas, treating a thousand li as nothing, to share with him their goodness. But if he does not love what is good, the people will say, " Yes, yes ! I know that already." The sound and look of that " Yes, yes ! " will drive people more than a thousand li away. If the scholars remain at a distance, more than a thousand li away, then slanderers, flatterers, and eye-servers will gather round. When one dwells amongst such, although he may wish to govern the state well, can he

attain to this?'" Of course, it is not asserted that love of goodness without any other preparation is sufficient for the carrying out the highest ends of government. The discussion was with one who had been a disciple of Mencius. But what Mencius desires to impress upon us is true, viz., that moral unfitness and a mind given to immorality and frivolity, even when combined with the most brilliant endowments and practical ability, never does aught but injury to the public service. A nobler, truer, purer, and therefore more lovely character will adorn any position, even if there remain many technical qualifications to be desired.

390. Three kinds of circumstances which formerly hindered men from taking office (p. 321). "Some one asked, 'Under what circumstances did the superior men of old take office?' Mencius answered, 'They accepted it in three cases, and declined it in three. If they were received with every mark of respect, and experienced appropriate treatment, and their discourse had some result, they accepted it. If their work had no effect, they departed, notwithstanding that there was no diminution of the respect offered to them. The second case was when, although their proposals had no immediate result, yet they themselves were received with the highest marks of respect and appropriate treatment; then they took office; but were this behaviour diminished, they departed. The third (and least important), if one morning there were nothing to eat, and at evening nothing to eat, so that for hunger he could not leave his door; and the ruler on hearing of this said, "I cannot carry out his method at large nor follow his counsels, but I am ashamed to let him die of hunger in my territories;" then he may indeed receive the alms (offered), yet only sufficiently to avoid death.'" This naturally only finds fulfilment amongst the candidates for the higher offices in the state, when these are men of character and fame. But in real life other factors come into operation—as family, friendship,

&c., which exert great influence upon the taking or declining of office.

391. The example of Confucius (p. 258). "Confucius
took office upon trial. When the trial was sufficiently
long for the carrying out (of his ideas), and that carrying
out ceased, he went away; therefore it was that he never
stayed anywhere three full years. Confucius took office
where he saw that their practice was possible, a position
where his reception made it possible, a position where he
received official support." Confucius held it to be his
duty to use that in which he was superior to other men to
serve them with. He knew well that he could only raise
another to his own ideal when he himself was living up
to it. In this consisted his greatness. But it is plain,
from the testimony of contemporaries, that his failure
arose not simply from defects in his moral principles, but
also from their exaggerated form. Ancient forms should
preserve the spirit of antiquity or be reformed. That is
the defect of all dead conservatism.

392. Places for poor aspirants (p. 259). Mencius said,
"One does not seek office on account of poverty, but yet
at times it is so. A wife is not taken for the sake of her
attention, yet at times it is so. He who takes office on
account of poverty, denies himself honour and remains in
an inferior position, denies himself wealth and remains
poor : what is suitable for such a one ? To become a
doorkeeper and strike the watchman's staff. Confucius
was once keeper of the stores ; then said he, ' My accounts
must balance; there is nothing more.' Once he was manager
of the public fields ; he said, ' Now to have oxen and sheep
fat, strong, and of good size—that is all.' To speak of
high things when in a low position is a crime. To hold a
place in the administration when one's principles (Tao)
are not carried out is a disgrace." This extract is the
necessary complement to Art. 390. This extension is
worthy of consideration. There only death from hunger
was to be avoided, whilst here a continual office may be

entered on, in which one's highest duty is to hold one's tongue. The attention is to be directed exclusively to the nearest duties, and the state may go its way. Sheep and oxen can also be fattened under a tyrant. According to the proper result of the Confucian system, every participation in the rule of a tyrant, even in his domestic economy, must be avoided. According to the ancient Chinese ideal, these poor aspirants might engage in business or agriculture, and wait a favourable opportunity. Naturally it is not so in a constitutional state, where the law is above the will of the ruler. There one's duty is to carry out firmly the law, even under the worst of sovereigns. Still in such lands there will be found often enough judges and counsellors bending to every breath of wind from the throne.

393. "The gift of introduction" is necessary (p. 143). (Cf. Art. 387.) This has now become a regular purchase of office, an evil which poisons the whole current of Chinese public life.

2. DUTIES IN OFFICE.

(a.) General Duties.

394. Due honour to the sovereign (p. 168). "To urge to difficult deeds is called, in reference to the sovereign, respect; to develop the good and to repress his evil is paying due honour to him. To say, 'My sovereign is incompetent,' is to defraud him." This is an important ethical position, to find the true way of honouring the sovereign in seeking by all loyal means his moral progress. How very different would have been the course of universal history had earth's many sovereigns only had such advisers around them! It does not seem that parliamentary freedom has done much to help towards this. In place of a despotic sovereign, we have the more dangerous tyranny of parties, in face of which the above passage is but empty words. (Cf. Arts. 291 and 407.)

395. A minister of decided character "does not permit himself to be sent for like a servant" (p. 90). (Cf. Arts. 320, 188.) To do so would be to yield much of the dignity of his office, which gives him a relative independence, and enables him to exercise over his sovereign more or less of influence, sometimes even of restraint.

396. Speedy compliance with commands conformable to rule (p. 89). "The Book of Rites says, 'If the father calls, do not delay (but straightway obey); when the sovereign's command calls, do not wait for the carriage.'" In both cases strict subordination is due. This is most important in all kinds of service, if the failure of the leader's plans is to be effectually prevented. In China the power of the father is more absolute than that of the Emperor.

397. What has been learned is to be practised in office (p. 43). (Cf. Arts. 99, 80, 392.) "Mencius had an interview with the King of Ts'e, and said, 'If a saloon is about to be built, you surely let the inspector of works seek great timbers. When he has found these great trees, the king rejoices, in that it corresponds to his purpose. If the carpenter hews them so that they are too small, the king will be angry, in that it fails to correspond to his purpose. Now a man desires in his full age to carry out what he has learned in youth. If the king say, "Let go what you have learned and follow me," how shall he behave then? Had we here a rough gem, although worth twenty-four ounces of gold, you would surely confide it to a lapidary to cut and polish it; but in reference to the government of the state you still say, "Only let go what you have learned and follow me." Why do you make such a difference from your conduct in giving the lapidary your gem to cut and polish?'" Mencius is not here consistent in his teaching. Any one who is about to build a house will previously come to an understanding with the builder about its plan; likewise with the lapidary about the form of his gem; it is only the carrying out of the work that is left to their hands. It should be thus also in the govern-

ment. The sovereign and minister must be of one mind
about the general plan of government, or at least have
come to some understanding about it, even when the
minister is the ruler and the sovereign a mere puppet.
This being granted, then the minister should be afforded
the utmost freedom in carrying out the plan.

398 to 405. The particulars of these Arts. will be found
in the first and second Books of Mencius. In these are
delineated the politics of small states. Mencius advocates,
in opposition to these as exemplified by Kwan Chung, a
policy for the whole realm. Kwan Chung was the most
able minister of the period embraced in the " Spring and
Autumn Annals " of Confucius ; he raised the state of Ts'e
to the highest position amongst the other vassal states,
but did not secure for it imperial power over them. This
appeared to Mencius as a political fault. Confucius took
another view, and several times praised him highly. There
was a difference in the time of these two politicians.
Confucius desired to strengthen the Chow dynasty, but
Mencius had already given it up : he wished to bring
forward some other able dynasty into the imperial position, and purposed to reserve for himself the position of
independent prime minister. In the carrying out of this
plan, however, he had no more success than Confucius.

(b.) *Duty in Word.*

406. The superior minister "will not speak of profit,"
which works destructively. (Cf. Arts. 162 and 342.) By
profit men are not improved, but mostly morally ruined,
because their selfishness is ever increased as their eye is
sharpened to perceive opportunities of profit.

407. The happiness of all consists in humanity and
righteousness, which should therefore have great stress
laid upon them (p. 88). "No man of Ts'e speaks to the
king about humanity and righteousness ; is it that they
do not regard humanity and righteousness as excellent ?

In their hearts they say, 'How can it be done, to speak
with him about humanity and righteousness?' That is
a lack of respect which is unequalled." (Cf. Art. 394.)
We must not too quickly give up a man as lost to good.
Self-conceit and a love of our own ease, if not also a con-
temptuous estimate of others, lead us to do this. He
who possesses in himself anything better than another has
thereby a mission in the world. (Cf. Arts. 409 and 391.)

408. The rectification of the sovereign is to be sought.
(Cf. Arts. 202, 230.)

409. Ministers must be silent where prudence dictates
(p. 243). "A minister knew beforehand that his sovereign
would not be advised by him; therefore he was silent
and took his departure." (Cf. Art. 133.) Everything has
its limits, even exhortation. If frequent speech bears no
fruit, then absolute silence becomes a duty. If another
will not let us save him, it is permissible to look to our
own safety. But even this only when the welfare of the
country imposes no other considerations.

(c.) *Duty in Deed.*

410. The virtuous minister is not to be blinded by external splendour (p. 372). Mencius said, "He who advises
great people estimates them lightly and considers not their
pompous manners. Halls several storeys high, with the
beams of the roof projecting several feet, would not be so
built if I had my way. Food spread before me over (a
table) ten cubits square, with some hundreds of waitresses,
would not be so ordered if I had my way. Great festi-
vities, drinking parties, state hunts, with a train of a
thousand carriages, would not be arranged if I had my
way. With all that, they (the princes), like myself, have
no sympathy; all that I care for is the discipline of the
ancients. Why should I fear them?" One commentary
says here, "These three retrospective statements are the expression of scorn." Another says, "Mencius here measures

other people by his own height; we do not find such
vehemence in Confucius." A third remarks, "Mencius
arrived at this because as a holy man he could not transform the people through his virtue." We see from this
that the Chinese know how to get rid of that which they
do not like. There is no doubt, however, that Mencius
was somewhat embittered owing to his deep researches
into antiquity. His words in the text seem a little sharp,
but his meaning is good. Contempt for external pomp
and splendour can well exist side by side with proper
reverence for the position of the prince.

411. Stands boldly in opposition to the ruler.

412. Will not anticipate the sinful desires of the princes
(p. 314). "The sin of him who furthers the wickedness
of the sovereign is small; the sin of him who anticipates
the wickedness of the sovereign, and goes to meet it, is
great. The officers of our day anticipate all the evil of
the sovereign, therefore it is that the modern officials sin
against the princes." The commentary says, "The difference consists in this, that in the first the sovereign con-
ceives the idea and the minister carries it out; in the latter
the sovereign has not yet laid hold of the idea, and the
minister leads him on to it, prepares him for it, i.e., anticipates his evil." The minister is thus the author of the
evil, and not merely an involuntary helper. To degrade
oneself to this last is abhorrent, but it is simply criminal
to excite one to evil, and lead them on in its practice,
when the duty of the minister is to work out with all his
energy the morally good.

413. Is faithful in the smallest demands of duty. (See
quotation in Art. 392.) He who enters upon an office
should fulfil its requirements with all fidelity. In this
Confucius was a good example. The endeavour after what
is higher is not excluded, but must never be pursued at
the cost of duties close at hand.

414. Does not seek power and territory to further the
private aims of the sovereign (p. 316). " Mencius said,

'He who now serves his sovereign says, "I may for my prince extend his territories and fill his treasuries;" such is now called a good minister, but of old would have been called a robber of the people. If a sovereign is not established in the right way (Tao), nor his will (aim) in humanity, the endeavour to enrich him is nothing but to enrich a Kee (a tyrant). "I may for my sovereign conclude agreements with other states, so that the battle must be won by us;" such is now called a good minister, who would of old have been called a robber of the people. If a sovereign be not established in the truth (Tao), if humanity be not his aim, then the endeavour to make him successful in war is nought but to further a (tyrant) Kee. Although one following the course of the present day without altering its customs should have the empire given him, he could not retain it for a single morning.'" Unfortunately the policy condemned by Mencius has to this present day received greater consideration than the opposite, which he commends. Financial administration, and that characteristic of modern states, military power, claim a higher place than morals and religion even in so-called Christian countries. Theoretically the ideal aim is recognised, but practically it falls into the background, whilst material interests and increase of power are nowadays the great objects of government.

3. FAILURE.

(a.) Causes of Failure.

418. Only occasional visits to the ruler, and these neglected by him (p. 285). "It is not to be wondered at that the king of Ts'e is so unwise. If a thing is the easiest to grow of all in the world, if you set it one day in the heat and then ten days in the cold, it cannot grow. I very seldom have an audience; as soon as my back is turned there come the cold elements; had I even called forth some shoots, what could happen to them?" This

conflict with opposing elements, this counter-working
which all true work meets with, which is even called forth
by it, or at least quickened by it, can only be estimated
by the skilful labourer. All theories—and not only those
in the department of politics—must undergo many modifi-
cations in their carrying out in practical life—many ship-
wrecks ere the high sea is crossed.

419. Ministers not working in harmony (p. 181).
" Were all the ministers of the king virtuous men, with
whom could he do evil? Were they the reverse, with
whom could the king do good? What can one single
excellent minister do for the king?" This extract unites
into one many former sayings. The solitary man, even if
one of the most excellent, is but a little fragment, an
atom in the universe. But yet it would be wrong for
him to allow himself to be discouraged by the mere consideration of the uselessness of such working. Spirit
works upon spirit in an intensive and incalculable way—
electro-chemically, we may say. But without firm conviction, without faith, nothing is of any use.

(b.) Failure Leads to Resignation.

420. On the overthrow of justice by the sovereign.
Mencius says (p. 196), " When innocent scholars are put
to death, the officials may take their departure; if the
people, being innocent, are slaughtered, the scholars may
well remove themselves thence." In political life it is
very important to consider the signs of the times. It
soon comes to the endangering of one's life by continuing
in office without being able thereby to advantage the
state.

421. When stern counsels find no listener (p. 94).
" Mencius said to Ch'e Wa, ' You, sire, resigned a governor-
ship and requested the office of criminal judge, which
appeared as if you sought it as affording an opportunity
of speaking your mind. Now many months have already

elapsed; could you find nothing to speak about?' Ch'e
Wa then remonstrated with the king but without any
result, so he resigned his office and took his departure.
The people of Ts'e said the motive of Ch'e Wa was good,
but that of Mencius himself was not to be discerned.
Some one told Mencius of this. He said, ' I have heard
that he who is in office gives it up when he cannot fulfil
his duty; he who urges the ruler with words departs
when he attains to no result. I myself have no office; I
have no word to speak necessarily; may I not, therefore,
act voluntarily and without constraint in my intercourse
with others?'" High officials, especially ministers of
. state, have no option but either to follow the sovereign or
to take their departure if the ruler will not determine
upon receiving their advice. (Cf. Arts. 390, 424.)

422. When he proves it an impossibility to help the
people (p. 93). "Mencius came to P'ing-luh and said to
the governor, ' Would you, sir, execute one of your spear-
men who three times on one day should lose his place in
the ranks?' ' He answered, ' I would not wait for three
times.' ' Yet you, sir, have several times lost your place in
the ranks. In bad times and famine years the old and
enfeebled amongst your subjects were driven to the
ditches and canals; the able-bodied who were scattered to
the four corners of the earth amounted to some thousands.'
He replied, ' That is not what Kew Sin (his own name)
had to care for.' Mencius replied, ' If now some one
receives from other people oxen and sheep to feed the
same for them, he must seek pasture and grass for them;
if he thereon sought and found not, would he not give
them back to their owners, or would he stand by and see
them die?' Kew Sin replied, ' That is my fault.' On
another day Mencius had an audience with the king and
said, ' Your humble servant knows five of your majesty's
governors, but the only one of them who perceives his
faults is Kung Kew Sin.' After he had related the above
to the king, the king said, ' This is, then, the fault of me,

unworthy.'" It is singular to find it always insisted upon
that sovereigns are answerable for the well-being as well
as for the good behaviour of their subjects. Unhappily
this is far too frequently forgotten both by higher as well
as lower officials; great social injury is the result, and
thus are excited political ferment and discontent. Where
there is existing distress to be removed, each one readily
appeals to lack of instruction, or powerlessness, or to some
one who formerly must have preceded, &c. Such subter-
fuges manifest a deficiency in personal sympathy, and an
ignorance of that divine charity which desires to help all.
It is striking yet pleasing to find that Mencius always
treats the relation between the ruler and the governed as
pastoral. In this we have a very fruitful idea. He who
cannot grasp such an idea is not fitted for bearing rule.
Many modern sovereigns and ministers comport themselves as if the people only existed on their account. It
is a proof of a deep sense of the moral duty one owes to
the people when a great minister gives up his office simply
and solely because he cannot advantage the people.

423. On being treated in an unbecoming manner by
the sovereign, unless this be merely passing neglect (p.
310). "When Confucius was chief-justice in Loo he
remained unused; then followed the sacrifice; as no roast
flesh came to him, he went away without taking off his
cap of ceremony. The ignorant think that he did this on
account of wishing for the flesh; the thoughtful conceive
him to have done it because propriety was lacking. But
Confucius preferred to go away on account of a small
offence rather than seem malicious. The masses cannot
properly understand what the superior man does." The
first reason, that he was unused, that the sovereign did
not care for his counsels, was his real motive, but it offered
nothing to lay hold of. This he met with in the assembly
for sacrifice. It was but a slight offence, but it was characteristic, and afforded the wished-for opportunity. The
crowd only saw the cause nearest them without recog-

nising a deeper reason. It is important for the historian
to consider these. The difference in the judgment passed
upon the conduct of great men consists mostly in the
shallowness or profundity with which their motives are
grasped. By these conceptions the historian or biographer
really characterises himself.

(c.) *Failure Resulting in the Dethronement of a Sovereign.*

424. Only a minister who is a relative dare do this (p.
268). "The king of Ts'e asked concerning chief ministers
of state. Mencius said, ' Concerning which chief ministers
does your majesty ask ? ' The king said, ' Are there different kinds of chief ministers ? ' 'There are several chief
ministers of noble relationship and others of a different
surname (to the king).' The king said, ' Permit me to
ask about those of noble relationship.' He answered, ' If
the sovereign has great faults, they ought to make remon-
strances; if this is repeated without receiving any attention, they may change (the occupant of) the throne.' The
king was moved and changed countenance. Mencius said,
' Let it not make the king angry. The king asked his
humble servant, and I dared not say aught but the truth
in reply.' The king's countenance became composed. He
then asked about the other chief ministers of another
surname. He replied, ' If the sovereign has faults, they
remonstrate with him; if this is repeated without receiving
any attention, they will depart (resign).' " The idea so
plainly defined here is good, and it is a proper limitation
of the doctrine of revolution. (Cf. Art. 370.) The relatives
of the sovereign must naturally feel every way concerned
in preserving the future of the dynasty. Unhappily, such
palace revolutions have generally ended with murder.
They are only justifiable when grounded not merely upon
political considerations, but upon actual enormities committed by the reigning sovereign. It is also requisite
that this should not be done by illegal and immoral

P

means, and privately, but by an abdication of the crown, after which a harmless private life may be led. Thirdly, this change of sovereigns must receive general and public recognition.

425. Yet this may happen in the case of other ministers from a higher point of view (p. 343). "A disciple remarked, 'E-Yin, the prime minister, said, "I cannot endure the disobedient" (to principle, Tao), and he banished the emperor to T'ung (the graves of his ancestors). The people were much pleased. When the emperor became a worthy, he brought him back, and the people were greatly pleased. If a worthy be a minister and his sovereign be not a worthy, may he thus banish him?' Mencius said, 'Were the real aim of E-Yin followed, it may be done; without the aim of E-Yin it is usurpation.'" The history is in the Book of Documents (Shoo-King). E-Yin (see Art. 271) was an old and approved minister of state, who, properly, had founded the Yin dynasty, for he helped the father of this emperor to the imperial dignity. What his view was in banishing this young emperor he showed after three years. But the like experiment has also its dangerous side, and in the present day could hardly be carried out anywhere. There would be an abundance of suspicions, and thus of inward disturbance. The best means of counteracting the madness of a tyrant are to be found in the moral incorruptibility and firmness of the ministers, especially the highest, and the sound feeling of the people. Towards this, true religion and morality help far more than any other recipes for political improvement. On the putting to death of a sovereign, see Art. 374. The thoroughness with which Mencius treats of the relations between the sovereign and his ministers shows plainly the high importance he attached to the same. It forms, and not unreasonably, the proper centre of his teaching. In political life, everything clings closely around the sovereign and the ministers, or, according to modern notions, around the lawgiver and the administration,

which latter contains within itself both courts of justice and government. According to Mencius, the sovereign is the only lawgiver, although the conception of the laws generally proceeds from the ministers. But the lawgiver, according to Eastern custom, is never himself subordinate to the laws, but possesses in regard to them unlimited freedom. His will has no legal or justly imposed limits. In spite of this, however, the greatest despot is bound by moral principles. These it behoves rulers to keep clear and proclaim conscientiously. It is well to keep this in mind, that we may be able to judge rightly of the method of Mencius regarded in its entirety. The teaching which he gives to absolute rulers is of a deeply ethical nature, but so piercing at times that we must feel astonished at the grand freedom which then prevailed. We see this in the bold appearance of the leaders of Socialism, Communism, and Sensualism. The teaching of Mencius aims at this, that the moral law, embodied in the persons of virtuous ministers, shall oppose itself energetically to the absolute authority of dissolute rulers. The minister should not be the blind co-worker with his sovereign, but the representative of the people, the incorporation of the moral law of human existence and of general social life. We are somewhat reminded by the above of the position which the prophets of the Old Testament held with regard to the kings. At the same time we bear in mind the important difference between the moral government devised by Mencius and the theocracy of those prophets. These were never the ministers of the kings, and always preserved their freedom in regard to them. They were equally free in dealing with the people, to whom they maintained the sternest preaching of repentance. The prophets did not receive the law from without, as did Confucius from antiquity, but spake as they were moved by the Spirit of Jehovah, therefore the very Spirit of the Lawgiver: they deepened and explained the teachings of former times. The latter alone applies to Mencius.

In opposing the governors of his day, he did not consider that the ministers of a despot can never preserve the independence and freedom requisite for carrying out his teachings. Mencius himself spoke so boldly because he was out of office at the time. Yet, farther, Mencius overlooked the importance of renewing from beneath. The evil ways and requirements of the people were never illuminated by him in the sense and spirit of the prophets. He held that all reformation of social life should proceed from the Government. Of how little use that is without the conversion of the people generally we may learn from the history of the Jewish people under Joash, Hezekiah, and Josiah. It may appear strange that the point of this discussion of Mencius is turned against the sovereign, so that even his execution is justified, whilst the death of a guilty official, although just mentioned (Art. 332), is never advised. Only his dismissal appears to be justified, and no details are given of this. The resignation of the officials, on the other hand, seems to be pretty fully discussed. This democratic feature, as we may call it, of Mencius is certainly worthy of note. Confucius would have often shaken his head at these teachings of his bold successor. The teachings of so important a moral character as Mencius apply very closely to the circumstances of his own time. Yet he surely found few amongst the officials who corresponded to his ideal : his own disciples even appear to have been of very little importance.

Book III.

THE RESULT AIMED AT IN MORAL DEVE-LOPMENT—THE ORGANISATION OF THE STATE.

CHAPTER I.

NATIONAL ECONOMY IN PRODUCTION, COMMERCE, AND TAXES.

(a.) Production.

426. RIVERS and streams to be confined in proper limits (p. 126). "Formerly, in the time of Yaou, when the empire had not been reduced to order, the great waters streamed seawards over their limits, so that a great inundation took place. Grass and vegetation grew luxuriantly, and birds and wild beasts were innumerable; the five kinds of grain were not grown, and the birds and beasts pressed upon man. The tracks of the beasts and the footprints of the birds crossed each other throughout the middle kingdom. Yaou alone was distressed on this account; he raised Shun to be co-regent. Shun, through Yih, caused fire to be applied. Yih kindled the mountains and lowlands and burnt them up (the vegetation and grass). The birds and beasts fled and hid themselves. Yih cleared the nine streams, purified the Ts'e and T'ah, and guided them to the seas. He opened the Joo and Han, and regulated the Hwae and Sze, and guided them into the Keang (the great river). After that the middle

kingdom could obtain food. During this, Yaou went three times past his own door in the eight years or more, yet did not enter it." This passage always gives one the impression that the empire of China commenced at this time. In the accounts we have of Shun there is much that is fabulous. (Cf. those collected in Art. 265, also 298.) A good chart of the water system of ancient China is much to be desired. Many questions concerning the geography of ancient times must depend for solution upon local researches. The ancient accounts can only give us hints here and there. The territories of the Yellow and Great rivers contain many treasures of scientific importance, but the researches of Western scholars are necessary to bring them to light. The confining of the waters to proper limits was the very condition of existence in many of the Chinese states. At this day it would enrich and bless many states if Governments gave more thought to the reclamation of the many pieces of waste ground within their borders. The first possibly large outlay would amply repay itself in the following generation. China in this respect is in advance of many European states. In later days it became otherwise in China, especially through the influence of the little politics of the small states. A minister said to Mencius (p. 319), " My management of the waters surpasses that of Yu." Mencius replied, " You are in error, sir. Yu's management of the waters was correspondent to the course of the waters. Yu therefore made the four seas their receptacle; you, sir, make that to be the neighbouring states. The overflow of waters is called an inundation; an inundation is a waste of water, which humane people abhor. You are in error, sir." This management of the waters was only a measure adopted for momentary relief. For a thorough cure of the evil there needed apparently the co-operation of the adjoining states. The flood which was mastered was by no means a great one. Vain service, by which one's own state has been helped at the cost of neighbouring lands, has often been rewarded with orders in our own days. We may draw important conclusions from these two citations, namely, that the Government ought to care for the regulation of the course of the rivers, the making canals, &c. It generally lies in the interest of states to increase the area of habitable land and cultivated fields. Thus is the number of inhabitants increased. Of course this is more the case in industrial communities; but industry is subject to many fluctuations, and should therefore always have a sure agricultural background.

427. "A just subdivision of the land." (For details of this see Art. 438.) In China, from old times, the system of small farms obtained. This is of advantage for the increase of the population; it offers abundant work, and spurs on the people to industry and frugality. Large farms, indeed, permit of a more advanced management, but the profits are not so large, and are often absorbed. Many large properties are much neglected. The extension of the population, especially the improvement of agriculture on small estates, must ever be cared for by the state, as was the case in ancient China.

428. The appointment of the times for agricultural operations, facilitating the cultivation of grain and hemp, ordering of nets for fishing, care of forests, cultivation of silk, breeding of domestic animals (p. 6). "If the times of husbandry be not hindered (by enforced service for the state, in the army, &c.), there will be more grain than can be consumed. If no narrow nets are permitted in the lakes and ponds, there will be fish and turtles in abundance. If the axe and bill only at the right time enter the forests and wooded hills, there will be more timber to hand than is needed. If there be grain, fish, and turtles in abundance, and more timber than is needed, the subjects can nourish the living and bury their dead without entertaining wrong feelings towards any one. The nourishing of the living and the burying of the dead without showing wrong feelings is the beginning of the

imperial way (or principle *Tao*). If possessions of five acres of land are planted with mulberry trees, then those fifty years of age may be clothed in silk. If the time for fowls, pigs, dogs, and swine be not neglected, then those of seventy years of age may eat flesh. If the time be not let slip for fields of a hundred acres, families of several persons shall not suffer from hunger. If attention be given to education and the duties of filial and fraternal affection be inculcated, the white-headed will not carry burdens in the streets. It was never yet the case that the imperial dignity was not obtained when the people of seventy years old were clothed in silk and ate flesh, and the black-haired people suffered neither from hunger nor cold." The state ought to care for everything which is beyond the power of the individual or for which he lacks the needful information. Of course this is simply, as is stated in the text, in the things of physical welfare and moral culture, not in extravagances. Even in the case of adults there remains a difficult problem to be solved by an able Government. The caring for the nourishing, housing, and clothing, as well in time of peace as in time of war, should not be neglected by the State. Every instance of neglect gives rise to social questions fraught with danger. The administration must ever remain conscious of this problem, and keep their eyes open to the welfare of the people. The chief thing is that there should be offered a way of satisfying in a proper way those requirements which will not be denied. The Government has, therefore, not only to provide for the administration of justice and for education, but also, in the first place, for the necessary conditions of human existence.

429. The Government is answerable for the welfare of the people (p. 9). "The king of Leang said, ' Your servant wishes quite humbly to receive instruction.' Mencius said, ' Is there any difference between killing a man with a stick or a sword ? ' He answered, ' It makes no

difference.' 'Does it make any difference whether it happens by means of a sword or through the form of Government?' He answered, 'It makes none.' He said, 'In the kitchen is fat meat, in the stalls fat horses, but the people have the appearance of hunger, and in the open lie those who have died of hunger; that is called cattle preferred and men consumed. Men abhor the wild beasts because they devour one another; but when he who is the father and mother of his people in the exercise of his authority does not avoid the increase of domesticated animals and the devouring of men, where is his mother and father-hood for the people? Confucius said, "He who first made images had no posterity." Because he made images of men and used them (to bury with the dead). How then will it be with him who lets his people die of hunger?'" Great luxury always goes hand in hand with great misery. The upper classes are often unmindful amidst their refined enjoyments of the thousands they are leaving to languish in misery. Laws can do little to help these, only pitiful love can afford assistance. It is often a difficult question to decide how, but so long as things have not gone to extremes, the ways and means are to be found at least of bringing such into a better position as, apart from individual guilt or vicious lives, have been brought down in the world. That is man's duty.

430. Inspection of the state of husbandry in spring and autumn. (See Arts. 349 and 366.) "The saying of the Hea is, 'If our king does not journey, how can we obtain prosperity? If our king care not, how can we obtain assistance?'" As already mentioned, the emperor himself ought personally to oversee the progress made in agriculture, and punish all neglect of the same. To let good arable land go untilled is a sin against the state. To let the whole land become desolate through anarchy is a sin against humanity, for thereby people innumerable are plunged into misery, and the neighbouring states made

to partake of the trouble. From this point of view inter-
ference is often a duty of humanity.

431. No neglect of work to be tolerated (p. 113). " The
Duke of T'ang asked concerning the 'progress of the
state.' Mencius answered, 'The work of the people must
not be neglected. In the Book of Odes it says—

> ' By day go gather the grass,
> By night quick twist the ropes ;
> Make haste and mount the roof,
> For seed-time will soon be here.'

The spirit of the people depends upon their nourishment."
(Cf. Art. 32.) Unhappily the oversight of work is now
for the most part neglected. There are many idlers in
the world, both rich and poor, specially in Asia. Europe
has a superabundance also. Hunger and also affection
urge the majority of men to energy of action, either mental
or physical; but an evil minority is at work in social life,
just as decay works in nature. State policy is to disinfect
itself of this. The state essentially requires industrious
and skilful subjects. Indolence relaxes all energy and
leads the poor to crime, the rich to sexual enjoyment ; it
brings about physical and moral weakness, and finally
political ruin. This and nothing else was the ruin of all
the earlier civilisations. The state should also, on the
ground of self-preservation, urge or constrain all capable
of labour to work. He who has no need to work for his
daily bread ought to labour for the common weal in the
widest sense. He who has no mind for this had better
be sent across the frontier into Utopia.

(b.) *Commerce.*

432. The essential condition of this is division of
labour. In this place we have the argument against the
teaching of Communism, according to which every one,
including the sovereign, must look after his own needs
(p. 123). (Cf. Art. 346.) Mencius said, " ' Will, then, the

Communist first sow his own corn and then eat of it?'
Answered, 'Yes.' 'Will he first weave his own stuff and
then clothe himself?' 'No; the Communist clothes
himself in rough stuff (Koh).' 'Does he wear a cap?'
'Yes.' 'What sort of cap?' 'A plain one.' 'One
woven by himself?' 'No; one exchanged for grain.'
'How is it he does not weave it himself?' 'That would
cause neglect to his husbandry.' 'Does he require metal
and earthenware vessels for cooking and iron for a plough?'
'Yes.' 'Does he make them himself?' 'No; he exchanges
grain for them.' 'These objects being exchanged for grain
is no wrong done to the potter and worker of metal; and for
them to exchange grain is that anything to the husbandman?' 'Why is not the Communist also a potter and a
worker in metal and all things that he requires in his house,
so as to use them? Why is he so confused as to carry on exchanges with various handicraftsmen? Why does not the
holy Communist fear so much trouble?' He answered,
'The businesses of various handicrafts could not be carried
on along with agriculture. Can, then, the governing of
the whole empire alone be carried on along with agriculture? There is work for great men, and there is work for
little men. Farther, there is available for the use of one
person what various handicraftsmen have produced. If
each should provide for himself and then use them, the
whole empire would be brought into the streets.'" Were
men able to supply their own needs in their own houses
without the help of others, all commerce would be superfluous. But man is not only mentally but also physically
destined for social life. A well-ordered state is thus
necessitated by his external relations, and it is a yet
greater necessity of his nature. For such a state one
member is united to another and all incorporated into a
harmonious organisation, actually and not theoretically.
It soon follows that even the individual state has not
sufficient in itself for its own needs, but that the whole of
humanity must enter into relations with every part. In-

ternational commerce thus increasingly develops itself.
All commerce arises from man's necessities. One seeks
to supply one's own lack from the superabundance of
others, and at the same time to dispose of his own superfluity in like manner. This is true whether of natural
products or of industrial manufactures. The part of the
Government is to provide that this exchange shall be
carried out properly. In China this was not only looked
after in the bulk, but the Government appointed also
streets for exchange, mountain-passes, markets, and such
like. (Cf. Arts. 428, 434.)

433. The motive to commerce is the worth of the product; therefore the same will not be artificially fixed
(p. 132). " If the Communistic method were followed (said
a defender of the same) there would not be two prices in
the market and no deceit in the state. Even if one sent
a half-grown boy to the market, no one would take advantage of him. Linen and silk of the same length would
correspond in price, likewise hemp and silk of the same
weight, so also the five kinds of grain in the same quantity,
and shoes of the same size. Mencius answered, 'The
inequality of products is their peculiarity (quality), whether
it be double, fourfold, tenfold, a hundredfold, a thousand-
fold. If you make them all equal, that would throw the
whole empire into confusion. Put shoes of delicate work
and common shoes at the same price, would the people
make them? If these Communistic doctrines are
followed, people will be led to deceive one another;
could one use them for governing a state or a family?' "
The quantitative value is the simple value to the con-
consumer ; this is different to the value in exchange.
Fine work requires more time, and therefore represents
greater value than common. The price must be fixed
accordingly ; but in estimating the price another factor
must also be taken into consideration besides labour and
usefulness, namely, beauty. This will depend partly upon
the influence of fashion and partly upon the taste of the

individual. The value of usefulness is also a compound element which may arise either from a momentary or permanent necessity, from one single requirement, or from several in union. Again, the price varies with the practicability of the work. Such work as can be undertaken by any one without preparation has naturally the lowest price; such, on the contrary, as can be effected by gifted hands and under special circumstances has a much higher value. We may call this the principle of rarity. The same applies also to natural products. Briefly we may say the price is determined by the material, the labourer, the usefulness, the rarity, the task, and the purse (of the buyer). The mistake of regulating the market value by a fixed scale has been committed by many Governments. Nothing but disadvantage to the public generally can result. The price can only regulate itself on a sound basis when production and exchange are free, *i.e.*, not constrained by a number of regulations. Oppressive laws interfering with industry, especially taxation, hinder the free development of commerce. Monopolies need not be entirely abolished, yet they ought to be characterised by brevity of duration, *e.g.*, the perfecting of a new invention ; afterwards they should merge in the stream of general competition. Yet the closest watching is requisite of this general competition to tax as highly as possible every absolute deception. That the greatest adulteration prevails most where there is the freest action allowed to commerce Mencius does not seem to have anticipated. Individuals cannot possibly protect themselves on all sides in the present complicated relations of trade, so much the more, therefore, could and should the Government look after this.

434. Of chief importance for commerce are markets, bridges, &c. (p. 193). The prime minister of Ch'ung carried people across the river in his own carriage. Mencius said, " That is kindness ; yet without understanding how government is to be carried on. When the foot-

bridges are prepared in the eleventh month of the year, and bridges for carriages in the twelfth month, the people will not have to wade across. If the government of the superior man be well balanced, he may have people removed from his path; how can he carry every one across the river ? If, therefore, the ruler wishes to please everybody, the time will not be sufficient." The favour of people is often both sought and obtained in an improper manner. The only care of the Government is that everything in the land be ordered in the best manner. Exceptions only hold good in special cases. There will always be room to prevent everything going on in a mechanical routine. It was improper for a prime minister to become a hackney coachman; although in a special case of urgency it would redound to his honour to use his state carriage to help on a poor subject. If the case was as Mencius relates it, one of neglect on the part of the Government, the business of the Government was to apply the great remedy that so each individual might help himself. China of old was far in advance in the building of streets and bridges, although now she has fallen behind other countries. The peculiar importance of easy and rapid transit, commercially considered, to places far removed from each other, and for the development of the empire itself, is quite unrecognised in modern China. Railways and steamboats are the natural outcome of what the Governments of antiquity undertook. Here we may express our wonder that the many thousand merchants of high civilisation, the customs officials, and officers in the Chinese service, together with all the ministers, consuls, and others, in so many years, have not been able to bring the Chinese mind to recognise the absolute necessity of these things. Whatever civilisation has hitherto obtained from China by way of concession is without exception due to the superiority of our arms ; as good as nothing has been obtained as the result of diplomacy exclusively. In relation to commerce we may remark that both the factors already mentioned, production and value, are greatly influenced by means of communication, which make the widest distribution of commodities possible. 435*a*. Luxury and extravagance are to be prevented (p. 338). " Let the consumption correspond to the season of the year, let the use be according to propriety; then the goods cannot be used up." This is one great help to the Government. Mencius supposes that the people live temperately and economically, as indeed is the case with the working classes in China up to the present time. It is general also with the Government and the nobility. Confucius never ate what was not in season, *i.e.*, which did not belong to the season of the year. That is still considered right living in China. The other advantage is economy. Of course this is only the case with some kinds of food, as vegetables, fruit, &c. If the use is seasonable, there will be neither covetousness nor prodigality. Here again we have an important hint for the political economist. As in a family to spend more than the income must result in misery, so it is in the state if the consumption is more than the production, and when the means for a supply of foreign produce are thereby limited. This is not the only reason for endeavouring to obtain a superabundance of products. The chief thing is that a certain equality in the consumption be brought about. If amongst a thousand inhabitants a hundred revel in abundance, two hundred live moderately, four hundred have barely enough, and three hundred suffer from hunger or privation, wanting those things which can support their strength and preserve their health, this is a wrong which demands rectification. Extravagance is always to be found amongst the lower classes; it shows itself periodically when wages are good. It is to be seen in the general use of stimulants, which have never been proved by physicians to be repeatedly necessary. What is the good of constant tobacco-smoking ? A constant application of a stimulus to the nerves only produces nervousness, of which there is a great deal too much. The general abuse of alcohol peoples the institutes for the imbecile and mad. Strengthening and nourishing food might well be more used in the place of these. Then again there is luxury in clothes to be considered. This, especially amongst the women of the humbler classes, ought to be highly taxed, and inconsistent dressing be publicly censured. Otherwise, this evil will go on increasing until its perpetrators get the upper hand. Then, when everything that is thought manly consists in sensual enjoyment and outward appearance, the humblest will have the same right as the noblest, and the embittering results of social democracy be fully established. Mencius had another view of what is desirable, and so have we.

435b. "In times of need the cattle should not receive that nourishing food whereby man can be sustained" (p. 5). (Cf. Arts. 345, 429.) The royal hounds and swine are mentioned here. These last were being fed with good grain, in order to make their flesh tasty for the royal table. Even now there is many a useless beast well fed whilst men are allowed to perish.

(c.) Taxes.

436. The tenth for the necessary requirements of a civilised state (p. 316). "A minister said, 'I wish to take the twentieth, how would that do?' Mencius replied, 'That is the way (Tao) of the Mih (Barbarians). In a state of 10,000 households, would it do to have only one potter?' 'No, there would not be sufficient vessels to use.' Mencius continued, 'In Mih they do not grow all the five kinds of grain, but only millet; there are no walled towns, public edifices, temples, and stated sacrifices, no presents of silk and entertainments for princes, no ministers and officials by hundreds: on this account the revenue of one twentieth is sufficient. But to live now in the middle kingdom and do away with human (duties),

relationships, to have no rulers (superiors), how would that do? With only a few potters a kingdom could not subsist, how much less without a ruler? If it be wished to make the taxes lighter than the plan (Tao) of Yáou and Shun, we shall have a greater and lesser Mih; if it be wished to make them heavier than the plan of Yaou and Shun, we shall have a greater and less Kee (tyrant).'" A civilised state has not only natural, but also artificial requirements. For the circumstances of that time the tithe was the most appropriate form of tax. In modern states it would be found most oppressive. Then the agricultural labourers, peasants, were the principal payers of taxes. The handicraftsmen had their special imposts. The whole of the *literati* were excepted, and the people who had no property or business were also exempt. Capitalists did not exist. Thus is to be explained the tithe, the almost universal form of the taxes of antiquity.

437. The tenth is better taken in the form of labour (socage) than in a direct share of goods (p. 117). "The rulers of the Hea dynasty enacted the giving of fifty acres to each family, and a tax to be levied on them; the Yin dynasty, seventy acres and socage; the Chow dynasty, one hundred acres and a share of the produce; in reality they all gave one-tenth. . . . Lung-sze said, 'For regulating the land there is no better system than socage, none worse than taxes. By the tax system it took permanently the general average of several years. In good years, when the yield of grain is immense, much may be taken without oppression; yet the amount taken is small. In bad years, when the yield is not enough to cover the manuring of the field, the full amount must still be taken. He who should be as the father and mother of his people makes them dejected, because, after a whole year's industrious toil, they cannot obtain enough to support their parents. Then they borrow to assist them, till old and young are scattered about in canals and ditches (perishing of hunger).

Q

Where is there a father or mother's feeling for the people?'
... The ode says, 'May the rain first come down upon
the public field and then upon our own.' Only where
socage is is there a public field. From this passage we
see that the Chow dynasty had socage." These Chinese
acres, or mow, were about the same in the gross, because
the unit of measurement varied. The advocacy of the
socage system under the Sung dynasty by Mencius is to
be explained by the fact that he only considered that
system from the ideal side, whilst he kept in view the
injury done by the other two systems. The chief objection
to taxation arises when the superabundance of a good year
is quickly paid away to foreigners. Fluctuation is generally
shown in the revenue from the land, which vitally affects
all business, and in the full extension of the commerce of
the world, brings about most rapidly an equality between
deficiency and supply. In that case taxation can also be
equalised, and the tax recommends itself. It is singular
that this is spoken of as the oldest form of taxation.

438. The ancient agrarian system (p. 119). "The Duke
sent his minister to consult about the system of dividing
the land into nine parts. Mencius answered, ' As your
ruler desires to carry on a benevolent Government, and
has chosen and appointed you for that purpose, you must
make this of chief importance. A benevolent Government
must commence with the boundaries. If the boundaries
are not correct, the division into nine parts will be unequal
and the revenue in grain irregular. It is on this account
that, under tyrannical rulers, corrupt ministers neglect the
boundaries. If, on the other hand, the boundaries are
correctly laid down, you may sit down and decide the
portion of the land-tax. . . . I recommend for the open
land a ninth part as socage land, but in the midst of the
state a tenth, which the residents themselves must be
induced to give up of themselves. From the chief governor downwards, each official must have his clear field.
This clear field consists of fifty acres. Males not included

in families are to have twenty-five acres. On occasion of death or of removal, there is no going out of the district. In the fields of a district those of each group of nine are friends to one another in going out and coming in; they help one another, guarding and watching, and supporting one another in sickness. The people thus live in mutual harmony. A square li makes nine squares. A group of nine covers nine hundred acres. The centre is the public field, eight families have each one hundred acres of their own. They cultivate together the public field. When the public work is finished, then they first venture to attend to their private affairs. This is the way the countrymen are distinguished from savages. This is an outline, the actual achievement of which rests with the sovereign and you, sir.'" It appears that by the socage system two and a half acres were allotted to each family for buildings and garden, although they only had to culti-vate ten acres instead of taxes. This was the tenth of the hundred. In the share system one hundred and twelve and a half acres came to each family, of which they had to give up the produce of twelve and a half, which is one-ninth. The difference consists in the two and a half acres for house and garden, which, mentioned in the commentary, here escapes memory. This, however, is only a feint to help on the somewhat lame system proposed by Mencius. According to another statement, the people held of the best fields one hundred acres; of medium, two hundred acres; of bad, three hundred. The good field lay one year fallow, the medium two years, the bad three years. The exchange of workers took place every three years, so that in three years the three kinds of fields were managed by each peasant. Of the second and third kind there were only one hundred acres cultivated, so that the remainder lay fallow, and the piece cultivated this year lay fallow next year. Mencius clearly shows by his preference for the socage system that he had an ideal social existence in his mind. He would, as is shown in the text, bind together the families in closer bonds, that each should not exist for itself, but cultivate a spirit of union. It might have been foreseen that such constraint would cause dissensions. In public works in general there is unhappily a tendency to magnify one's own power as much as possible. Only under very primitive circumstances is the socage system practicable, or upon special occasions when the spirit of common action is strongly aroused, and a unique demand arises for speedy assistance. But it cannot long continue, still less assume a permanent form. If the corresponding means of exchange are ready, and there be no lack of workers, it is better for every Government to receive for the labour its value in products of other labour or an equivalent in gold, than to provide for its own requirements free labour. Thus both parties are served. Mencius having chosen the worst out of three previous systems is a sign that he was not a great economist, and was also a novice in social politics.

439. The doubling of taxes, "taking one-fifth" instead of one-tenth, is strongly condemned (p. 181). (Cf. Art. 487.) Of three kinds of taxes, only one at a time is permissible (p. 367). " There are taxes of linen and silks, a tax on grain, a tax on labour. The superior man uses one of these and leaves the other two ; if he demand two of them, the people will suffer from want; if he exacts the three, then father and son are separated (*i.e.*, families cannot exist)." Mencius is always considering how the people may be protected from the exactions of extravagant despots. These three kinds of taxes were all paid by the same people, the peasants. But the taxing of only one article would certainly prejudice its production, if others found sufficient demand, especially in the neighbouring states. An equable partition of tenths, or a tax in lieu thereof, would have answered far better, or even Mencius's pet plan of socage.

440. Market taxes, &c. (p. 75). "Mencius said, 'Is there a ground-rent to be paid in the market without a

tax on goods, or inspection without any rent ? all the merchants in the empire will be delighted, and desire to have a store in the market. If at the passes there is an inspection of persons without taxes, all travellers will be pleased and wish to pass over those roads. If the husbandmen give socage service but no taxes, then all the peasants of the empire will rejoice and desire to plough in those fields. If there be only ground-rent, but not poll or house tax, then all the people of the empire will rejoice and wish to be his subjects.'" The Commentary in the Chow-li remarks, "that in markets and towns rooms were taxed according to size. Taxes on dwellings were first introduced in a time of national decay. Many princes exacted socage from the public field and a tithe from the private fields also. Houses without a plantation of mulberry-trees in the garden had to pay the tax on dwellings, and people without occupation the poll-tax." Mencius was disinclined to complicated systems of taxes, but in doing away with the misuse he rejected much that was good. The tithe was unjust as soon as it had to be taken from one's personal requirements. Mencius supposes that every one has first provided for his necessity. This may be in the simple relations of a thinly peopled state, but not in modern times, when foreign commercial relations are important factors in questions of taxation.

441. Customs duties to be abolished (p. 357). " Of old there were frontier posts to guard against violence ; now they have frontier posts to exercise violence." Every one is agreed that frontier duties, not to speak of inland taxes between one district and another, as is now the custom in China, are an inconvenience to travellers and a great hindrance to commerce. Unhappily neither the wisdom of China nor of the West has been able to devise means for abolishing them ; that is to say, nothing has been found to take their place. It is also necessary that the abolition of these be simultaneous and universal. The state which precedes others in this path will suffer serious

financial injury, of which foreigners reap the advantage. Antiquity is no argument in such things for our days, seeing that the principle could not be unconditionally applied in the time of Mencius. (Cf. Arts. 166, 437, 440.)

442. Marshes and ponds ought to be kept common (p. 38). "The management of affairs by King Wan in K'e was of old thus: the peasants gave a ninth as a tax, the officials had hereditary revenues, at the markets and passes there was inspection without duties, the use of marshes and weirs was unrestricted, criminals were not punished in their wives and children." The weirs served to form ponds for preserving fish. We may conclude that in the time of Mencius the princes knew how to keep the fishing for themselves. In China of to-day it is free, and is carried on with energy.

443. The leading principle is that true wealth does not consist in gold and silver (p. 368). "Mencius said, 'The prince has three kinds of most precious things—the land, the people, the business of governing. He who counts pearls and jewels as the most precious, calamity will overtake him." Whilst true in the first place of the private enrichment of princes, this is an important lesson to finance ministers in regard to national economy. The accumulation of gold will not give a country or a monarch superiority over others; but the best management of the useful products of the land, the advancement of morality and intelligence amongst the people, with enlightened and liberal government. Where these prevail, there is no danger from within or without. Mere monetary wealth soon brings trouble. A curious account is given of the origin of taxes (p. 104), in which is indicated the idea that the greed of sharp traders led to their imposition.

CHAPTER II.

NATIONAL EDUCATION : ITS THEORY, SCHOOLS, TEACHERS, METHOD, AND MUSIC.

(a.) Theory.

444. MORAL culture as well as physical is indispensable to the state (p. 127). "There is a way with men; enough to eat, warm clothing, comfortable residences, without education, makes them like beasts." This tendency unhappily shows itself in many so-called scholars, whose education has lacked the moral element. The culture of the intellect and the acquisition of information cannot supply this deficiency. Simple material prosperity cannot long continue in a state unless moral purity and truth are widespread amongst the people.

445. Education is not a suppression but a drawing out (p. 199).[1] "Mencius said, 'He who seeks to subjugate men by goodness will never succeed in subjugating them. He who educates them by goodness will bring the whole realm into subjection. If the hearts of all in the whole realm be not subjugated, the imperial power is unattainable.'" The Government must always have the power to legislate in favour of what is good, but it is to its interest very rarely to exercise this power. The more other factors work to this end, to which the people voluntarily listen, the deeper will strike the roots of the authority of Govern-

---

[1] This seems a parallel to a very common saying, "You cannot make men virtuous by Acts of Parliament." Moral suasion alone will produce real goodness. External virtue, though convenient to society, is destructive to the individual, making him a "whited sepulchre."

ment. Those other factors are the Church and its missions. Sometimes, however, these will so fail that the good, the truth itself, seems as an authority external to the people and in opposition to the individual, and fear or some lower motive is needed to force them to accept it. At the first opportunity a reaction will take place, and an endeavour be made to break the unbearable yoke. It is otherwise where timely instruction and suitable education have brought about their reception. Thus is aroused a love for and joy in the good. Persuasion is the natural, ethical, and the only religious way.

446. "Therefore the people fear good government (that is, the united will which compels to good the individual will of the subject), but it loves good instruction" (p. 331). The people will not lightly venture to oppose authority, but are easily coerced or intimidated, as are children, with whom, in addition to firm discipline, are needed not only training and teaching, but also threatening.

447. Guidance of the people by "the personal example" of their ruler (p. 330). (Cf. 193.) The personal example of those in authority and sovereigns is a most impressive teaching for the people, who follow it as children like to imitate what they see in adults. The imitation of the nobility is indeed nowadays carried to extremes. The evil is more copied than the good. It is every way better when the true and the good are the pattern, and the will of God is the only rule. But few lay hold on this.

448. The lower soon appear like the upper classes (p. 196). "Mencius said, 'If the sovereign be benevolent, then every one is benevolent; is he righteous? then every one is righteous.'" The sovereign should, therefore, be properly not only the representative of the power of the state and of the law, but also the embodiment of morality. That is his high calling, which even in our own day and circumstances is of highest importance.

449. Importance of propriety and education to the life of the state (p. 167). "The misfortune of a state is not

that its walls and fortifications are incomplete, and its arms and armour are not abundantly forthcoming; the injury of a state is not that its fields are not increased and its possessions are not accumulating. If the upper classes have no propriety and the lower no education, revolutionists will rise up, and the final catastrophe is not far off." This is directed against the oppression of the upper classes. They ought to show propriety (or consistency). If the officials of a state generally were to preserve propriety towards every one under all circumstances, that by itself would much further the education of the people. Education in China has permeated all sections of the community far more than in Europe. If we contrast the conduct, speech, and intercourse with each other of the lowest class of people in China and Europe, we shall find our assertion amply confirmed. The cause of this is that the Government of China from the earliest period has regarded the education of the people as its chief duty. It is true that the courtesy of the Chinese of to-day is very hypocritical. It lacks the genuineness of a sound morality and a pure religion. There is therefore no occasion to place the morals of the Chinese above those of Christianity, as has been done by some superficial scholars. We will only refer to the fact that the Chinese have already recognised and cultivated many important elements of good government which in other states have remained neglected, spite of better influences. We must, alas! also refer to the press, which holds so high a position in the education of the popular mind. How little of propriety reigns in this region towards those who think otherwise! Is this rude, malicious, scornful, dogmatic tone that of modern cultivation? It matters not what the party, all are similarly affected. The public weal can only be furthered when those who seek to advance it really respect others who also seek to promote it (although by other means and in other ways), and treat them with at least learned propriety.

450. The education of the people therefore characterises

the Government (p. 71). "By seeing the customs we may know the kind of Government." (Cf. Art. 180.) It sounds paradoxical, but it is true. It is the relation of the pupil to the master. From the behaviour of the former one can well estimate the ability of the latter. But the pupil can never be greater than his master.

451. An uneducated people is useless even for war (p. 315). "Mencius said, 'The people, being uninstructed, to use them for war is said to be bringing the people to destruction.'" Text and commentary here both leave us in doubt as to the kind of instruction meant. According to the examples in the Book of Documents (Shoo King), we should take it to mean instruction as to the cause and aim of war. But the general application is also admissible. It is education alone which distinguishes the soldier from a wild animal of the worst kind.

452. The result of education is prosperity (p. 337). (Cf. Arts. 142, 359, 435.) Education is the cultivator of all that is noble, and shows itself not least in its power over the lower passions. Where education increases sensual enjoyment, by adding a refined zest to it, it is no longer the education intended by Mencius, but belongs to the school of Epicurus. This has a tendency to destroy and not to increase prosperity. It is well we should inquire what is the aim proposed and striven for in the much-belauded education of our day.

(b.) Schools.

453. Of several kinds, viz., boarding, military, elementary, and high. (Cf. Art. 428.) Mencius said (p. 118), "Establish boarding-schools, gymnasia, and elementary and high schools for the education of the people. Boarding, i.e., nourishing; high, i.e., advanced education; gymnasia, i.e., military exercises (the bow). The Hea dynasty called theirs high schools; the Yin, gymnasia; the Chow, boarding-schools. Elementary schools were

common to the three dynasties. By all of these were the
duties of men made plain. If the duties of men are
made plain by the upper classes, there will be the attachment of the people shown by the lower. Should an
emperor arise, he will certainly take example by this, and
thus you will become the teacher of the emperor." The
Commentary says, " Wealthy people had a school in their
hall. Twenty-five families would unite for a public
school, and five companies for a local school. Those
mentioned in the text are local schools. Next, model
schools were established in the imperial residence, which
were then imitated in the provinces. All these were of
the same kind, but they differed in name. In the boarding-schools the old people were at times entertained ; and
in the gymnasia military exercises were practised, especially prize-shooting (archery). According to the text,
the aim of these schools was to develop a symmetrical
education." The scholars were prepared to fulfil all social
obligations. We ought here to keep in mind the views of
Mencius as to human nature, as laid down in Arts. 1–35.
The education of humanity only requires other instruction
and exercise in order to assist the development of the
pure humanity, which, according to Mencius, is ethico-
religious. Nowadays instructors frequently cannot " see
the wood for the trees," and teach in consequence many
specialities which are of no practical value, but are
destined to be forgotten. The necessary moral and religious fundamental training may be considered under two
aspects—that which is not simply individual but keeps
in mind the social duties, and the vocation for one's life
as a citizen, of which only the first steps are to be acquired,
which it is most probable each pupil will require later on
in life. The special education for any department of life
can then more. rationally commence with the choice of a
vocation. The education of the people supposes an unin-
terrupted progress in learning, which is brought about in
many ways throughout life.

454. Permanence of the orthodox school (p. 377).
Mencius said, "From Yaou and Shun to T'ang there were
over five hundred years. Men like Yu and Kaou-yaou
saw and recognised it (the truth) ; such as T'ang heard of
it and recognised it. From T'ang to King Wan there were
more than five hundred years. Men like E-Yin and Lae
Choo, they saw and knew it. King Wan heard of it and
knew it. From King Wan to Confucius there were more
than five hundred years. Men like Tae-Kung Wang
and San E-Sang, they saw and knew it. Confucius
heard of it and knew it. From Confucius till the present time are one hundred years. One is so little removed from the age of the Holy One (the Sage), is so
very near to the place of his residence. Is there then no
one ? Is there none to transmit them ? " Hence we see
that the chief representatives of Chinese orthodoxy were
the most important of her emperors, thus indicating that
the nature of that orthodoxy was political economy.
That this has all along continued so conservative arises
from the fact of its strong moral basis, which again is
founded upon the nature and destiny of man. The time
in which Mencius lived was a period of political, not of
literary decay. Mencius had many contemporaries of the
first rank. Of the founders of new dynasties which arose
after Mencius, not one became sufficiently famous to be
classed with the examples of antiquity. Although there
has been no lack of great changes in form, there has been
an underlying clinging to the traditional. The creative
power perished when the empire was consolidated. China
has had so long a continuance as an empire because no
rebel in case of success had any new plan to bring forward, but simply sought to revivify the ancient. This
success only lasted for a time, till a new rebellion again
overthrew a decrepit Government and repeated the process.
The latest rebellion of the Taipings alone was national and
boldly reformatory. It failed, not because of the opposi-

tion of so-called Chinese stagnation, but from the absolute incompetency of its leaders.

455. Shun was "the founder; he appointed the first minister of education" (p. 127). (Cf. Art. 326.) This office is therefore one of great antiquity, and of importance if the state will receive instruction. In a sound state of political life education must not be neglected; it ought not to be left to the crotchets of an individual, but be carried out so as to keep in view the requirements of the mass, whilst providing for the special needs of individuals. The Government may prescribe the examinations with regard to the requirements of the state, and it is its duty conscientiously to watch over these, but it ought carefully to guard against any division of interest between itself and the families of the empire. School and home ought ever to stand in closest harmony. Parental authority is established and an outlet is furnished in the energetic pursuit of a political career. If the parental authority be overthrown, that of the state falls also; there then remains no moral right, but only that of might. School life in China at the present day is very much neglected. There is no discipline, and there are neither preparatory institutions for teachers nor examinations of these. The state only examines those who offer themselves at the official examinations, and apportions their degree. Each one can see for himself how he may best provide himself with what is required. The office of a teacher is a thoroughly free and open profession. But free inquiry is entirely stifled by the way in which preparation is made for the Government examination. Choo Hi is sanctioned as the exponent of the Classics, after whom every Chinese must form his opinions; every opinion that deviates from his is legally wrong. Of late years the Chinese for the first time have had the opportunity of taking wider views, but are seldom in the position to do so. There, in the examination, lies the chief obstacle to the unprejudiced inquiry into anything foreign.

(c.) Teachers and Scholars.

456. Reception of scholars (p. 369). "Mencius said, I having opened a class, go not after those who leave, and reject not those who come. If they come with such a heart, they will be at once received." Mencius, therefore, received every one who came to him to learn without examining their character. The context says that a sandal was missing from the inn. Mencius repudiated being answerable for his pupils. At the same time he hints at the improbability of his scholars doing anything of the sort. Possibly it was simply a school joke that they had perpetrated. Confucius does not appear to have received scholars so easily.

457. Various kinds of scholars (p. 374). "When Confucius could not obtain men of moderation, to whom he might have communicated his views, he was obliged to take bigots and ascetics. The bigots quickly laid hold of things; the ascetics would not do many things. Did not Confucius desire to have moderate men? It was because he could not get them that he thought of the next class. The conversation of the bigots was high-sounding; they said, 'The men of old! the men of old!' But if we compare their conduct, it did not correspond. If he could not obtain bigots, he tried to get scholars who would not engage in anything impure, in order to communicate his views to them. These were the ascetics; they came after the others." Confucius thus taught one so-called correct school. It is noteworthy that the same types in all ages form the orthodox. The moderate men are rarely met with. The bigots, or dogmatists, develop more energy, we now see, amongst the Ultramontanes, whilst Protestants, as far as they are orthodox, take up the side of asceticism.

458. Refusal of conceited men (p. 354). "A disciple asked, 'When the regent's brother came within your door he should have been treated with propriety. Why did he

receive no answer?' Mencius said, 'He who questions
me, presuming on his nobility, or his talent, or his age, or
his services to me, or upon old acquaintance, will not be
answered.' The regent's brother did two of these things.''
Modesty is requisite in a learner, specially in a student
of ethics and statesmanship; still greater is this requirement for religion. Mencius would have to expel most of
the high-school students of the present day. The desire
for wisdom, and especially for knowing how to govern, is
not so great as appears at first sight.

459. Proselytes from other schools (p. 367). "Mencius
said, ' They who flee from Socialism go over to Sensualism;
they who flee from Sensualism go to the Orthodox. If they
go over to that, they ought to be at once received. Dis-
putants now deal with the Sensualists and Socialists as if
pursuing a stray pig ; even when they are already in the
sty, they follow after them and bind its feet.' " The idea
is plain. Socialism naturally begins with the ideal; it
pursues the highest aim, but it cannot long sustain itself
on high, but sinks down into miserable Sensualism.
Modern Socialism has already passed even this point.
Thence it raises itself and sends back many of its adherents to orthodoxy. Man as a moral and religious
being can find no satisfaction in the abyss of sensuality.
It leads many to destroy their nobler self; but the crowd
only follow such for a time, until they come to a consciousness of their actual state. It is usually only an
ideal or even an illusion which the mass of men pursue;
when undeceived, faith awakens and they find that orthodoxy alone secures their safety. Unhappily many mistakes
are made by the orthodox party at such times. One does
not like to see "the swine" again in the fold, but fears
that they may once more break away, so proceeds to bind
their feet, that they can neither stand nor walk. The
idea is, within the sphere of the school (the Church with
us) we ought to keep plenty of room. The "pure" doctrine is the rope wherewith feet are bound. In contrast

to this let men see from without and find tolerated within the richest variety. Life will have motion. Many of the world's chief herdsmen find the abundance of their swine or sheep very inconvenient for oversight; instead of fresher pasture, give dry hay or husks, and the herd gets fat upon it—possibly these shepherds yet more so. Only rest, rest in the stall! they say.

460. Irreverence of an earlier scholar (p. 188). One of the earlier scholars of Mencius came in the train of a minister to Ts'e. He came to see Mencius. "Mencius said, 'Do you come, sir, to see me also?' He answered, 'Why does the master utter such words?' Mencius answered, 'How many days is it since you came hither?' He said, 'Some.' 'Some! Is it not then right of me to utter such words?' 'My lodging was yet unprepared,' said he. 'Have you, sir, heard that one visits his chief after his lodging is prepared?' He said, 'I have sinned.'" In most cases we may know the tendency of a man's disposition if we can but observe what he does first of his free will, and what course he takes. In our own day many things are done for the sake of propriety, because one dare not leave them undone, but they are not the outcome of the heart.

461. Great reverence shown by the scholars (p. 130). "In former times, three years after the death of Confucius, his scholars prepared to return to their homes. They entered and bowed themselves before Tsze Kung. Standing opposite to each other, they wept till they all lost their voices and then returned home. Tsze Kung built afresh a dwelling upon the site of the grave (of his teacher Confucius), and lived there alone three years, after which he returned home." It is a fine trait that the scholars remained together three years after their master's death, and thought over what they had been taught. It was like the imperial mourning for a father. Yet Tsze Kung doubted this. This mourning was not observed by all the seventy disciples of the master, but only by a small

number. Still this remains a unique fact in his history. It could only be possible when the disciples had known their teacher for many years, and had been taught by him not only intellectually but also morally. In modern times that is extremely rarely the case, and then only for a very short time. The lack of reverence of our day lies chiefly at the door of the teacher, who too often fails to bring into prominence the ethical side of the master's vocation. We see here another indication of the greatness of Confucius; he was, indeed, the superior of Mencius.

(d.) *Methods of Education.*

462. Twofold (p. 324). "Mencius said, 'Education has many methods. I hold it (often times) unsuitable to teach (a man), and thereby I teach (him).'" The commentary paraphrases this, "I hold the conduct of a man to be impure, therefore I decline to teach him. The man feels this, he reforms himself, he learns to exercise humanity and righteousness. This is also one of my methods of giving instruction." This method smacks somewhat of stoical pride, but in some cases it may be justified. Where there is a sense of shame, it is rarely that a friendly admonition to virtue is entirely lost. To the light-minded an earnest discourse does no harm. In both cases a cold silence might increase enmity and break the last link. Love and sympathy are the best teachers. Only amongst scoffers is silence usually in keeping, and always amongst decided enemies.

463. Fivefold (p. 349). "Mencius said, 'The superior man teaches in five ways. 1. There are some he influences like a timely rain. 2. With some he perfects their virtue. 3. With some he brings out their talents. 4. Of some he answers the questions. 5. Some he teaches privately. These are the five methods which the superior man uses in teaching.'" The newer method would base these five ways upon psychology, after as many elements

R

of the life of the soul—Sensibility, the Will, Imagination, Intellect, and Reason. Such schemes have their advantages, but do not help us much, and often give us mere words instead of a living idea. Every teacher with a moral purpose will influence his pupils in various ways, each according to his individuality. The master who has his model quite ready for all shows that he is but a pedant. Mencius always keeps humanity as a whole in his mind, and lets peculiarities find their place naturally. The first, thoroughly awake to instruction, receive it eagerly and joyously. The second have more aptitude for the ethical, and yield themselves to right guidance. The third have a special inclination for this or that theoretical or practical department, and press on in that direction. The fourth are intellectual, critical natures, who require answers to their questions, lest through suppressed doubts they should end in uncertainty. The fifth are those who specially attach themselves to the master and allow themselves to be urged on by him. Naturally the thorough scholar and higher education are here supposed.

464. Levelling downward " by compromises " is to be rejected (p. 350). (Cf. Art. 80.) This especially relates to thorough scholars. To the good one may bend or condescend, but never pay compliments to the perverted or to the corrupted.

465. The ideal is to be kept before one (p. 297). " Mencius said, ' When E (the great archer) taught any one to shoot, he directed his attention to the full drawing (of the bow), and the attention of his pupils must be directed to the same. A great master-workman who teaches any one does it with the compass and square, and his pupil must also use the compass and square.' " The learner must receive from his master an idea of what is to be done in his department. To that his endeavour must be directed entirely until he is able to accomplish it. In this way he will keep his zeal excited and avoid the self-satisfaction which ever accompanies superficial attainments.

466. Instruction gives ideas, but not the ability to carry them out (p. 356). "Mencius said, 'The joiner and wheelwright can give a man the compass and square, but cannot make him skilful with them.'" This is an important consideration when we wish to estimate the work of the teacher. There must also be a correspondence between the ability of the teacher and the willingness and ability of the scholar in order to reach the highest result.

467. The farther education in life (p. 196). "Those who have ability train those without ability, the gifted train those without gifts; therefore men rejoice at having skilful fathers and elder brothers. If the able scorn those without ability and the gifted those without gifts, then the difference between the skilful and the incapable does not amount to an inch." The commentary says, "If the skilful do not fulfil this their vocation, they become as fools, and reckon themselves with those of no ability." That higher knowledge or civilisation should effect the education of those of lower attainments is not only agreeable to nature, but also a moral duty. Only in this way can the differences and difficulties of social life be overcome. That in its widest sense is the idea of missions. As long as a mission only uses peaceful and benevolent means, it stands justified in the forum of civilisation and science.

468. Nominal enlightenment (p. 363). "Mencius said, 'The talented used to make men enlightened through their enlightenment; now they make men enlightened by their obscurity.'" The commentary says, "Enlightenment takes place by means of morality (Tao Te)." Thus the so-called enlighteners of our time may measure the worth of their teaching. To impart knowledge to the people so as to fill them with doubt is not enlightening them in the sense of Mencius, but darkening, because it removes them from the moral duties of men. Without a moral and religious education the intellectual only injures men, because it lends dangerous weapons to immorality, selfish-

ness, and wickedness. Endeavours for the good of others, in a religious and moral sense, have never led them to destruction, but to nobler enlightenment. It is only human ambition which likes to lead to darkness instead of light. Let men consider the difference. In all ages there have been blind leaders of the blind, not only amongst Pharisees and Scribes, but amongst teachers, lawyers, officials, ministers, and sovereigns. All great revolutions show darkness on the side from which enlightening ought to come, and light that breaks forth out of the darkness of the once despised.

(c.) *Music.*

Philosophic Conception.

Music plays an important part in popular education in China. Only the Socialists vigorously oppose it. Confucianists ascribe to it great influence upon the minds of the people, and thus upon social life and the Government. Confucius is more copious on this subject than Mencius.[1]

469. Its nature is joy (p. 190). "The nature of music is to rejoice in these two (filial and fraternal duties). When there is joy these increase ; when increasing, how can they be discontinued? If they cannot be discontinued, the feet dance and the hands gesticulate unconsciously towards them." It is not so absurd as it appears at first sight that music should bring men's hearts into union with moral government. Melody and rhythmical movement are external signs of that which sways the heart. That a decided tone pleases us and certain harmonies carry us with them has indeed an external cause in the relations of their vibrations, but a deeper still in the constitution and disposition of our souls.

470. Its influence perfects the national life (p. 26). "A

[1] Cf. The Digest of Confucius (p. 82).

minister visited Mencius and said, 'I had an audience of
the king. The king spake with me about his love of
music, and I had no reply to make: how is it with the
love of music?' Mencius answered, 'Had the king a
great love for music, what would the state of Ts'e lack?'
Another day Mencius had an audience of the king and
said, 'The king once spake with his minister about a love
for music; is it not so?' The king changed countenance
and said, 'I cannot love the music of the ancient kings,
but I love that which suits our own day.' He replied, 'If
the king had great love for music, what would be lacking
to the state of Ts'e? The present music would be like
the ancient.' 'May we hear how that is?' Mencius said,
'Which is real enjoyment, to enjoy music alone or with
others?' 'There is nothing like enjoying it with others.'
Mencius said, 'Which is enjoyment, to enjoy music with
a few or with a mass?' He answered, 'There is nothing
like enjoying it with a multitude.' Mencius said, 'Permit
your humble servant to speak to the king about music.
Your majesty is now having music here, and the people
hear the clang of the royal bells and drums, the fifes and
flutes, and all say with aching heads and wrinkled brows
to one another, "Our king loves to have his music; but
why does he bring us to such extremity?" Father and
son do not see each other. Brothers, wives, and children
are separated and scattered abroad. This is nothing else
than that you do not share your pleasure with the people.
Now, had your majesty your music here, and the people
that heard the clang of the royal bells and drums, and the
sound of the fifes and flutes, said cheerfully and pleased,
and with pleasant countenances, one to another, "Our king
is not ill, else how could he enjoy music?" This would be
nothing but your enjoying yourself in common with your
people.'" From this place it appears plainly what position
in ethics is assigned by Mencius to music. Ruler and
subjects should be in harmony, and music be the expression of the common joy. We have thus also a doctrine

of social harmony. In the above Mencius departs somewhat from his master Confucius, who ascribed to the ancient music a magical effect upon the revivifying of state life, but denounced the modern music as destructive to the mind.

471. Therefore Mencius could say (p. 71), " By listening to the music we know the virtue (of the sovereign)." (Cf. Art. 180.) Properly, the music, like the rites, must be approved by the sovereign, if it be not appointed by him. The music for festal occasions, especially for the great sacrifices, was appointed by the sovereign formerly, but in the time of Mencius mostly by the princes. Besides this there was the popular music abounding in song. The classical Book of Odes collected by Confucius contained many such popular songs. Much may be understood of the popular opinion from the music of the day, formerly also the kind of government, because the people then were in close dependence upon it. The character of Chinese music is determined by the compass f, g, a, b, c, d, e, f. In the most ancient times they knew the intervals of fifths. The octave is unknown in China, all music being arranged to a scale of five notes. Harmony was unknown, but melody, rhythm, and the peculiar tones of different instruments are distinguished. With music the art of dancing was often united. Music itself was never taught in Chinese schools. Confucius himself was musical, as were some of his disciples. Mencius does not seem to have been distinguished in this respect. In other ancient philosophic writings of China examples were given of great musical feats. Music ought not to be undervalued as a means in educating the people. Man generally has a delight in music and song. Only care should be taken to improve the taste, and not let it be lost. In this respect the views of Confucius contain a degree of truth. Where simply good music is loved, there, as a rule, good thoughts will be cherished and prized. The thoughtful can apply this to the music of our own day.

472. Theory of music (pp. 161, 165, and 36).
473. Instruments.
474. Performances.
475. Concerts.
476. Ancient and modern music are alike.
477. Discussion concerning the old bell (p. 248).

CHAPTER III.

THE NATIONAL DEFENCES.

(a.) *Firmness at Home.*

478. PARTY strife is the ruin of the state (p. 175). "A man must first disgrace himself, then it will happen to him from others; a family must first destroy itself, and then it will happen to it from others; a state must first stab itself, then it will happen to it from others." Internal dissensions precede external ruin. Where this is not the case, assaults of foes serve to arouse new life. The inner divisions are often forgotten for a while in presence of a common danger, but too often for the first time when it is too late.

479. Not fortified towns but law-abiding moral order affords protection (p. 84). "Mencius said, 'The time of Heaven is not like the advantage of earth; the advantage of earth is not like the harmony of men. If a fortress (a walled town) of three li circumference, with outworks of seven li, be besieged and assaulted but not taken, it was the time of Heaven for the besieging and assaulting. But the not being taken indicates that the time of Heaven is not like the advantage of the earth. A fortress by no means deficient in height, surrounded with moats by no means deficient in depth, whose arms and weapons lack neither strength nor sharpness, whose stores of grain are not lacking in abundance, if after all given up, this indicates that the advantage of earth is not like the harmony of men. Therefore it is said, A people is not

protected by the throwing up of frontier forts, a state is
not defended by steep mountains and ravines, the whole
realm is not held in loyalty by the advantage of arms.
He who has found the moral law of the universe (Tao),
many assist him; he who has lost it, few assist him."
The commentary says, amongst other things, "The ancients
divided the land, not the people." At this time the
princes wished to keep the people to their own boundaries, so they erected the frontier fortresses, *i.e.*, they
wished, in a lawful way, to hinder the people from
wandering about, and to cause them to settle down in
definite dwelling-places. How many means of restraint
have been sought by Governments when they have lost
the chief means! Small states have always exhibited the
same symptoms, and have perished absolutely in their
littleness. Now that we have the great states, we see the
same thing on a larger scale. Each is envious of the
other, always at work fabricating more destructive arms,
building stronger fortresses, seeking to increase their
inhabitants, yet thinking very little, indeed, about the
inner harmony, which is more important than aught else.
But, says Mencius, the chief thing is principle (Tao). The
strongest forts are often lost through a lack of moral
union in the defenders. Proper military preparations are,
of course, not excluded, but these are often overrated to
one's destruction; they are no guarantee against treachery,
deceit, and neglect.

480. A Government which is active in doing good need
not fear the enterprise of neighbouring states (p. 50).
"The Duke of T'ang asked, 'The people of Ts'e are forti-
fying See. I feel on this account great alarm; what is best
to be done?' Mencius replied, 'If (the Duke) does good,
his descendant in later generations will attain the imperial
dignity. The superior man founds the inheritance, offers
the clue which can be continued in the future. When
the completion of the work arrives it is from Heaven.
What has the ruler to do with that (neighbouring state)?

Be active in doing good, and that is enough.'" Were states to seek to excel each other in good, in arrangements to secure peace, life would be more restful and useful. But attention is solely directed to power and dignity, rarely to the deep moral purpose of national and political existence.

481. The state must receive teaching from all sources (p. 173). "The small states take the large for their example, yet are ashamed to receive their commands; that is as if a scholar were ashamed to receive the directions of his master. If one is ashamed of this, there is nothing better than to take King Wan for an example. If he does this, he will be certain, with a large state in five years, or with a small one in seven years, to obtain the rule over the whole empire." For King Wan's way, see Art. 268. Pride and caprice are ever united with pupils, old or young. The best way to become free of the teacher is industrious study, by which alone one arrives quickly and easily at one's aim. States which will not learn often receive blows from their stronger instructors, neither are lesser corrections wanting.

(b.) Defensive against External Foes.

482. External foes and calamities serve to vivify the state (p. 323). "If there are within no conservative families and worthy counsellors, and abroad no inimical states and external calamities, that state will generally come to ruin." By these the energy of the state is incited and the self-satisfied repose, and effeminacy, by which most of the old civilisations have perished, will be averted.

483. In danger the ruler must either immediately flee or make a firm stand, even to death (p. 51). "The Duke of T'ang asked, saying, 'T'ang is a small state; although exerting all my strength to serve the large states, I cannot avoid the inevitable; how may this be done?' Mencius answered, 'In former times the great king (founder of the

Chow) dwelt in Pin; the barbarians made incursions into
it; he gave tribute of skins and silks without being able to
get rid of them. He gave them dogs and horses, pearls and
jewels, without getting rid of them. Then he assembled
the old people and spoke to them as follows, saying,
"What the barbarians covet is the land. I have heard
that the superior man does not injure men with that by
which he nourishes them. What difficulty will it be for
my two or three children to be without a ruler? I will
leave you." He left Pin, crossed the Leang mountain,
and founded a town at the foot of the K'e mountain, where
he dwelt. The people of Pin said, "He is a humane man;
we must not lose him." They followed after him like
crowds hastening to the market. Or you may say, The
land belongs to the generations following, an individual
cannot alter this; I will rather die than give it up: I ask
the ruler to choose between these two courses.'" Modern
times are not without examples of princes abdicating,
though not with the result of the Chinese sovereign. The
reason being that modern abdications do not take place
from a love of the people, but as a last means of self-
preservation for rulers abandoned by their people. If a
ruler can trust himself to his people, the conflict is to be
preferred, in case there is a possibility of victory and of
maintaining the same; otherwise it is more humane to
flee. Self-destruction is romantic but barbarous.

484. Defensive measures (p. 50). "The Duke of T'ang
asked, saying, 'T'ang is a small state between Ts'e and
Ts'oo; shall I serve this or that?' Mencius replied, 'I
cannot grasp this proposal. There remains only one way.
Deepen your moats, improve the walls of your forts, and
defend them together with your people. Prepare to die,
and let not the people depart: in this way you may
succeed.'" History proves that a small state, where the
people love their government, has often successfully resisted mighty powers, and defeated them with great loss.

(c.) *War.*

485. Lust of conquest will not prosper (p. 20). "'If the king (of Ts'e), therefore, prepares arms, endangers soldiers and officers, excites discontent among the princes, does this give you joy in your heart?' 'No,' said the king; 'what joy can I have in these? Thereby I only seek that which I covet.' 'May I hear what it is you so greatly covet?' The king laughed and said nothing. Mencius continued, 'Is it because your rich and sweet food is insufficient for your mouth, your light and warmth insufficient for your body?' . . . 'No, not on that account.' 'Then,' said Mencius, 'one can understand what your majesty covets so much; it is to extend your territories, to have Ts'in and Ts'oo at your court, to govern the middle kingdom, and to keep the four (frontier) savage regions in hand. To endeavour by the means you are using to obtain your desire is like looking for fish in a lofty tree.' The king said, 'Is it as bad as that?' He replied, 'It is worse; for if you seek for fish in a high tree, although you do not find any, there will be no evil result following. To seek what you desire by what you are doing, and to direct all the energy of your spirit to it, must have an evil result.' He said, 'May I hear how?' He replied, 'If the people of Tsow fight with those of Ts'oo, which does your majesty think will conquer?' 'The people of Ts'oo would conquer.' 'Therefore the small cannot contend in war with the great, nor the minority with the majority, nor the weak with the strong. The land within the four seas contains nine times a thousand li; Ts'e only consists of one such part. To seek with one to overthrow the eight, what difference is there between this and Tsow going to war with Ts'oo? It is even opposed to radical principles.'" This monarch, therefore, was preparing to seize the empire by force of arms. Mencius often urged the princes to strive earnestly after the imperial dignity, but always in the way of peace.

He who wishes to carry out anything by external power must carefully calculate the opposing forces. Without considerable spiritual superiority an eightfold power cannot be conquered, but the very attempt is fraught with ruin. Ts'e reckoned upon the lack of union amongst the other powers, but found out its error later, and experienced signal discomfiture. (Cf. Art. 489.)

486. War hinders the increase of population (p. 5). "The king of Leang complained to Mencius that, in spite of his anxious thought on behalf of his people, the population of his state did not increase, nor that of his neighbours decrease. Mencius answered, 'Your majesty loves war. . . . That is why the land is depopulated.'" War costs not only precious lives, but also arms and provisions. It takes away from production the best strength, and hinders it likewise, whilst consumption is increased. The injury and the destruction is yet worse if the land is invaded. Spite of all which, statesmen have as yet discovered no remedy or way of preventing wars.

487. A war of conquest is really manslaughter (p. 181). "If the fighting is for land, the slain fill the open fields; if the fighting is for a town, the slain fill that town. This is what is meant by 'increasing the territory and devouring the flesh of men,' a crime for which death is insufficient. Therefore skilful warriors should undergo the most severe punishment, next those who unite princes in alliances, afterwards those who extend the area of moorland and burden the people with uncultivated territory." Mencius suggests many questions in regard to the history of the world. What have all the great conquerors of past times, down to Napoleon, done for the good of humanity? Millions of lives have been sacrificed, civilisation has retrograded, and the history of the world still taken another course than that proposed by the conqueror. The conquering state is generally ruined by its greatness. Righteousness exalteth a people, yet more a throne. But such great convulsions are necessitated when states keep

so much aloof from one another, and so develop angry opposition. It is with peoples much as with the atmosphere; where well-ordered equality of temperature prevails, all is soft and mild; where opposite temperatures come into direct opposition, storms result.

488. It destroys the balance of power between states (p. 315). "Mencius said, 'The land of the emperor contains about a thousand square li; without that it would not be sufficient for the entertainment of the princes. The land of a prince contains about one hundred square li; without that he would not have enough to maintain the statutes of his ancestral temple. When Duke Chow was invested with Loo, it was one hundred square li; the territory was not insufficient, but it was limited to one hundred li. . . . . Now Loo is five times one hundred square li. What do you think, sir? Were an emperor to arise, would Loo be diminished or increased? A humane man would not do it were it simply the taking from one and the giving to another, how much less ought one to do so by the slaughter of men?'" Loo had formerly annexed nine states, but soon after itself suffered the same treatment. It saddens one to see how often like occurrences repeat themselves in history in a slightly different form. The history of China of that period might well serve as an example and warning to modern Europe. The present smaller states will not much longer be able to enjoy their independence. It would show us that in the formation of any great power no general European or universal peace is possible. China had first its small, then its large states. In Europe there is a greater because a national difference. There is a great importance in this, but also a dark side. As long as selfishness is the leading motive of politics, state boundaries cannot be absolutely settled. If we finally arrived at a monarchy like that of China under the Tsin dynasty, B.C. 250, even this would not secure enduring peace. How many rebellions has China experienced since that time! The ruling dynasty

has been changed more than twenty times. Still we need
not despond. The kingdom of God alone remains eternal;
but that consists in righteousness, peace, and joy in the
Holy Ghost. States only exist by virtue of those eternal
virtues which they exhibit. We think in the first place
only of that which Mencius has so well brought forward
here. Especially ought we to remember his two fundamental ideas of humanity and righteousness. These are
eternal virtues. They show their lasting nature in that
they cannot be exhausted upon earth.

489. Annexation should only be when the inhabitants
are favourable (p. 45). "Mencius said, 'If the dwellers
in Yen are pleased at being annexed, then annex it.
Among the ancients there was one who so acted; it was
King Woo. If the people of Yen are not pleased at being
annexed, then do not annex it. Amongst the ancients
there was one who acted on this principle; it was King
Wan.'" (Cf. Art. 41.) The king annexed it, and the
result is seen (p. 46). "When the people of Ts'e had
conquered Yen they annexed it. The princes of the realm
took counsel how to save Yen. The king of Ts'e said to
Mencius, 'The princes are advising how to attack me. How
ought they to be treated?' Mencius replied, 'Your servant
has heard of some one with seventy li who exercised the
government over all the realm; that was T'ang. I have
never heard of any one with a thousand li who feared
others. Now the ruler of Yen was tyrannising over his
subjects; your majesty went and punished him; the people
regarded it as their own saving out of water and fire, and
received your troops with baskets of rice and vessels of
soup. But they killed their fathers and elder brothers, and
laid their sons and younger brothers in fetters, destroyed
their ancestral temple, and carried away its precious
vessels; how could this prosper? The whole realm fears
with reason the power of Ts'e. Now with territory doubled
and no humane government exercised, that sets in motion
the arms of the whole empire. If the king hastens to

issue an order for the release of the old and young, to leave the precious vessels in their place and position, to set up a ruler after taking counsel with the people of Yen, and then withdraws, so may the halting (of the troops of the allies) be attained.'" The king did not do so. Yen revolted, and Ts'e suffered a reverse, losing also its prince and much land. Yen, in fact, owed its safety to the envy of other states at Ts'e's acquisition of territory. So it is in this day in the case of several weak states.

490. Even a war of punishment may be avoided (p. 354). "In executing punishment the superior authority makes war upon the inferior. Hostile states do not punish each other." (Cf. Art. 367.) (P. 356.) "Punishment of the states is called correction. If each wishes itself to be corrected, why does it require war?" The misery is when states do not correct themselves. For this is needed the universal dominion of morals and religion. Of course, neither this nor that external form is meant, which often enough have caused war, but the reality of them. That war amongst the peoples ought to be abolished is as impracticable as the desire to do away with all capital punishment. To seek to diminish crime and to make punishment just and humane, is possibly attainable. Many wars might be prevented by suitable means. Even if all states did not join it, a generally recognised authority might be established and recognised, to whose decisions differing states might have recourse, or which in case of refusal might with other states act as the executive, but all private endeavours do nothing to help toward this.

491. War is generally to be deprecated (p. 354). "There are no righteous wars. Instances there are of one war better than another." (Cf. Arts. 488, 154, 490.) Mencius is highly to be regarded in this respect, that he always advocates a policy of peace. In this respect he is at one with all the chief state philosophers of the Chinese.

How unlike these to the Greeks, who idealised robbery and violence, in both small and great, above everything! Yet many scholars regard the Greeks as far higher, if not the very highest, exponents of humanity. The ideas of the Chinese offer a great contrast to these, especially in political economy. The Greek conception is that of a town council by the side of the grand statesmanlike intuitions of the Chinese.

S

CHAPTER IV.

HOME POLITICS.

*(a.) The Identity of the Interest of the Government
and the People.*

492. THE Government, as well as the laws, is for the
welfare of the people (p. 165). "There are now rulers
with benevolent hearts and a reputation for humanity,
yet the people do not receive any benefit from them, and
they cannot be examples to future generations, because
they do not use the (Tao) practice of the earlier kings.
Hence it is said, 'Good in and by itself is not sufficient
to establish a Government; law in and by itself cannot
carry itself out.'" The laws of the state represent a will.
Its difference from the will of an individual is that it is
the will of the community, the Government for those
governed. As thought has universal laws, so has the will.
As every thought is not right, but only in so far as the
law of thought therein finds expression, so has the will
laws which are the standard for its realisation. Not every
will corresponds to the law of man's right will. But as
"the thought" is to be distinguished from thinking, so
"the will" from willing, or, more clearly expressed, "that
which is willed," just as thought corresponds to "that
which is thought." The will of the Government, as that
which is willed, is the law for the state. Both the will
and that which is willed belong together. But the carrying out of this is not so secured; that requires the mind
or will of the subjects; the law must also become some-

thing willed by them. Because this is never fully the case, the law requires external enforcement. This it finds only in the personal representative of the law, who effects the carrying of it out with more or less power. This power stands in an inverse ratio to the will of the subjects. We may also say that the force which the state exerts towards its subjects indicates the difference between the will of the Government and the will of those governed. In the department of politics this law never becomes so carried out as its sense properly requires. The state consists in reality of several single beings, and its power cannot so watch over all of these as would be necessary to carry out the formulated will of the law. Thus it forms to itself by degrees a modified, and possibly tolerably practical, mode of proceeding. Ministers with the best intentions cannot help the law beyond this. A sound state policy requires a personal representative of the law. The people must feel, and where possible see, that its welfare depends upon the stability of the law and the Government. That which is legally willed thus becomes the will of the people. The step from this will to its fulfilment is then easier, although it is very seldom that there is a complete correspondence between that which is willed and that which is done.

493. " The people are the chief consideration in the State " (p. 359). (Cf. Art. 57.) This appears self-evident, yet it is but rarely understood:

494. Therefore the destitute must be cared for (p. 38). " The widowers, the widows, the childless, and orphans form the poor folk of the realm, and have no one to whom they can complain." King Wan cared first for these four kinds of people when he announced the humanity (or benevolence) of his Government. The Ode says—

> ' It goes well with the rich,
> But pity these poor solitary ones.' "

The Government has always to provide for the common

weal. But in considering the whole it must not lose sight of those who, without state help, must perish. This is often too long neglected.

495. The "old to be nourished" (pp. 179–336). (Cf. Art. 142.) Mencius does not mean that the state is to support all the aged, but to see that this be done by their relations. That was attained formerly by encouraging useful occupations. This might even now be recommended with advantage. Where it happens that the heads of families cannot support all who depend on them, it is the duty of the Government to inquire the cause and to find the requisite assistance. Where such cases can be treated in detail, the individual can generally be enabled to help himself; but where the evil is widely extended, the poor worker with the best will cannot devise expedients; he can neither see what to do nor has he power to do it.

496. "Help to be given the people when necessary" (p. 261). (Cf. Arts. 195 and 343.) In preserving the people the Government preserves itself. The home policy can by gentle discrimination secure many friends. For other questions the people generally care little and understand less. Only it should be a wise care for the poor, as much as possible exercised through poor persons, because such better understand the cases and more easily find a favourable hearing. These could be controlled by well-to-do people of higher position.

497. General sympathy (p. 77). "The earlier kings had a sympathetic heart, and therewith also a commiserating government. He who with a sympathetic heart exercises a commiserating government may govern the whole empire as if turning it round in the hand." Sympathy opens the heart, sternness closes it. Still great energy is required with the sympathy to form and carry out great plans; the good of the people is the moving cause, and the people, provided they are not passionately excited, have a keen perception of this.

498. Reciprocity. For such a Government the people willingly die, but they abandon the unsympathetic (p. 48). " Tsow had an engagement with Loo. Duke Muh of Tsow asked Mencius, saying, 'Of my officers there remained thirty-three men killed, and none of the common soldiers died. To punish these in the way of discipline cannot be done, but if not, then they maliciously saw their leaders die without standing by them; what, then, is best to be done?' Mencius replied, 'In times of want and years of famine, there were of your subjects the old and the weak lying about (dead) in the moats and canals, the strong, who were scattered about to the four quarters, several thousand persons. Yet your magazines were supplied and your treasuries filled. None of the officers made a report. Thus the neglect of the superiors is cruelty to the inferiors. Tsang-tsze (a disciple of Confucius) said, "Stop! stop! what goes from you comes back to you!" Now the people have only returned their conduct to the officers. Do not blame them. If you exercise a benevolent government, this people will be attached to their superiors and die for their leaders.'" A similar thing has been heard of in modern European armies, *i.e.*, that soldiers have shot their own officers in the battle. Rigid discipline need not exhibit itself in brutality. Specially should all set over men respect their subordinates. That is the secret of all power over others, consideration for the least, and participation in their experiences. With this, energy in the carrying out of principles may well be united. As long as the upper classes think that they are a class of men by themselves, and the lower classes are only for their service, the gentle human feeling of these latter will be outraged. Then there is the constant danger of an explosion, a revolution, brought about by the uprising of suppressed human nature.

499. Means by which the Government may win the love of the people (p. 176). "Procure for the people what they desire, and do not offer them what they abhor." (Cf.

Art. 357.) This is a general statement; specially are mentioned—(1.) The scholars are to be won by honour to the excellent, gifts to the skilful, place to the distinguished. (2.) The merchants by exacting only ground-rent without taxing of merchandise, inspection without payments. (3.) The travellers, inspection at the boundaries and frontiers without taxes. (4.) The agriculturists by socage service without taxes. (Cf. Art. 440.) Mencius also would have the state keep in mind its purpose of civilisation, and that taxation must supply the requisite means. A too great lightening of taxation would be most prejudicial to the state, could not long continue, and must be very dearly purchased. But a Government profits the people when all that is exacted turns to the advantage of the administration. Such is the principle in vogue throughout Asia and in part of Eastern Europe. It sometimes seems to be the chief idea at times in the budgets of constitutional states. It is worthy of note that in China great importance was attached by the Socialists to military preparation.

500. "The rendering of service to individuals is to be deprecated" (p. 194). (Cf. Art. 434.) Time is too short for it, and it indicates weakness in the Government. It is, we have seen (Arts. 492–499), an object of home government to attach the subjects, individuals as well as large masses, to itself, but much depends on the way in which this is done.

501. The use to be made of the people should be the very best (p. 330). Mencius said, "Let the people be employed in a way to secure their happiness; although wearied they will not murmur. Let them be killed in the work of preserving their lives; although they die they will not murmur against him who causes their death." This again is universally true. No one loves toil for the sake of toil, or death for its own sake. It requires the aim to be made very plain, which is only to be obtained through this means. If the aim is generally desirable,

one can put up with very unpleasant means of attaining
to it, even if many have to be employed. But a mistake
is often made in the choice of means. In politics it is not
every aim that sanctifies the means.

502. Prosperity shared with the people (p. 39). "The
king said to Mencius, 'I have a passion for something; I
love wealth.' He answered, 'In old time Duke Lew loved
wealth. The Ode says—

> " He hoarded up, he gathered in,
> He packed up dried flesh and grain
> In bags and sacks.
> He thought, The mustering of the people brings glory.
> Halberds, bows, and arrows were prepared,
> Shields, spears, battle-axes, and hatchets;
> Then he marched forth."

Thus those who remained had stacks and stores, those
who marched had provisions packed ; then it was that he
first felt able to begin his march. If your majesty loves
wealth, let it be mutually shared with your people.' " (Cf.
Arts. 426–443.) A ruler who only amasses private wealth
mistakes his position and loses the affection of his people,
causing mistrust and envy by this splendour. How different when his state is his treasure and his subjects his
jewels.

503. Rejoicing with the people (p. 4). "King Wan used
the strength of his people to make his tower and lake, and
yet the people rejoiced, calling the tower the 'Wonder
Tower,' the lake the 'Wonder Lake;' they rejoiced that
he preserved his stags and deer, fishes and turtles. The
men of old enjoyed themselves together with their people,
therefore they could rejoice." Joy in the joy of fellow-
men is a very noble joy. To wipe away the tears of the
poor and sorrowful and to give them laughter instead is
a higher kind of enjoyment than that procured by costly
paintings and sculptures. In the present day private
parks are much in vogue. Seldom is it that the possessors
find pleasure in these, or time to enjoy themselves in them;

the public look through the gates and lament that so beauteous a spot lies useless to the neighbourhood. Generally there cannot exist for long in any community an arrangement by which the greater part does the work and only the remainder derives its pleasure from it. Human nature has, in consequence of the unrest which results from its indispensable labour, a need for amusement that cannot be repressed, for obtaining some kind of enjoyment, the desire for which is of equal importance with the strength to labour. Where the majority find this impossible, then the mass begins to ferment, and a revolutionary explosion follows. Each right desire requires a careful directing towards the noble and beautiful, so that it be not degraded into mere sensuality and vulgarity. Here is the problem for the Government, which both can and will form the taste of the people for enjoyment by its own pleasures.

504. The contrast to this, when the pleasure of the monarch is treated as a crime in the people (p. 30). " Mencius said to the king of Ts'e, ' When I arrived at your borders, I inquired about the great prohibitions before I ventured to enter it; and I heard that inside the border gates there was a park of forty square li, and that he who killed a deer in it was held guilty of the same crime as he who killed a man. Thus those forty li are a pitfall in the midst of the state. Is it not natural for the people to hold them to be too large? The park of King Wan contained about seventy square li. Grass-cutters and wood-gatherers visited it, pheasant and hare catchers visited it; he held it in common with the people. Was it not natural for them to regard it as too small?' " Under King Wan hunting was free, truly a political means of preparing his elevation against the Yen dynasty three thousand years since. Even now hunting is free in China in the open field, specially in uninhabited districts or on the mountains. This subject is treated (p. 28) in the same way as music (Art. 47c).

505. Sympathy in joy and in sorrow (p. 33). The king of Ts'e had an interview with Mencius in the Snow Palace. The king said to him, "Have men of distinguished virtue this pleasure also?" Mencius replied, "They have; and if others obtain not the same, they condemn their superiors. They are wrong in condemning their superiors because they cannot obtain pleasure. But to be ruler of the people and not to share enjoyment with them is also wrong. He who rejoices in the pleasure of the people, in his pleasure the people also rejoice. He who is grieved at the sorrow of his people, in his sorrow they also grieve. To rejoice with the whole realm, to sorrow with the whole realm, and yet not to obtain the imperial dignity, has never yet happened." The argument is striking. The upper classes, specially those who have possessions, have indeed a legal right to the enjoyment of their own. Those who can only look on have no right to condemn these. But right has its limits in humanity : as soon as it becomes inhuman it passes over into the opposite. Not only from the standpoint of humanity, but also from that of wisdom, is it incumbent upon those in a high position to preserve an accordance of feeling with the feelings of the lower classes. If the noble and the right—the truly human— are not cultivated whilst there is the opportunity, then the passions, the wild forces of nature, break loose. Equality in our common humanity with firm maintenance of differences of rank is essential.

506. "Enjoyment of beauty with the people." (Cf. Art. 312.) Mencius meant that each king should rejoice in his own wife. Were this the case with all those in authority, marriage throughout the land would be happier than is frequently the case. This point is one of extraordinary importance for the state. The more happy marriages, the more contented families. These are the foundations of the state. It is necessary to direct the attention of noble minds to this point; the matter must, however, be gently handled.

(b.) The Political Factors.

507. The state organisation in its constituent parts. The individual is the ultimate element (p. 171). "Mencius said, 'The people have a common saying: "The empire, the state, the family," is what all say. The basis of the empire is the individual state; the basis of the state is the family; the basis of the family is the individual.'" This is first said of the emperor, who through his state governs the realm, through his family his state, and through his individuality his family (family here in its wider sense). Here Mencius thinks not of quantity but of the right quality. The head of the state must be a person who has proved himself, and is approved, in the narrowest circle, head of the family, and in the widest as head of the state. Only to such an individuality will all the various elements of the empire bend. This is the condition of internal peace and prosperity. Beyond this it is signified by the above passage that the organisation of the state does not rest directly upon the family; there is something beneath that. Where there are no longer feudal states, the realm requires some other bond of union between the great families and its colossal and complex self. The more there are of such great families, and the more closely their interests are intertwined, so much the more vitality has the state in itself, and the stronger its position towards what is external. But if these are exclusive and stand in an inimical position to each other, the whole is in confusion. If the family be not regarded in its individual members, each is absorbed in the whole, and there will soon be a lack of decided characters. Each should be, even for his own sake, a thoroughly educated, morally developed individual. This last position ought not, however, to be attained by opposition to the rest, but by means of its well-regulated unity.

508. Great families (p. 171). "Mencius said, 'The

administration of government is not difficult. One must
not offend against the great families. To him to whom
the great families incline, the state inclines; to him to
whom the state inclines, inclines the whole realm. The
virtue-inculcating teaching of such a one will spread as a
result over all, over-filling the four seas.' " These families
were in China what the powerful noble families of Europe
once were. Now, in the place of these, we may and must
place the corporations and associations, especially those
of a political nature, whose influence is in some respects
greater than that of the earlier noble houses. A Government can seldom remain neutral towards all parties. It
has too great an interest in the result to stand quietly by
watching for the end, resolved to be contented with it.
It requires a leading principle and a majority to make its
success possible. Therefore it must unite with one or
other party. An intelligent Government ought never to
let itself be torn in pieces by party passion; it must yet
more seek to incorporate the elements of truth held by its
opponents, spite of the one-sidedness of party. Only thus
can it hope to attain an enduring victory. The greatest
political mistake of a ruling party is to persecute the
others by means of external power. That is a misuse of
power. Let one treat opponents, as far as the difference
is one of conviction, with gentleness and consideration.
Only actions, never opinions, should be held as criminal.
(But many words are the same as actions.) An Opposition
can only hold together so long as it maintains truths
which have not obtained recognition by the ruling party.
So, for instance, the Confucian political economy has
appropriated the essentials of the Socialistic, and is fuller
and more powerful for the struggle it has undergone. So
it is in every department of social life. It is not a weak
eclecticism, but a living growth here advocated. Every
new addition works upon the old truth, rejuvenating it or
lending it new life : the type is the same, but there
is somewhat new in every part. This is a law of the

organic life of natural, spiritual, social, and political well-being.

509. Conservative elements (p. 323). "If there are no conservative families at court . . . the state will come to ruin." (Cf. Art. 482.) Concerning the parties in the ancient political life of China we have but few hardly intelligible intimations, which form a subject for the discussions of sinologists. That the conservative element is most important for a healthy political development will not be quite evident to some of the "party of progress." But we must distinguish between the true conservatism, which will only hold fast to traditions proved good, and its caricature, which endeavours to perpetuate everything ancient without examining it. Although China has, in the present day, fallen into this last error, it was by no means the meaning of Mencius. He simply was not sufficiently clear in guarding against it. Every organism which ceases renewing itself, dies out, becoming inorganic. This renewing must take place by way of growth, as the development of the original type; thus it busies itself in casting off all that is unnecessary and a mere excrescence. Too-hasty progress often breaks away from the old stem without any growing life in the new graft. The result is long delay or retrogression, until that which has been lost is restored.

510. "Faithful officials." (Cf. Arts. 375 *et seq.*, 106, 331.) Without trustworthy officials the Government halts. For training such, the ruler, even with the best intentions, is manifestly insufficient. Only when among the subjects and officials each faithfully fulfils his own duties can success be secured. The temptations to unfaithfulness proceed mostly from the people. China is not the only state now suffering from this evil.

511. "Harmonious interaction of the upper and lower classes." (Cf. Art. 359.) Every one in the state must do his duty; not merely his legal duty, which may be done as a matter of policy, but the moral duty, the inner require-

ments of the law of the mind. There is too much lack
of this. In times of moral corruption, the Government
blames the subjects, the subjects the Government. Both
are so far in the right that common repentance is needed.
Here lies also the great importance of religion to the state.
The morality of the state is a kind of average, although
the Government must take a higher moral standpoint
in order to be able to effect the education of the people.
The Christian religion has a higher moral standpoint than
the state. The ordinary morality is presupposed, but the
moral feeling is deepened, and an ideal striven after that
corresponds to the highest—the divine claims in man.
This perfection striven after is, however, never attained.
In individual cases religious people may sink below the
level of the common morality. The state has public
opinion in addition to legal punishment for such cases.
The religious body (the Church) has also its discipline, its
excommunication, whereby she can publicly declare her
moral character to all who have fallen below her moral
standpoint. In a great Church body there must be formed
smaller associations with this end in view, after the religious standpoint of the individual. These can exert discipline over each other. Through these by degrees the
general moral tone is improved and elevated. The Christian religion can never be thereby exhausted. She seeks
a fellowship of love with the Heavenly Father, through
the Saviour, who has revealed the divine love in His own
fulness. But the more intimate the fellowship with God
becomes, the more perfect becomes the human personality
which is created after God, and thus too the general moral
conduct is perfected. Then the moral conduct proceeds
in a natural way from within, instead of being a mere
external acquired form. The multitudinous errors that
have been made in the past prove nothing against the
truth and importance of this matter.

512. Proportionate distribution of honours and incomes
(p. 249). "Mencius was asked the arrangement of digni-

ties and emoluments determined by the house of Chow?"
(1100 B.C.) (p. 250). "The emperor had a domain of one
thousand square li. His chief minister had land equal in
extent to a prince; the other ministers as much as a count;
great officials as much as barons; dukes and princes had a
territory of about one hundred square li. The ruler of
this had ten times the income of a chief minister; these
four times as much as the other ministers; these again
double the amount of the great officials; these double of
the middle - class officials, and these double the lower
officials; these had the same as the palace servants. The
income of these was equivalent to what they made by
their own field-work.[1]   Counts had a territory of seventy
li. The income of the ruler was tenfold that of a chief
minister; he had three times as much as the other ministers;
these double the amount of great officials, &c., as above.
Barons had a territory of fifty li; yet there were the
same four grades. He who had not fifty li had no access
to the emperor. These smaller holders of estates were
attached to some prince to whom they joined themselves.
In a territory of fifty li the ruler had an income tenfold
that of a chief minister; he had double that of the other
ministers, &c., as above. A husbandman received the
produce of fields of one hundred acres. The chief husbandman received the manure for one hundred acres,
which supported nine people; the next classes supported
eight, seven, six, and the lowest, five persons. The income
of the ordinary servants in the palace was regulated by
these varieties." According to the Chow Li, the emperor
had formerly 11 chief ministers, 68 of the second class,
and 269 other ministers, 1150 great officials, 4496 middle
class, and 19,507 lower officials. Dukes and princes received an income equal to that of 2880 persons; counts

[1] If we take the values of the present day as a guide, for the sake of realising the difference apportioned to the different ranks, we shall find, taking a low estimate, the lowest official receiving, say, £12 per annum; the middle, £24; the highest, £48; the ministers, £96; the chief minister, £384; the duke or prince, £3840. Field-work is variously remunerated in the different provinces at from 15s. to 25s. per month.

equal to 2160, and barons 1440.[1] If Mencius had not
disposed of these arrangements by other considerations,
there was yet in antiquity a fixed scale of dignities and
incomes. Mencius tells us that the princes had voluntarily upset this (p. 249). "The particulars of that arrangement (Chow) cannot be learned, for the princes, disliking
them as injurious to themselves, have all made away with
the records of them." They hoped to do better for themselves. The officials did as the princes nowadays; the
mandarins have only a trifling nominal income, and are
dependent upon fees or perquisites for their necessary
expenses. These fees are very pliable or elastic, and
include a mass of illegal impositions. These and the
further corruption resulting from the sale of offices have
poisoned Chinese political life to the very core. A new
and righteous regulating of the whole finance system
is one of the fundamental conditions for a healthy and
prosperous political future. Unhappily it is frequently
overlooked; a solid moral principle is the great prerequisite.
When a baron expends as much as a monarch and a
subordinate official as much as a minister, it is natural
that their proper income should be insufficient. They
seek other assistance in order to be able to meet this
extravagance. To confine themselves strictly within
proper limits is no longer understood by most. There is
then a moral perversity combined with a sickly public
opinion. Social and political injury are the result.

513. Maintenance of the moral and social bonds (p. 19).
"I treated my aged as aged, and so reached to the aged of
others. I treated my young as young, and so reached to
the young of others. Thus may the whole realm be made
to turn round in the open hand." In the Ode it says, "An
example to his gracious wife, it reached even his brothers,
and reflected itself in the families and in the land. The

---

[1] At first sight this appears inconsistent with the text; but if we remember that nine persons constituted
a family, we shall find that 2880 ÷ 9
= 320: in other words, the dukes received 320 times as much as supported a labourer's family.

language only takes up such a mind and applies it to all."
Each man stands in manifold relation to his fellow-men,
not only in reference to age, which is laid hold of here,
but also as husband and wife, father or mother, son or
daughter, sister, friend, master, or servant, &c. These
distinctions are to be recognised and fulfilled by each one
in his special position, so as to set an example to all others.
We have seen in earlier Arts. what Mencius taught concerning these individual relations. It is important that
we keep clearly before us this fundamental idea of Confucian politics. Therefore no levelling is permitted of
these social distinctions, but a moral elevation and carrying
out of the same. On this account there should be more
care taken in the present day in the education of youth.
"Think what thou art and what thy neighbour, and
conduct thyself so that you may be an example for all
who may be likewise circumstanced, and put yourself in
the place of another!" If this were always everywhere
the rule, an ideal state would be arrived at.

514. "Alternations of order and disorder are unavoid-
able" (p. 155.) It has ever been so during the existence
of the Empire. The beginning of each dynasty was good,
the end of it was evil. So is it throughout the world.
Frequently both follow quickly upon each other. Rarely
has the disorder been brought about by external misfortune ; generally it results from destruction of morals,
which poisons the social relations or overturns them, and
thus destroys the health of the national life. The evils
themselves are always otherwise caused, springing generally from some other nearer source, and requiring other
means for their healing. Rightly to recognise the root of
self-announced evils, and to make these harmless in the
right manner, belongs even to-day to such people as the
Chinese call "holy." But, alas! these very rarely appear.
We have now through the Gospel certain, and at the same
time thorough, knowledge of many chief evils which were
hidden from the ancients, of which they indeed felt the

evil result, but whose seat and healing they sought in the
wrong direction. Still Christianity has not made the
changes our article speaks of impossible. The mind of
Christ governs far too few men, and of these sways the
hearts of but few. The more abundantly that becomes
the case, the better condition will be attained by means
of these vicissitudes. Compare a century of the history
of various states for a proof of this.

515. The chief source of injury to home politics (p. 358).
" Mencius said, ' If confidence be not placed in the humane
and excellent, the state will become empty and void.
Without propriety and righteousness there will be confusion of the upper and lower classes; without good
administration and management the wealth will not
suffice for the expenditure." It is supposed that the state
has a sufficient number of men of ability in whom confidence may be placed. The higher moral education must
therefore have become pretty general. The second point
unites righteousness with propriety; this is very important.
Righteousness is cold and exclusive; propriety softens its
hard appearance. So with the first point; excellency or
skill without humanity or benevolence, whilst in many
cases commanding respect, rather repels than attracts
men. In the third case, the carrying out of the principles
of government is associated with the care for the daily
business of the state. The Government must not only
regard what comes before it from day to day, but must
also keep in view the culture problems of political life.
These three are worth laying to heart.

516. Lack of principle is the worst evil (p. 166). "If
he[1] who is above has no principle (Tao) to examine (his
government by), those below have no law to keep, the
court will not believe in principle (Tao), the handicrafts-
man will not trust his measure, the superiors will trans-
gress against righteousness, the common people against
the penal laws. That the state stands firm is then only

[1] *i.e.,* the sovereign or minister.

T

the result of a happy accident." [1]   Man lives not by bread
alone, but by ideas and the ideal.   He who overlooks this
often deceives himself in his reckoning.   There remains
for the Government a principle to carry out; not to leave
individuals entirely to their own ideas, but to pursue one
recognised fundamental idea for the whole state.   This
ideal gives coherence to the units, it elevates and energises
the whole.   This must not be a Utopia, but must stand
in correlation to the nature and destiny of man, especially
with the social and political side of man's nature, and
with his destiny, physical, moral, and heavenly.   In a
Christian state it would be a descent below the position
of the heathen empire of China were men to remove the
religious principle from politics.   It is unreasonable to
desire that religion should rule the state, and a mistake to
seek to govern the state simply according to the requirements of any religion.   Both these are attained first in the
fulfilment of all things, the kingdom of God in its majesty.
It is an anti-Christian endeavour under the pretence of the
Christian religion to wish to govern in the state from the
Church side.   Jesus Christ has provided for His kingdom
only the Word of truth, the power of the Holy Ghost, and
not external power.   Human pride and love of dominion
please themselves in ruling, even when one must take the
police as spiritual to help for a religious purpose.   It is a
misuse of the authority of the state to issue religious
prescriptions, to mix other inimical departments with
religion, as is witnessed by the really hurtful confusion
of our day through the mixing of science and religion.
Verily the Evangelical Church is being most perceptibly
injured thereby.   Only the religiously awakened are fitted
to teach religion—men borne along by the deeper religious
convictions, whose preaching comes from faith, and whose
faith is their innermost experience.   Neither matricula-
tions nor university degrees help to the attainment of

[1] The unhappy state of Ireland in 1881 may serve as a comment upon
these words.

this. Simple peasants and labourers may possess more religious intelligence than many who stand high in the ranks of the learned. As between men, an intimate and friendly relationship is not dependent upon a well-grounded knowledge of anatomy, physiology, &c., so still less is fellowship with God, the inner Christian life, dependent upon the scientific acquaintance with these things. One should cultivate these and inquire into them entirely unimpeded by ecclesiastical statutes, and only in accordance with the laws of truth. There may even be provided scientifically taught preachers for the circle which desires them, and can enjoy what such offer. But the people require homely fare. They need direct instruction as to their religious and moral duties and necessities. Science is for the intellect, and for that alone. Man requires food for his soul, which comes from God, and will be nourished only by the divine. Spite of all the advances of chemistry, men still prove their food by the taste. So, spite of all advances of science, they will go for spiritual food to faith, and not knowledge. If these considerations seem to lie a little apart from the text, let us look again at the short verse, and then compare with it the already evident workings of the struggle of civilisation.

Made in the USA
Coppell, TX
18 July 2022